White Enclosures

On Decoloniality

A series edited by WALTER D. MIGNOLO
and CATHERINE E. WALSH

On Decoloniality interconnects a diverse array of perspectives from the lived experiences of coloniality and decolonial thought/praxis in different local histories from across the globe. The series is concerned with coloniality's global logic and scope and with the myriad of decolonial responses and engagements that contest coloniality/modernity's totalizing violences, claims, and frame, opening toward an otherwise of being, thinking, sensing, knowing, and living; that is, of re-existences and world-making. Aimed at a broad audience, from scholars, students, and artists to journalists, activists, and socially engaged intellectuals, On Decoloniality invites a wide range of participants to join one of the fastest-growing debates in the humanities and social sciences that attends to the lived concerns of dignity, life, and the survival of the planet.

Piro Rexhepi

WHITE ENCLOSURES

Racial Capitalism and Coloniality along the Balkan Route

DUKE UNIVERSITY PRESS Durham and London 2023

Designed by Aimee C. Harrison
Typeset in Portrait Text Regular
by Westchester Publishing Services

LIBRARY OF CONGRESS CATALOGING-IN-PUBLICATION DATA
Names: Rexhepi, Piro, [date] author.
Title: White enclosures : racial capitalism and coloniality along the
Balkan route / Piro Rexhepi.
Other titles: On decoloniality.
Description: Durham : Duke University Press, 2023. | Series: On
decoloniality | Includes bibliographical references and index.
Identifiers: LCCN 2022026606 (print)
LCCN 2022026607 (ebook)
ISBN 9781478019282 (paperback)
ISBN 9781478016632 (hardcover)
ISBN 9781478023913 (ebook)
Subjects: LCSH: White nationalism—Balkan Peninsula. | Muslims—
Balkan Peninsula. | Romanies—Balkan Peninsula. | Racism—Balkan
Peninsula. | Ethnology—Balkan Peninsula. | Balkan Peninsula—Ethnic
relations—21st century. | Balkan Peninsula—Ethnic relations—Political
aspects. | BISAC: SOCIAL SCIENCE / Sociology / General | HISTORY /
Europe / General
Classification: LCC DR24 .R494 2023 (print) | LCC DR24 (ebook) |
DDC 320.56/909496—dc23/eng/20220804
LC record available at https://lccn.loc.gov/2022026606
LC ebook record available at https://lccn.loc.gov/2022026607

For Theo

Contents

Acknowledgments

I am deeply grateful to everyone who has supported me throughout this praxis. I thank my family, friends, and mentors over the years, including Dr. Marina Fernando at City College of New York who first introduced me to decolonial thinking, doing, and being. Without Julian Liu and Tjaša Kancler, this book would have been impossible: Julian introduced me to queer of color critique, while Tjaša pushed me to think of geopolitics from the body. Andreas Bräm has helped me stay on track by providing emotional support every time I was ready to give up. Much appreciation and gratitude to my friends and colleagues Antonio Da Silva, Melika Salihbegović Bosnawi, Terrence Rothline, Mahdis Azarmandi, Ajkuna Tafa, Seemi Ahmad, David Yakubov, Lisa Jemina Maria, Adem Ferizaj, Saffo Papantonopoulou, Salman Sayyid, Jeremy Walton, Catherine Elizabeth Walsh, Ahmet Alibasič, Mukesh Mehta, Marlene Gomes, Orjeta Gjini, Orhan Sadriu, Laura Zhuta, Lekë Salihu, Alyosxa Tudor, Hossein Alizadeh, Reed Seifer, Jasmina Sinanovic, Velina Manolova, Shirly Bahar, Art Haxhijakupi, James Mcnally, Shaha Hyseni, Klejdi Këlliçi, Jamie Bowman, Luis, Cristina, Ana Maria and Mariana Da Costa, Professor David Judge, Amir Knežević, Raed Rafai, Elis Gjevori, Jeta Mulaj, Jeta Jetim Luboteni, Madlen Nikolova, Bojan Bilić, Vjosa Musliu, Martin Hasani, Samira Musleh, Romana Mirza, Paola Bacheta, Esra Özyürek, Behar Sadriu, Leyla Amzi-Erdogdular, Noa Kerstin Ha, Dijana Jelača, Sabiha Allouce, Leah Pamposo, Zora Kostadinova, Marina Chornyak, Marina Gržinić, Sandra Zito, Ilgu Özler, Sanja Bojanić, Ervin Hatibi, Enis Sulstarova, Katarina Kušić, Kasia Narkowicz, Edona Fetoshi, Stephen Pampinella, Dženita Karić, Lorik Berisha, Tire and

Irfan Hoxha, Mary Marques and Duncan Morimoto Brown, Nick Booth and Marko Levreković, Bjorn Elf, Emil Yng, James Neil, Paul Justin Scott, David Henderson, Mitko Lambov, Agnesa Ziba-Bicaj, Alex Irwin, Annmarie Gayle, Linda Gorçaj, Doron Frishman, Keyvan Aarabi, and Andrea Fuzek, as well as my supportive friends, students, and Northampton Community College colleagues Ken Burak, Alexander Allen, Nathan Carpenter, and Christine Pense. This book is dedicated to my son, Theo; my parents, Arziko and Qazim; and my siblings, Teuta and Tomor Rexhepi.

Introduction

In the early summer of 2017, in the Loznitsa neighborhood of Asenovgrad, a small town in southern Bulgaria, a fight broke out between the city's Bulgarian kayaking team and local Roma and Muslim residents. The conflict began when residents who sought to save a drowning Bulgarian woman were met with racist slurs by members of the kayaking team who happened to be practicing in the lake. Eight Roma residents from Loznitsa were subsequently arrested and charged with violations, but no charges were made against the members of the kayaking team, who left the incident unscathed. A spontaneous racist rally denouncing "Roma aggression" erupted the day after, in which local Bulgarians were quickly joined by far-right groups from other parts of the country and marched into town. Attempts by Loznitsa community members to organize a protest were prevented by local police officials, citing security concerns. In the following days, the police increased their presence in the neighborhood in order to closely monitor journalists and human rights activists who had arrived in the city as the incident gained national attention. Within a couple of weeks, racist rallies against Roma aggression had spread across Bulgaria.

Prompted by Prime Minister Boyko Borisov, who had built his political career by speaking bluntly for years about the dangers of the demographic rise of Muslims and Roma populations as "bad human material" (*Telegraph* 2009) multiplying in the peripheries of Bulgarian towns and cities, local Asenovgrad authorities began conducting background checks, installing security cameras, demolishing homes, and evicting the Roma and Muslim residents from Loznitsa. In the meantime, the Ministry of

FIGURE INTRO.1.
Demolished
homes in the
Roma Muslim
neighborhood
of Asenovgrad,
August 2017.

Interior celebrated the opening of a new police station with traditional Bulgarian dances and with European Union (EU) and Bulgarian flags to celebrate police officers who had worked side by side with workers sent to demolish "illegal constructions." When I returned to the neighborhood at the end of August, more than thirty homes had been destroyed, and demolitions were continuing.

I talked to Muhave, a local resident in her sixties, who sat in front of her ruined home and pulled out a paper dating back to socialist Bulgaria affirming her right to dwell there. "I was born and raised here," she said. "My family has been here as long as we remember and now we are told that we are illegal and arrived in the last twenty years with a caravan." In a rushed decision after the incident, the municipal assembly started a process of redesignating the once-public land where the mostly Roma Muslim community lived for private development. Residents argued that the privatization of public land earmarked for residential dwellings was undertaken selectively for the purpose of displacing Roma Muslim communities. Some of Muhave's neighbors had started to demolish their own homes in order to save building materials.

By the end of summer 2017, the demolition of homes in Roma and Muslim neighborhoods had spread all across Bulgaria, including two of the largest Roma communities in the country: Zaharna Fabrika in Sofia and Pobeda in Burgas. Displacements were accompanied by accounts of unchecked violence—in some instances instigated by the police and in others by fascist formations close to the ruling coalition government. Municipal authorities were told to focus on "cleaning" and fencing their towns and cities. At the Bulgarian National Assembly, members from a wide range of political parties, from the right to the left, sought to capitalize on widespread racist rallies. Angel Dzhambazki, from the far-right Bulgarian National Movement Party (IMRO) then in the governing coalition, called for the euthanizing of those arrested in the Asenovgrad incident. Ivo Hristov, from the opposition Bulgarian Socialist Party "for Bulgaria," after arguing that the "gypsy enclaves" were a demographic "explosive material" that were "threatening Bulgarian national security" as they had also become the "hearth of Islamic fundamentalism in Bulgaria," commented that, like the Albanians in Yugoslavia, the Roma are the "capsule detonator that is going to blow up Bulgaria" (National Assembly of the Republic of Bulgaria 2017). That phrase—"Albanians in Yugoslavia"—referred to an earlier public concern prevalent in socialist Yugoslavia about the fast demographic growth of Albanians considered by both socialists and nationalists alike as a strategic move by Albanians to claim Kosovo in the future.

The demographic threat debates, reminiscent of the discourse during the disintegration of neighboring Yugoslavia, appeared on the Bulgarian national stage as the EU was lifting work restrictions on Bulgarians and an exodus of highly skilled Bulgarian workers combined with overall decline in birth rates resulted in a drastic population drop. With the arrival of Syrian refugees seeking passage through the Balkan route, political parties began fomenting a "de-Bulgarianization" panic by combining selective data sets to show a rise in Muslim, Roma, and Turkish minorities and a decline in white Bulgarians. In the media, intellectuals warned the public that the influx of refugees and the rise of minority populations would turn Bulgarians into an "extinct exotic minority," frequently framing the Syrian refugee surge as "a new Ottoman invasion." Meanwhile, the prime minister, who had previously praised the vigilante border patrols that had emerged to supposedly defend Bulgaria and Europe from refugees, promised to finish erecting a fence along the EU Bulgarian-Turkish border. Between 2015 and 2020, the government charted various demographic policies that ranged from defending the border and birth control for minorities to the infamous 2019 proposal by the defense minister Krasimir Karakachanov called a "Concept of Changes in the Integration Policy of the Gypsy (Roma) Ethnicity in the Republic of Bulgaria and the Measures for their Implementation" that called for free-of-charge sterilization for Roma women along with the demolition and displacement of Roma communities to training camps for "integration." The political manifesto of Karakachanov's party, the IMRO, which was part of the government coalition, also called for reservation camps for Roma people modeled after Indigenous US and Australian reservations that would generate their own income as tourist attractions.

Bulgarian and international media have for the most part attributed the escalation of racist violence to the "populist" political platforms that have produced the EU refugee crisis, Brexit, and the presidency of Donald Trump in the United States. Yet the slogans "For Europe" and "United we stand strong," like the politics of the Bulgarian far right, closely mirror those of the EU and the Bulgarian government, which launched its presidency of the Council of the EU in January 2018 with a call for increased border control and migration management in line with the EU-Turkish deal of 2016. A few weeks later, during the fascist Lukov March held in Sofia in February 2018 in honor of the World War II Bulgarian Nazi-allied leader Hristo Lukov, inspired by the US-based *Identity Evropa* movement, European and Bulgarian marchers carried signs that read "Together for Europe" (see figure Intro.2) while chanting for "a stronger Europe with strong borders."

The normalization of postsocialist racist politics has gone hand in hand with the EU and NATO's eastern expansion. The ruling coalition partners of GERB (Граждани за европейско развитие на България; Citizens for European Development of Bulgaria) in Bulgaria from 2009 to 2021, known collectively as the Patriotic Front—the National Front for the Salvation of Bulgaria (NFSB) and the IMRO—were all center-right

FIGURE INTRO.2. Neo-Nazi Lukov March, Sofia, Bulgaria, February 18, 2018.

parties with close links to fascist and vigilante groups committed to the Euro-Atlantic enclosure with stylistic rather than substantial differences. Bulgaria's politics are not unique to the Balkans and the broader postsocialist landscape. In Hungary, Poland, Slovakia, Slovenia, and Croatia too, racist, antimigrant, and misogynist agendas align with political parties in power, such as the Hungarian government's policy of "procreation, not immigration." All have organized around the idea of a united Europe under threat of demographic decline because of an influx of migrants and Muslims, ideas generally recuperated by World War II anti-Semitic heroes renewed after socialism. Much like the EU, they invoke Europe as a postnational Pan-European geopolitical entity tied by common history and geography and defined through race and religion. Far from being "Eurosceptics," they consider their postsocialist integration into Euro-Atlantic security and capitalist economy as the backbone of their ascendance and see the sealing of borders as a fulfilment of a post–Cold War promise of a globally gated white enclosure.

The EU has exceeded their expectations by overhauling its asylum policies, which have now produced a public-private carceral conglomerate amounting to a growing industry that has bolstered its spending for border security from €5.6 billion ($6.3 billion) for 2014–2020 to €21.3 billion ($24 billion) for 2021–2027. A good amount of that money has landed in the hands of governments along the Balkan route accompanied by the European Border and Coast Guard Agency (known as Frontex). There are now refugee carceral camps in every country across the Balkan route with standard revenue streams from the EU that are funneled through government subcontracting of local and mostly private construction, surveillance, security, tracing technologies, and transportation services and the larger humanitarian-industrial complex that are meant to provide food, sanitation, and health and social services. The emergence and growth of a carceral capitalist conglomerate of policing, pushbacks, or confining refugees along the Balkan route go beyond the profit incentive that comes out of security services, processing suppliers, aid workers, cleaners, and cross-examiners to also extract precarious migrant labor underwritten by profit margins that are hardwired by the histories of racial capitalism and colonialism that constitute what Encarnación Gutiérrez Rodríguez (2018) calls the "coloniality of migration" of both EU and US geopolitical bordering of wealth and whiteness. Recent "rapid border intervention" agreements with countries aspiring to become EU member states have sought to negotiate their freedom of movement within the EU at the expense of policing the movement of migrants along the Balkan route: Montenegro (February 2019), Bosnia and Herzegovina (January 2019), Serbia (September 2018), and Macedonia and Albania (both in July 2018).

In October 2020, the EU contracted the state-owned Israel Aerospace Industries and Israel's largest private weapons manufacturer Elbit to design a wholesale drone surveillance system for tracking migrants along the Greek coast and the Bulgarian-Turkish border based on their effective use in the ongoing siege of Gaza in the occupied Palestinian territories. There is now an ongoing effort by EU officials to either cover up border violence by classifying migrant torture reports or attributing them to specificities of nation-state border policing as a supposedly separate realm of sovereignty. In one such instance, EU officials classified details of the Croatian border police beating migrants, dismembering their fingers, and pushing them back into Bosnia with shaved and spray-painted crosses on their heads so that drone surveillance could monitor their movements in the forest. In another instance Frontex covered up pushback images captured by its own surveillance planes showing the Greek Coast Guard dragging migrant boats into Turkish waters; Frontex was subsequently forced to release the images as part of an internal antifraud investigation (Christides et al. 2022).

The overall logistics and border technologies that have now come to dominate surveillance, incarceration, and the sealing off of populations into enclosures rely on technologies developed in settler-colonial contexts. Unsurprisingly, the United States and Israel not only provide examples for enclosures but are also front-runners in the automation of carceral regimes, having developed expansive industries that export services around the world. Crossing sites along former colonial zones of contact that are now seen as weak links of the expanding Euro-Atlantic enclosure constitute their main revenue. Rather than consider these enclosure sites along the transatlantic peripheries as mere outcomes of military-border corporatism or transient populist electoral platforms, this book situates the Balkan route in the larger context of the coloniality of racial capitalism and borders.

I started with Loznitsa as a departure point because I want to draw attention to how seemingly small and situated acts of enclosure around a Roma Muslim community in the outskirts of a peripheral Bulgarian town are linked with the ongoing transformations of Western "white replacement" conspiracies into Euro-American white enclosure policies. These transformations raise fundamental questions about the nature of enclosures, not only as contemporary coagulations of white, colonial-capitalist accumulation of wealth within Euro-American spaces through sprawling and interconnected border regimes around the US-Mexico crossing, the EU-Mediterranean passage, and the Balkan route but also as colonial formations of race bent on bolstering white demographics at its edges.

ENCLOSURE AS THE NEW GEOPOLITICS OF WHITENESS

The Balkan route has now become a geopolitical enclosure for surveilling, sequestering, sorting, torturing, and incarcerating migrants, part of what Achille Mbembe calls the emergence of an "archipelago of carceral spaces" across global peripheries (Universitaet zu Koeln 2019). While these spaces are now visible around the world, this book focuses on the Balkan route—not because it is a unique site of carceral capitalist regimes but because it is an overlooked site of connected global histories of race and coloniality that inform ongoing georacial imaginaries of a world-white enclosure. If the US-Mexico border has served to symbolize and structure the geopolitical racial frontier for the Americas, wherein the "Third World grates against the first and bleeds" (Anzaldúa 1987, 25), the Balkan route and Mediterranean crossing represent the "two main geographical, cultural, and racial threats [in] long-standing European tropes: one located in the Global South, with African migration representing the quintessential racial difference from white Europe; the other emanating from the Middle East, where Muslim migrants embody the religious/cultural opposition to Christian/enlightened Europe" (El-Tayeb 2008, 651). Despite attempts to understand the connected and global nature of these borders through their "compartmentalization into nation-states," as Roberto Hernández (2018, 3) points out, they are "nonetheless refracted in our contemporary geopolitical ordering" as the underside of European modernity/coloniality (Quijano 2000; Mignolo 2002). Blurred mandates of white vigilante groups and the vectors of the state at the US-Mexico border, like the ones on the Bulgarian-Turkish EU-non-EU border, all form part of the geopolitical attempts of walling whiteness. The screams of "you will not replace us" in Charlottesville, Virginia, and the panic over the changing demographics in Europe and the United

States are not simply the percolation of fears about "white extinction" but the logic of worldwide white supremacy preemptively legitimizing the violence that this fear unleashes. To the decolonial ear, the vocabulary and imaginaries that have accompanied Western millenarist apocalyptic declarations about the "end of the world as we know it" sound awfully familiar. Racist angst emanating across transatlantic territories tells us that the West is incubating new removals in order to sustain its white world b/orders: ideologically, demographically, and economically. If colonial cartographies inform the mapping of borderland zones across Euro-American peripheries, race functions as "a logic of enclosure" as a "processes of racialization aim[ing] to mark population groups, to fix as precisely as possible the limits within which they can circulate, and to determine as exactly as possible which sites they can occupy—in sum, to limit circulation in a way that diminishes threats and secures general safety of the species" (Mbembe 2017, 35).

When white supremacists in the West make reference to the Bosnian and Kosovo wars—from Anders Behring Breivik's 2011 manifesto "2083—A European Declaration of Independence," which calls for the extermination of Muslims and Roma from the Balkans, to the Christchurch terrorist in 2019 drawing inspiration from the Bosnian genocide—all form part of renewed Reconquista ideologies that dominated white internationalist battalions in the war on Bosnia and Kosovo and saw themselves as the new crusaders and conquistadors defending Europe and Christianity at its Balkan borderlands.[1] Their race imaginaries are identical to border points policed today by Euro-Atlantic enclosure policies. Rather than suggesting these are entirely new political realities, I think through these processes in this book as expanded modern/colonial racialized relations of power because the ways in which these histories are reactivated today to remake race through the imposition of border regimes across global borderlands suggests a much more protracted geopolitical undertaking of white supremacy in both scope and shape, one unique neither to the EU nor the United States but part of a larger Euro-Atlantic coloniality.

White Enclosure traces Euro-Atlantic politics of borderization along the Balkan route as a way of bringing attention to peripheries of white supremacy, where processes of race and border making are intricately and historically tied to the ways in which whiteness and coloniality function within the inner core of Euro-American spaces.[2] It examines the integration of postsocialist people and spaces into the Euro-Atlantic alliance as a strategic spatial sedimentation of racial difference between the redeemable and integrable whiteness of the postsocialist former br/other and the irredeemable impasse of the postcolonial others. Here, the spatial integration of postsocialist territories into the white enclosure serves to both secure borderlands and recruit white Eastern European workers as means to tackle demands for cheap labor and the decline in racial demographics.[3] I theorize this process in the book as *geopolitical whiteness* or the post–Cold War recalibration of Euro-American colonial/capitalist race making in relation to ongoing territorial enclosures of whiteness wherein the Balkan route serves as a racial cordon sanitaire of *colonial difference* in the current geopolitical coordinates of coloniality. The Balkan route reemerges here not as a separate set of supposedly independent nation-states submerged in interethnic conflicts but as collaborative, interdependent, and protracted forms of modern/colonial regimes of power that facilitate the filtering of refugees for the Euro-American inner core through parallel processes of interpolicing their own racialized populations.

Acknowledged or not, postsocialist subjects understand that joining the enclosure comes with the mandate of supporting and sustaining white supremacy and defending its borders at its edges, its rhetoric of rights, its politics of racelessness, and especially its "fantasy of whiteness," which "draws part of its self-assurance from structural violence and the ways in which it contributes on a planetary scale to the profoundly unequal redistribution of the resources of life and the privileges of citizenship" (Mbembe 2017, 45). The frequently promised but continuously deferred state of Euro-Atlantic integration in the region plays out through various political scenarios, where the privilege of EU and NATO membership contrasts with memories of recent genocidal violence, postsocialist poverty, and the precarious position of refugees at their borders—reminding the remaining aspiring populations of the violence reserved for those who remain outside their gates. The mandate of policing the borders of the enclosure at its edges is thus presented as an auspicious opportunity to be saved once and for all through integration into white supremacy while also redeeming Euro-Atlantic coloniality in the name of ostensibly "regional," but actually racial, stability. That the left across the region today has become complicit in the enclosure, be it around small communities such as Loznitsa or around the Balkan route, is not because it continues to conceptually treat race as an outcome of capitalist exploitation or because it relegates debates about modernization into the safe socialist past where colonial institutionalized hierarchies of race go to hide their tracks. Rather, to confront racism politically in the current context would require recourse from the volumes of nostalgic attempts to salvage the ruins of second-world color-blind socialism as well as its postsocialist dead ends.

My goal in this book is not to suggest what such recourse might look like but to think *decolonial Balkan routes* through the perspective of racialized and colonized communities as front and center of regional histories and their connections to larger geographies of liberation. The main focus of the first part of this book is on those people, movements, memories, and methods that defy the increased violence of Euro-American enclosure along the Balkan route. The goal here however is not to "study or report about social movements, actors, and thinkers," as Catherine Walsh (2018, 85) points out, but "to think with, and, at the same time, to theorize *from* the 'political moments' in which I am also engaged." A great deal of attention in this part is also given to what Catherine Hall calls "reparatory history," as a way "to think about the wrongs of the past and the possibilities of repair" (2018, 203). My work in this context means not taking for granted the connections between post-Ottoman racial formations in the region, their color-blind and secular seepage into socialist structures, and mandates of modernization and their return today as raceless projects of Euro-Atlantic integration. Decolonial praxis has been foundational in reconsidering the Balkan region through the coloniality of power, being, knowledge, gender, and race as a way of delinking from the spatiotemporal coordinates of Eurocentric epistemic infrastructures (Mignolo 2007; Mignolo and Wash 2018; Maldonado-Torres 2007; Quijano 2000; Lugones 2008; 2010; Grosfoguel 2011). Madina Tlostanova's work (2013, 2012, 2015, 2017a, 2017b, 2019a, 2019b) has been particularly helpful in thinking from the ruins of socialist modernity and the uneven postsocialist capitalist development built on the precarious labour of racialized and colonized communities and industries that have thrived on their displacement and destruction. I am equally influenced in thinking through these processes in the global context of racial capitalism and the ways in which they intersect with histories of migration, racism, and carceral economies (Robinson 2020; Gilmore 1999; Bhattacharyya 2018). In this sense, I approach the carceral economies of refugee confinement and Roma displacement along the Balkan route not as a mere outcome of "neoliberal" or "late capitalist" austerity measures (Wang 2018, 19) but as histories of racial capitalism underwritten by colonial mappings of population, place, and time.

While the geopolitical designation of borders has been enacted by Euro-Atlantic security structures, their questioning on the ground has been generally disrupted by queer and trans people whose embodiments, desires, dilemmas, and destinations for a different and possibly decolonial politics of solidarity open new fugitive flights from the enclosure while also *shifting the geographies of reason* (Kancler 2016). These interventions are important, particularly since gender and sexuality have been the intimate jurisdictions of post-Ottoman and postsocialist "saving" missions, frequently by dis/orienting local populations toward the gendered matrix of colonial/modern power. Maria Lugones's work on the "modern colonial gender system" (2008, 16) and "the process of narrowing of the concept of gender to the control of sex, its resources, and products" (12) has been especially helpful in thinking through the post-Ottoman gendering of Muslim populations in particular, given their perception as bearers of deviant genders and sexualities. In the second half of this book, I look at how the mandates of modernizing and nationalizing post-Ottoman Muslim populations in the Balkans were not just guided by the geopolitical racial reconfigurations of the world but were also invested in ordering, secularizing, and sanitizing the locals through new social, medical, and educational codes that sought to create a distinction between normative and deviant gender/sexual embodiments. Here I look at how the racial reconfiguration of gender and sexuality served as spatializing and secularizing processes of modernization, where the orientation of post-Ottoman Muslim subjects toward Europe was contingent on the straightening of their ambiguous sexualities. My goal here is not to suggest that these were top-down gendering processes since emerging industrial elites were deeply invested mediators of modernity/coloniality. What I am arguing is that the association of sexual deviance with the Islamic past became the post-Ottoman modern/colonial imperative through which the Muslim man was saved and secularized by reclaiming and returning to his supposed pre-Islamic European/white heterosexuality. This post-Ottoman return to race through (hetero)sexuality has shaped modern embodiments of secular masculinity as restless and perpetual acts of chivalry contingent on overcoming the double temptations of the tainted past, deviant desires, and Islam. In thinking about the expanded afterlives and *durabilities* (Stoler 2016) of these modern/colonial projects, I am also interested in how sexuality reemerges in the postsocialist moment to mediate new saving projects through "sexual rights," this time not by promoting heterosexuality but ideals of sexual diversity aligned with homonormative Euro-American epistemologies and embodiments. In both instances, the subjectivization of borderland bodies through sexuality is not only "created by the emotional residue of an unnatural boundary," as in the US-Mexico context, but also secures white supremacy by seeking to straighten and sort out "the squint-eyed, the perverse, the queer, the troublesome, the mongrel, the mulatto, the half-breed, the half dead; in short, those who cross over and pass over, or go through the confines of the 'normal'" (Anzaldúa 1987, 25). Thus, the second half of the book links the geopolitical to the body politic by looking at how the enduring effects of colonial histories and racialized relations of power engender particular kinds of subjectivities through sexuality as the more intimate site, where Euro-American geopolitics are enacted in and through bodily b/orders.

"EASTERN EUROPEAN" EXCEPTIONALISMS

One of the premises of this book is that Eastern Europe is not an exception to but a peripheral extension of European coloniality. While the geopolitical mapping of a white enclosure has seemed self-evident for a while now, its actual enactment and enforcement across peripheries remains overshadowed by national histories and epistemic hegemonies that obscure their connections to modernity/coloniality while also making opaque peripheral movements and solidarities. Writing this book has required reconsideration of those histories while also paying close attention and tracing the reactivation of other, more reactionary pasts that have served the larger postsocialist and (post)genocidal racial realignment of Eastern Europe with Euro-American trajectories of "integration." This has meant working against the pervasive leveling of violence on postsocialist racialized communities as interethnic conflict while also acknowledging their colonial origins and entailments through decoloniality. But to think through decoloniality in the Balkan borderlands means to unsettle broader Eastern European exceptionalism about coloniality despite the fact that racial, religious, spatial, and epistemic proximity to Europe and whiteness has served as the historical measure of modernity adopted to racialize those who do not fit what Fatima El-Tayeb (2016) calls the "normalized, Christian(ized, secular) whiteness" of Europe. Both post-Ottoman and post–Cold War narratives of "unification" with Europe and the West remain potent narratives of progress whereby the racial and religious markings of the Balkans as European are understood as white and Christian, with the Ottoman and socialist pasts figuring as temporal misalignments from the European path. While attempts are made to continuously suggest the history of the region as white, there is also unsurpassable difference in the presentation of the local Roma and Muslim population as tainted Europeans whose integration into enclosure is presented as simultaneously desirable for security but impossible racially. Even seemingly "critical" accounts of the Balkans reproduce this spatiotemporal arrangement of race and religion, as is the case with the often quoted *Imagining the Balkans* by Maria Todorova, who claims that "the Balkans are Europe, are part of Europe, although, admittedly, for the past several centuries its provincial part or periphery" (2009, 17), a "concreteness" read through its "predominantly white and Christian" population (455). But this viability, legibility, and legitimacy of whiteness is confronted by the very existence of the Roma, of the Muslims and refugees, whose epistemic erasure and ongoing physical removal have been foundational for Euro-Atlantic white integration. Like European discourses of racelessness (El-Tayeb 2011; Bouteldja 2016; Dabashi 2015) that abstract race in the service of colonial amnesia, "the deceased 'second world'" (Imre 2005), is eager to exclude itself from its own colonial-present pasts. This is frequently done by projecting postsocialist populations as victims of Western European colonialism or what Tlostanova calls a "double colonial difference" (2009; 2015), which converges, and at times copies, Euro-American colonial categorizations of race so it applies to local racialized populations while also erasing the more complex constellations of colonial power and the ways in which white and Christian populations connect to European modern/colonial expansion. For this narrative of second-world color blindness and colonial-present past to work, there has to be a continuous erasure of Roma and Muslim populations in both the symbolic and structural sense. When Salman Sayyid argues that "the relationship between the emergence of Islamophobia and the crisis of Europeanness is exemplified by the way white revanchism has taken hold in East Central Europe," where "the persistence of Islamophobia and its entrenchment in public discourses throughout the region point to the ways in which it cannot be simply understood as an expression of prejudice" (2018, 435), what he means is that the very acceptance of Eastern Europeans as white Europeans and their subsequent inclusion into the Euro-Atlantic enclosure is conditional to systemic violence, assimilation, and genocide on Muslim populations.

With the racialization of postsocialist laborers in Western Europe and racist attacks on migrants and minorities across the EU, however, there have been attempts to address former Eastern European racism (Böröcz and Kovács 2001, 28; Račevskis 2002; Tudor 2017, 2018). In "The Unbearable Whiteness of the Polish Plumber and the Hungarian Peacock Dance around 'Race,'" for instance, József Böröcz and Mahua Sarkar illustrate how "the arrival of relatively large numbers of displaced people seems to have provided an excellent opportunity to the governments of Eastern Europe to stake out their claim, once and for all, to essential, unquestionable whiteness" and that "the discursive denigration of the 'Arab,' 'Muslim' 'migrants' "somehow shore[s] up the essential whiteness and Christian-ness of Hungarians (east Europeans)" (2017 314). These important interventions open new questions as to the extent to which Hungarian racism (for instance) can be considered a solely postsocialist phenomenon. The history of Hungary as a coconstitutive part of the Habsburg empire suggests the corroboration of whiteness is a historical formation of earlier Hungarian encounters with "others." The Habsburg colonization of Bosnia assured Hungarian and Habsburg whiteness vis-à-vis the majority-Muslim population of Bosnia while also strengthening its self-stylized image as "protector of Christianity in Central Europe and the Balkans" (Ruthner 2008, 8) against the alleged continued threat of an Islamic or Ottoman invasion. More importantly for the analysis here, given that the Roma were racialized before, during, and after socialism as "outsiders"[4] who supposedly arrived together with the Ottomans (Vekerdi 1988), to what extent were the racialized differences of the Habsburg empire decolonized during Hungary's socialism?

Hungary is no exception when it comes to complex constellations of coloniality in former Eastern Europe. The settler colonization of Kosovo by the kingdom of Serbs, Croats, and Slovenes after the Balkan Wars (Krstić 1928; Ristić 1958; Obradović 1981; Pribićević, Višnjić, and Vlajić 1996) relied on similar gradations of coloniality whereby the suspect whiteness and Europeanness of Serbs was validated by what Jovanović calls the Serb post-Ottoman "Reconquista" (2015, 95) colonization of Kosovo.[5] The nineteenth-century geopolitical mapping of the geographic, temporal, and racial borders of Europe that produced the Ottomans as an intrusion in the Balkans charged newly formed countries such as Greece, Bulgaria, Romania, and Serbia, and later the kingdom of Serbs, Croats, and Slovenes, with the re-Europeanization of post-Ottoman spatial and social relations.[6]

These racist worldviews that imagined the Balkans as the borderland battlefield where whiteness and Christianity had come into contact with nonwhite and non-Christian populations and "Islamic" influences in the post-Ottoman era were not just European concerns; they were joint Euro-American visions of a what the eugenicist David Starr Jordan considered "racial unity" of all white people. American Atlanticists of this period, such as Carlton Hayes, Ross Hoffman, and Walter Lippmann, believed that Christianity was the glue of Euro-Atlantic white civilization and supported various Christian missionary work to keep its Balkan buffer zone white and Western.[7] For most of them, the Balkans presented a site of security in the emerging Atlanticist movement that would gain momentum in both Europe and the United States during World War I, when the Balkan League solicited their support by projecting its geopolitical position as a guardian of the frontier of the white race and Christianity (see figures Intro.3 and Intro.4).

While European powers competed for dominance in the post-Ottoman territories, US Christian missionaries carried out the groundwork of saving, civilizing, and, when possible, converting local "pure races" such as the

FIGURE INTRO.3. A 1913 poster promoting the expulsion of Muslims from Europe following the victory of the Balkan League over the Ottoman Empire after the first Balkan War. The poster reads, "The expulsion of Abdi Baba and Fatime Hanim from paradise." It depicts a Bulgarian solider of the Balkan League with a fiery sword treading on the crescent moon while chasing a Muslim couple out of Europe.

FIGURE INTRO.4. "The Balkans against Tyranny," a Greek propaganda lithograph published on October 5, 1912, celebrating the Balkan military alliance among Bulgaria, Greece, Serbia, and Montenegro days before their declaration of war on the Ottoman Empire. The lithograph depicts the subjugation of the Ottoman Empire represented as a green dragon with yellow turban and bearded face with white Europa holding a cross in the background.

Albanians back into Christianity. Eugenicists like Jordan, who argued that the white race would degenerate because of mixing without serious effort toward global racial unity, believed that the unspoiled genetics of pure white races in the Balkans proved promising enough to preserve them, noting in the *Journal for Race Development* that there was "a large hope in the unspoiled wildness of the aboriginal Albanian" (1918, 134). Jordan supported Woodrow Wilson's presidential run based on an account that Wilson understood this global predicament and saw the "racial unity" of Euro-Atlantic civilization along identical racial lines. Indeed, the independence of much of the post-Ottoman and post-Habsburg nation-states in Eastern Europe at the Paris Peace Conference was, to a large extent, a racial realignment of these populations toward Europe. As Robert Vitalis (2015) points out in *White World Order, Black Power Politics*, international relations as a discipline and the League of Nations as its instrument emerged out of US intellectual concerns over interracial mixing and an imagined domestic and global race war. The subsequent population exchanges between Greece and Turkey in the 1920s overseen by the League of Nations was guided by this new racist thinking that created "racialized alignment of different groups with designated geographies of belonging, such as the assumption that incoming Muslims from Greece belonged to Turkey and likewise that the Greek Orthodox from Turkey belonged to Greece," which "signaled a modern fusion of the eugenicist logic with demography, mobilized through racialized thinking and statistics, and implemented as spatial segregation" (Iğsız 2018). Hayes, the most influential of the Atlanticists, believed that global racial segregation was imperative whereby US borders should be understood and secured as an extension of Christian Europe. Following World War II, Christian Atlanticists "cheered the creation of the North Atlantic Pact in 1949, a measure that they generally welcomed as a formalization of . . . security" (Alessandri 2010, 55–78).

The emergence of European- and American-supported Christian states in the Balkans in the second half of the nineteenth century provided boundary-drawing blueprints that designated new European racial frontiers and naturalized a binary differentiation of non-European and non-Christian outsiders and European and Christian insiders. The racist imaginaries that informed early state building are visible in virtually all of the Ottoman- and post-Ottoman-era independence movements of the time. Contemporary Euro-Atlantic integration projects depend on, and deepen, such histories and are enacted as sequences of events that envision merging with Europe teleologically as a preordained goal. The racial stratification of post-Ottoman populations was particularly powerful given that it introduced novel biopolitical forms of governance, offering opportunities for nation-building elites to test modern approaches to health, education, sanitation, and psychology with the mission of civilizing, ordering, and orienting the locals toward a fulfilling European life.

The centrality of race in the world system that emerged out of the post–World War I Paris Peace Conference can clearly be seen in the commitment of Woodrow Wilson and his European counterparts to preserve the "'white world order,' with its colonial and racial hierarchies [then] seen as being under threat from revolution, anticolonial agitation, and the rising power of nonwhite nations such as Japan" (Singh 2017, 52). The solidification of post-Ottoman nation-states in the Balkans during this period sedimented a buffer zone between colonizer and colonized, between Europe and non-Europe, as witnessed by the exchange of populations between Greece and Turkey and between Yugoslavia and Turkey in the interwar period and during the first decades of the post–World War II period.

Presocialist racial formations in the Balkans didn't disappear; neither were they entirely decolonized during socialism. As Vladimir Arsenijević points out, in regard to socialist Yugoslavia, "Even in the best of times, [Albanians in Kosovo] represented primitive and ridiculous piccaninnies and Uncle Toms . . . total outsiders in and to Yugoslavia" (2007). While Yugoslav socialism sought to address decolonization—a subject that remains underexplored—racist presocialist hangovers were common—not just in Yugoslavia but throughout the socialist bloc. Their reascendency into late socialism and injection into the wider Euro-American "clash of civilizations" discourse cannot be dismissed solely as a result of the late- and postsocialist politics of nationalism and interethnic conflict. This is not only because such a claim invalidates the unequal and racialized position of minoritized communities in socialist Yugoslavia and Bulgaria but because it occludes the continuities between presocialist racial and colonial practices and policies and socialist institutions. Yugoslavia provides a good illustration of this, especially given its self-fashioned preeminence as a leader in international decolonization that emerged out of Bandung, Indonesia.

The Institute for Balkan Studies in Belgrade, Serbia, provides a telling instance of this form of continuity. The institute was initially established in 1934 by King Aleksandar I Karađorđević as the Institut des études balkaniques to script, promote, and proliferate an epistemic cartography of the post-Ottoman Balkans by copying European anthropological methods onto the kingdom's own racial others. Shut down during World War II, it was reestablished between 1969 and 1970 (Samardžić and Duškov 1993) by, among others, Vasa Čubrilović. Čubrilović, whose presocialist career included a memorandum on the *Expulsion of the Albanians* (1937), argued that "at a time when Germany can expel tens of thousands of Jews and Russia can shift millions of people from one part of the continent to another, the expulsion of a few hundred thousand Albanians will not lead to the outbreak of a world war" (Mestrovic 2013, 44). Čubrilović's statement and the trajectory of his career prior to and during socialism not only complicate the rendering of socialist Yugoslavia as delinked from its colonial histories but they also illustrate the colonial logic of racialization that was not the exception but the rule. Similarly, the beloved and celebrated Yugoslav author Ivo Andrić, who received the Nobel Prize in Literature in 1961 and was a Yugoslav ambassador in Berlin in 1939, advised the Serbian government to pursue "the deportation of Moslem Albanians to Turkey . . . since, under the new circumstances, there would be no major impediment to such a move" (Elsie 1997). That expulsion and colonization were articulated in the larger context of European-wide efforts to cleanse Europe of its racialized others illustrates the collusion of Yugoslav colonial projects with European processes of anti-Semitism and racism.

The protracted racialization of Roma populations across different (post)Ottoman spaces betrays the supposed racelessness of socialism. In Bulgaria, for instance, while the Turkish and Pomak Muslim communities were, at least formally, granted citizenship and the right to vote, Roma Muslims were banned from voting with the Election Law of 1901, which was followed by restriction on Roma organizations and cultural, educational, and religious initiatives in the 1920s and 1930s that continued well into the 1950s, at which time the socialist state started forced mass name-changing and assimilation campaigns under the banner of "emancipation." The relative failure of the campaign prompted the Communist Party to erase the existence of the Roma people in its official discourse, muting any mention or reference to Roma in public records and media and, in some instances, walling off entire Roma neighborhoods.[8]

The effects of presocialist institutions and discourses on socialist modernizing are important in that they reveal the enduring afterlives of coloniality and racism throughout the Cold War. They helped create the various contemporary trajectories that produced race- and border-making as primary mandates of Euro-American modernity/coloniality. Ironically, such attempts result in exonerating the socialist second world of its many contributions to the augmentation of post–Cold War Euro-Atlantic border security race making. In this sense, postsocialist nostalgia for colonial-less and color-blind socialist progress frequently ignores the consideration that "colonial, precolonial, and postcolonial epochs are all possible defining features of postsocialist societies" (Silova, Millei, and Piattoeva 2017, 11). But it also erases decolonization struggles and solidarities between the then second and third worlds that were not premised on normative Cold War camps but approached decolonization as Pan-Islamic liberation. Since modernization informed both Cold War camps, their common contempt for Islam would not only compete in the methods and mandates of modernization but would otherwise converge to globalize an Islamic threat. Indeed, long before the Euro-American "war on terror," the larger context of the Soviet invasion of Afghanistan in 1979, the Bulgarian forced assimilation and eventual expulsion of Muslim populations between 1984 and 1989, and the Yugoslav trial of "Islamic fundamentalists" in 1983, the socialist world developed its own versions of an "Islamic threat" in the 1980s.

On August 26, 1982, Radio Free Europe journalist Slobodan Stankovič produced the hour-long program "Danger of Pan-Islamism in Yugoslavia?." "Hundreds of young Bosnian Muslims," worried Stankovič,

> were sent to various Islamic centers abroad (like Mecca or Cairo) to study the Qur'an. Although many of them were party members, they returned this time not as staunch Communists, but rather as fanatical Moslems—this time not as an ethnic group alone, but, which has been even more dangerous for the regime—as Moslems by religion. So instead of studying Marx's *Das Kapital* or Tito's works, these young Moslems study the Qur'an, celebrate Ramadan and seem to be spiritually closer to the Middle East Islamic leaders than their own party leaders. . . . The polemics about pan-Islamism in Sarajevo are not over. (Stankovič 1982)

Drawing on the intense public debates around the influence of the Iranian revolution in Yugoslavia, a main concern in the mainstream media at the time—*Danas* in Zagreb and *Književna reč* in Belgrade—was that Yugoslavia had established a bridge between Muslims in the Balkans and their coreligionists in the Arab world, endangering both sides of the Cold War camp. In these debates, Muslims in the Balkans appeared as the weak link, or the "green transversal," as it came to be known, a Muslim-populated belt that linked the Middle East with the Balkans and was considered a geostrategic threat to Europe. Today, the same spatial coordinates that defined the green transversal in the 1980s and 1990s was renamed the Balkan route.

The perceived danger of Pan-Islamism that followed the Iranian Revolution would become the root of an alleged Islamic threat that would come to dominate late twentieth- and early twenty-first-century global politics. Muslim Yugoslav activists who, in the 1960s and 1970s, situated themselves in the larger decolonizing politics of Josip Broz Tito's non-aligned commitments suddenly saw themselves referred to as fundamentalists.[9] Relative state tolerance toward the Mladi Muslimani movement organized around Alija Izetbegović's Pan-Islamist praxis would come to an end in 1983 with the arrest and trial of Muslim intellectuals involved in what came to be known as the Sarajevo Process (see figure Intro.5). The trials produced a wave of anti-Muslim discourse in late 1980s Yugoslavia, which, coupled with the economic crisis, student protests in Kosovo, and Muslims protests against assimilation programs and pogroms in neighboring Bulgaria, resulted in visible anti-Muslim political activity across the Balkans. Converging with the early onset of larger global discourses on the dual threats of Islamic fundamentalism and the clash of civilizations, Muslims in Bulgaria and Yugoslavia, alongside the Muslims of Afghanistan, Chechnya, and Dagestan, became a primary site of the early globalization of Islamophobia. Recent efforts to shift the focus on the Cold War from the "two-camps" reveal "locally diverse Cold War historical experiences rather than one that encompasses this reality of plurality in favor of some unifying scheme of ideas" (Kwon 2018, 214–15).

Yugoslavia's commitment to decolonization in the nonaligned world does however complicate the questions of race, racism, and coloniality.

FIGURE INTRO.5. The Sarajevo Process trials, 1983.

Jelena Subotić and Srdjan Vučetić (2019) illustrate, for instance, how Yugoslav communist cadres were ignorant of race and racism in their pursuit of leadership in the nonaligned world. Yugoslav leaders consistently failed to understand the racism at work in global politics or their white privilege. Here too, however, racialized communities within Yugoslavia such as Muslims, Roma, and Albanians were conspicuously absent from analysis. Yet the question of the Muslims in Yugoslavia in the context of the nonaligned world was a constant source of headache for Yugoslav diplomats shuttling between Cairo, Islamabad, and Jakarta, where Yugoslav communists deemed the constant pressure by nonaligned allies to address the question of Muslims in Yugoslavia a fascist undertaking (Miller 2017). Unlike the solidarity of Yugoslav leaders with the Non-Aligned Movement, which evaded the question of race and religion, the solidarity of Yugoslav Muslims with nonaligned decolonial movements in the Middle East and North Africa not only acknowledged racism within both socialism and capitalism but they actively denounced it.

Izetbegović's *Islamska deklaracija* (Islamic declaration), written and published at the height of Yugoslav involvement in the Non-Aligned Movement between 1969 and 1970, rejected both Western interventions into the Muslim world and third-world "nationalist movements in Muslim countries that replicate the logics of previous colonial logics" (Izetbegović 1990, 27). Writing from Yugoslavia, Izetbegović chided both the socialist and capitalist camps for their competition over who gets what of the Muslim world. Izetbegović's concerns for the "suffering of Muslims in Palestine or the Crimea, in Sinkiang, Kashmir or Ethiopia" that "arouse feelings of dejection and unanimous condemnation everywhere" (1990, 24) would reveal the limits of Yugoslav decolonial solidarity. These were different concerns than those of socialist solidarity and modernization between the second and third worlds, suggesting a different geography of belonging, resistance, and liberation from that of Yugoslav leaders.

There were also instances when Muslims influenced and negotiated leverage among socialist states competing for "modernizing" projects and oil deals in the Muslim world. Bulgarian arms sales and health services to Syria, Egypt, and Libya in return for a much-needed hard currency and oil were frequently underwritten by promises for better treatment of its Muslims given the ongoing protests of Muslims in Bulgaria (see figure Intro.6) against the large-scale, violent assimilation campaigns called the Bulgarian Revival Process. Ironically, Bulgarian national air

FIGURE INTRO.6. Muslims in Bulgaria protesting the ethnic cleansing policies of the "Process of Rebirth" of the Bulgarian government that required the changing of names and religion of the Muslim citizens and their ancestors. The sign reads, "We want our mothers' names." 1981.

carriers provided transportation for Libyan Muslims to *hajj* while Muslims in Bulgaria were largely restricted from making the journey. By 1989, the Bulgarian Communist Party proceeded with expelling approximately 340,000 Muslim citizens to Turkey. In Bulgarian public discourse, this mass expulsion continues to be called "the great excursion," implying a choice rather than state-organized displacement.

The more worrying aspect of socialist racial anxieties, however, was demographics. A constant concern of socialist authorities and academics in Yugoslavia, for instance, became the "tribal" family structures and high birth rates among Albanian and Roma populations who were frequently subjected to anthropological and ethnographic research on understanding the undercurrents of high birth rates (Radovanović 1964; Golubović and Dimitrijević 1967; Lutovac 1977; Mitrović 1985; First-Dilić 1985). The "ethnopsychological" (Marković 1974, 99) reproductive role of Albanian women in Kosovo became a prime target for socialist planning and biopolitical subjectivization. Roma Muslim women in Bulgaria became targets of these polices, as they were seen as both racially and religiously incompatible with the broader Revival Process assimilationist politics. If the Turkish and Pomak Muslims were at times seen as redeemable white "converts" to Islam, Roma people were projected as total outsiders. Moreover, the fear of racial mixing and popular resonance with Roma music in particular was closely and obsessively policed by Bulgarian socialist authorities. The popularity of Roma music in late socialism was feared for not only diluting the supposed purity and priority of Bulgarian folklore but was also considered a suspicious movement for alternative aesthetics and artistic expression that were perceived to recover, resonate with, and blur the boundaries of "Oriental" afterlives that post-Ottoman nation-states sought to break from. Nowhere are these anxieties of enduring racism toward Roma music as the last remaining renegades of (post)Ottoman politics of personhood, affect, sexuality, visuality, and overall straightened and whitewashed Bulgarian subjectivity more apparent than in the postsocialist popularity of Azis.

ON BODIES, BORDERS, AND RESTLESS OTTOMAN AFTERLIVES

In 2007, the Bulgarian Roma recording artist Azis placed a billboard in Sofia of himself kissing his then boyfriend Niki Kitaeca, a billboard removed shortly thereafter by Boyko Borisov, then mayor of Sofia. This was not the first time that Borisov had removed one of Azis's billboards. Borisov's political rise from civil servant in the Ministry of Interior in the early 2000s to prime minister in 2009 was closely tied to an earlier controversy and political debates centering on the removal of another of Azis's billboards in 2004. Azis had placed a billboard that revealed part of his bare backside promoting his song "How It Hurts" near the memorial of Vasil Levski, a Bulgarian national hero who had played a central role in the war of independence against Ottoman rule. Responding to public outcry for the disrespect Azis had shown by exposing his backside to the memorial of Levski, the Bulgarian people, and the Bulgarian church, Borisov sent firefighters and workers to ceremonially remove the billboard. The spectacular scene accentuated Bulgarians' racial and gendered anxieties over the larger historical heteronormalization and Europeanization of Bulgarian society right at a point in time when Bulgarians were finally being accepted and acknowledged as white and nominally Western—the same year that the country had been admitted as full member into NATO and had concluded EU-accession negotiations.

Following the incident in 2004, the celebrated Bulgarian talk show host Martin Karbowski invited Azis to his show. In a setting that seemed more like a public trial than an interview, Azis was brought in to face Karbowski, the publicist Kevork Kevorkian, and the philosopher Ivan Slavov. The conversation was framed around conspiratorial concerns as to whether Azis had been implanted into Bulgarian society—if he was "real" or the product of some sort of a provocative anti-Bulgarian laboratory. Slavov had brought a folder with pornography that he had collected in and around Sofia into the studio, problematizing the rising interest in anal sex in Bulgarian desire and insinuating that the proximity of Azis's backside to the memorial of national hero Levski may have been more than accidental. Slavov argued that this was part of a larger conspiracy not to liberate people's postsocialist sexualities but to feed them raunchy Roma perversity. Karbowski and Kevorkian interjected with questions directed at Azis, who looked visibly distressed and under attack. Wanting to further humiliate Azis, Kevorkian asked him if he had done this because of an inferiority complex about being Roma. When Azis defended himself by saying that he was not ashamed of being Bulgarian, Kevorkian asked, "Why don't you say that you are just a *cigan* [gypsy]?" (Karbowski 2004).

In the middle of the first decade of the twenty-first century, the popular attraction to Azis was perceived by establishment Bulgarian intellectuals as a threat to heterosexuality. As a Roma and a genderqueer person, Azis became the ultimate target of racist and queerphobic attacks. By the mid-2010s, there was a noticeable shift in both the subject matter in Azis's songs and videos and the ways in which public pressure was exerted on Azis. While his songs and videos had merged the sexual with the social, public outcry against them had shifted from accusations of having destabilized society's gendered-sexual order to charges concerning the "Arabization" of Bulgarian culture (Karbowski 2015). In 2015 in the middle of the refugee crisis, Azis's newly released single mourning the loss of his lover—"Habibi," Arabic for "my love"—went viral on YouTube. In another interview with Azis, Karbowski was now less concerned with the subjects of the song being a gay couple than with Azis's choice of an Arabic title for the song, which was a gesture of solidarity with the arrival of migrants along the Balkan route. Why had Azis not chosen the Bulgarian word for "my love"—*lyubimi*—asked Karbowski? Sporting a *kaffiyeh*, Azis responded by arguing that love is universal and that habibi just sounded nicer. Upset, Karbowski lashed out at Azis, accusing him of Arabizing Bulgarian culture and of turning Bulgaria into an "Arabistan." "Don't you think about these things . . . in the current situation?" continued Karbowski: "You are a cultural model." "Yes!" Azis responded defiantly. By invoking the current situation, Karbowski was alluding to the arrest and trials of Islamist radicals supposedly funded by foreign Arab organizations. Those trials and public fears about Muslim and Arab refugees passing through Bulgaria later led to a 2016 national law criminalizing radical Islam. They were in turn amplified by the WikiLeaks release of US embassy reports of a purported threat of the Arabization of Bulgarian Islam, claims that a portion of Muslim migrants arriving from Syria held Wahhabi views of Islam based on years of Western anthropological studies published on the dangers of radicalization of Bulgarian Muslims through "Eastern aid."

In the background, increased public paranoia over demographic decline of Bulgarians gave birth to the National Cause Movement (Движение за национална кауза), which uses the shorthand днк, Bulgarian for DNA, and concerns itself with "the cause of demography and the DNA" or the genetic preservation of the Bulgarian nation. In collaboration with the municipal authorities of Sofia and the Bulgarian Orthodox Church, through their campaign "Do It for Bulgaria" (later renamed "Do It Now"), the organization encourages Bulgarians to have more babies in return for free Christian baptisms, IVF treatments, and various perks and packages from sponsoring companies such as Philips Avent and Bebelan. In addition to the campaign's racist undertones, various promotional posters on social media and the streets of Sofia targeted women with misogynist messaging to increase their breasts to "size C without silicone" or depicted storks carrying Bulgarian flags celebrating March 3, the day of national independence from the Ottoman Empire.

I want to return to Azis because there are several overlapping fears that he disrupts. His solidarity with migrants; his choice of a Muslim stage name in the backdrop of a long history of forced name changes; and his troubling male/female, queer/heterosexual, white/Bulgarian/ Roma, Arab/European, native/migrant binaries combined with popular appeal for his *chalga* music were perceived as threats to the racial and religious purity of Bulgarians. In an opinion piece in *Postpravda* (2016), for instance, an author bemoans his popularity: "How, over the past decades, we've strayed quite a lot from the traditional bagpipes and angelic voices of Valya Balkanska and somehow stumbled onto Azis—a shocking, perverse, ever-changing hybrid of a person casually jumping between impersonations of Rihanna, Lady Gaga and a regular family man." His comparison with Valya Balkanska, born Feime Kestebekova in a Muslim family, is meant to contrast his refusal to follow the good minority mandated by the Revival Process, whereby a good Muslim, Turk, Pomak, or Roma are those who retain their forcibly given Bulgarian names and aspire to Bulgarian whiteness and cisheteropatriarchy by disavowing their Roma or Ottoman/Islamic affectations, afflictions, and affiliations.

Azis's queerness is dangerous precisely because he gestures away from hetero and white orientations, not just in responding to relational, intersectional, or incommensurate differences that could be understood as reinforcing binary opposites but also because he refuses Eurocentric inscriptions of gender and sexuality. His moves and music touch a particular historical nerve with aspiring Bulgarian and Balkan whiteness not only because he attends to (re)stored sensibilities that he awakens with his music, cross-dressing, and dancing but also because he challenges the colonially designated temporal and territorial coordinates that produce categorically different people in Bulgaria compared to the refugees who pass along the Balkan route. That Azis is heard in Belgrade and Beirut alike speaks volumes of the common post-Ottoman affective and aesthetic commonality that challenges racial/colonial b/ordering. The pressure to distance refugees or face accusations of "Arabizing" Bulgarian culture is not so much about xenophobic racism, as might be the case in the inner core of Euro-American spaces, but is about refugees' proximity and potential to resonate with the local racial other, the collaboration of which exposes the fragility of the supposed whiteness of the Bulgarian and Balkan people. But these anxieties are not just aesthetic; they are also phasmophobic fears of the return of expelled Muslims from Turkey, and the Middle East haunts the settled stability of a "nation" built on seized territory and time—not only of those ousted from Bulgaria or the Balkans but also through recovery of forced assimilation processes that once seemed certain in their success to forever purge or purify the immediate racial other. More importantly perhaps, and unapologetically so, Azis opens up questions that threaten the silenced, straightened, and whitewashed status quo around the ruined and removed lives of queer, trans, Roma, Muslim refugees and returnees who lurk underneath the veneer of Euro-Atlantic modern/colonial b/orders of Bulgaria and the Balkans. Many of them, as Madina Tlostanova argues, "are postsocialist and postcolonial others at once who will always be excluded from the European/

Western/Northern sameness into exteriority, yet due to a colonial-imperial configuration will never be able to belong to any locality—native or acquired" (2019b, 171).

Throughout this book, I have relied on decolonial, queer, and trans traditions of geopolitical thought that conceptualize bodies and populations as key sites of global power politics (Anzaldúa 1987; Dowler and Sharp 2001; Lugones 2008, 2010; Puar 2007, 2017; Fluri 2009; Massaro and Williams 2013; Tudor 2017; Smith 2017; Kancler 2016; Rao 2020) and the ways in which racialized and gendered populations come to contest the larger security infrastructures of the Euro-Atlantic enclosure. Keeping in mind that the infrastructural war on minoritized and migrant communities along the Balkan refugee route, the demographic panic over the reproduction and multiplication of racialized bodies, and the targeting of the rehabilitative strategies of migrant and minoritized bodies are neither recent nor exceptional mappings of Euro-Atlanticist territoriality but, rather, expanded race-making regimes of modernity/coloniality. Bringing attention to sexuality in this book has also allowed me to a look at moments and circumstances when colonial contradictions generated new social and spatial relations by refusing to live up to white European expectations and orientations that seek to reinforce the patriarchy by reducing women's bodies to incubators for the sole purpose of reproducing the nation under the threat of changing racial demographics in order to preserve white supremacy. Further, decolonization, "as a transformation of racialized consciousness, is always contingent on the radical reconstitution of normative gendered subjectivities precisely because gender provided the grounds of colonial subjection through corporeal refashioning" (Khanna 2020, 27). Considering the gender/sexual embodiments that continue to trouble the flattened, whitened, straightened, and secularized sensibilities conditioned by colonial/capitalism binaries is therefore not only important in confronting the intertwined workings of racism with coloniality but also in thinking through them as generative spaces for survival, radical care, and decolonial praxis.

Part of this project then is to unimagine the national and colonial arrangements of sedentary, straight, and stable notions of space along racial readings of territoriality and temporality that make enclosures seem like the logical fulfilment of forward-moving European "integration." Critical cultural geography in general and Doreen Massey's work in particular have been particularly helpful in rethinking the seemingly fixed and stable spatial relations to race and coloniality along the Balkan route and in reconsidering space not only as "a simultaneity of stories-so-far . . . within the wider power-geometries of space" but also in thinking about space along "the non-meetings-up, the disconnections and the relations not established, the exclusions" (2005, 130). I understand this approach to space and the broader geography of the Balkans in this book not only as a locale of multiple overlapping territorial regimes and as an object of Euro-Atlantic governance and enclosure but also as a potential route for collaborative peripheral and borderland praxis of resistance and re-existence.

BALKAN ROUTES TO DECOLONIALITY

Among the millions of people who traveled through the Balkan refugee route between 2010 and 2018 were the families of the famed Islamic scholars Muhammad Nasiruddin al-Albani and Abdul Kader Arnauti. Both were the last generation of Balkan born *muhacirs*, post-Ottoman Muslim refugees who traveled in the opposite direction through the same Balkan route toward the Middle East from the late nineteenth to the mid-twentieth century. On the occasion of the opening ceremony of the Abdul Kader Arnauti Center at the Faculty of Islamic Studies in Prishtina in 2015, his son Mahmud Arnauti, who had now settled in Kosovo, noted that like many Syrians arriving in the Balkans, he was not a refugee but a returnee coming back to his ancestral home.

The Arnautis had left the town of Istog in Kosovo with the arrival of the second wave of Serb and Montenegrin settler colonists in late 1920s, just as the initial emergency "Decree on the Colonization of the Southern Regions" issued in September 24, 1920, by the kingdom of Serbs, Croats, and Slovenes transformed into a more systematic displacement of Muslim-populated areas through evictions and expropriation of land that was now legal due to the law on the colonization of southern regions promulgated in June 11, 1931.

Arnauti's story raises several questions related to theorizations of post-Ottoman Muslim populations through Cold War–area studies segmented into different Middle Eastern and Eastern European categories, separating common histories of coloniality and solidarity. In other words, the return of people like Arnauti, now reframed as refuges of the Syrian war, erases the continuation of what Encarnación Gutiérrez Rodríguez (2018,

24) calls the "coloniality of migration." Rodríguez argues that "migration regulation ensures that the Other of the nation/Europe/the Occident is reconfigured in racial terms" and that "the logic generated in this context constructs and produces objects to be governed through restrictions, management devices, and administrative categories such as 'refugee,' 'asylum seeker,' or a variety of migrant statuses," allowing for the continued coloniality of migration through the "matrix of social classification on the basis of colonial racial hierarchies" (24). The attention on the Balkan route during the refugee crisis as an entry point for migrants and a weak link into the infrastructure of the Euro-Atlantic enclosure faces a challenge in its claims over the Balkan route as white territoriality. Here, the seemingly clear metropolitan distinctions between white and migrant become blurred, which is why postsocialist populations are continuously inveigled to both historically and racially distinguish themselves from refugees, even when such "refugees" are natives, as Arnauti's case suggests. Muslim communities in particular are pressured to promote a racial differentiation of Islam to prove their white pedigrees. In December 2016, at a ceremony marking the establishment in Brussels of the representative office of the Islamic Community in Bosnia and Herzegovina to the EU, the community's newly appointed head, Senaid Kobilica, sought to ease EU anxieties over the potential mixing of Bosnian Muslims with Arabs just as Bosnia was being assessed for Euro-Atlantic integration: "Bosnian Muslims, as indigenous Europeans, are committed to cooperation. We would like Muslims who live in Europe to understand and accept that they should be more concerned about their responsibilities than their freedoms," so that they can "earn their right to freedom" (Kobilica 2016, 22). Meanwhile, the delegation head, Bosnian grand mufti Husein Kavazović, insisted that as "the most numerous, original, and indigenous religious community of Muslims in Europe," Bosnian Muslims are ideally positioned to contribute to the development of an *authentic* European Islam because they "never adopted the practice of polygamy or marriage between close relatives" (2016a, 7–8), among other reasons. In closing, Grand Mufti Kavazović reminded his audience of mostly EU and NATO officials that Muslims in the Balkans "are neither Asians nor Africans, just like they are neither Turks nor Arabs" but are white Europeans whose Islamic institutions are modern European structures established not by the Ottomans but after the Austro-Hungarians' colonization of Bosnia in 1878.

The first three chapters in this book question these racial affirmations of whiteness and their colonial genealogies and ongoing mandates by bringing attention to overlooked moments and movements of Pan-Islamic solidarity and strategies of resistance in the lager decolonization processes of the Cold War. Looking at the collaborative work of Alija Izetbegović and Melika Salihbegović, chapter 1, "Nonaligned Muslims in the Margins of Socialism: The Islamic Revolution in Yugoslavia," illustrates how subterranean and subversive movements with itineraries and imaginaries that exceeded the capitalist-socialist binding Cold War "choices" sought to rehabilitate colonial damage and transcend the modern/colonial matrix. By focusing on Alija Izetbegović's *Islamska deklaracija* (Islamic declaration; 1969)—one of the more iconic outcomes of these subterranean relations and reflections—and Melika Salihbegović's revolutionary work, I aim to chart the alternatives to postcolonial nationalism these two thinkers engendered. Their dismissal of decolonization through modernization as a continuation of colonial relations of power in the Cold War resonated deeply with the political struggles of Muslims across the divides and became part of the larger scripts of Islamic solidarity that emerged in the late 1970s and 1980s. Here, I think of these unfinished projects that emerged out of the failures of postcolonial modernization as part of what Robbie Shilliam (2019) calls acts of "understated internationalism" during decolonization, as the performances and politics of peripheral people denied their capacity to partake in normative world making. The second part of the chapter illustrates how late Cold War and early post–Cold-War debates on the "Islamic threat" reactivated earlier colonial borderland cartographies and geopolitical racial imaginaries of white world making, with the war in Bosnia figuring not as an interethnic conflict as we are frequently told but as a genocidal attempt to eliminate Muslim populations from European borderlands. I think of this structural violence on Muslim populations in the 1990s as an early disciplinary reminder to reaffirm their racial bounds to Europe through whiteness as a way of securing their very existence along the enclosure.

Enclosures are not fixed and fortified entities. Though that may be the desired outcome, their making involves evolving, interactive, and porous sets of processes in which the geopolitical order is continually shaped on the imbrication of colonial, capitalist, and Cold War transnational infrastructures and institutions of knowledge along the production and b/ordering of memory. In chapter 2, "Historicizing Enclosure: Refashioned Colonial

Continuities as European Cultural Legacy," I turn to the curation of colonial sites and institutions in Bosnia in the last decade to examine the ways in which the occupation of the former Ottoman province by the Austro-Hungarian empire is today integrated in the European common memory, not as colonization but as a collective cultural legacy. Here, I think how the postwar refashioning of the siege of Sarajevo in 1990s and the genocide on Bosnian people are not sites of continuous colonial/capitalist violence but are darker chapters in the enlightened history of Europe, products of colonial amnesia and re-Westernizing of Bosnian history, situated within the confines of Euro-Atlantic territoriality. In the first part of the chapter, I examine how the reopening of the Habsburg-built National Museum brings into light past and present reification of European coloniality in Bosnia as a civilizing mission aimed to return Bosnians to their pre-Ottoman and presocialist "authentic" Western historiography. The second part looks at how these durable colonial references function as conduits of imperial claim making that rely on securing and securitizing colonially sanctioned genealogies and categories of whiteness through religious institutions. Here, I pay particular attention to the ways in which the Islamic Community recruits and promotes its Habsburg colonial origins as religious regulatory practices that designate acceptable forms of local practices of Islam by policing and rendering illegal divergent Islamic forms supposedly imported from the "Arab world." In thinking through the various forms of resistance to these narratives across the chapter, I illustrate how collective and individual attempts to *shift the geographies of reason*, to quote from Tjaša Kancler (2016) again, evoke movements and moments in time when they were part of larger geographies of liberation. For most of these attempts, the revival of both colonial ruins and a reactionary reading of history have not only depoliticized collaborative forms of resistance through reification of "cultural differences" but have also allowed the suspension of sovereignty under the pretext of a postwar instability. Indeed, the deferred and fragmented forms of sovereignty in Bosnia (and Kosovo) today secured through international missions and mechanisms of control are neither accidental nor sui generis exceptions of Westphalian order but rather reworked racial configurations of coloniality through suspended sovereignties.

While these logics of worldwide white supremacy have similar functions across the borderlands of the Euro-Atlantic enclosure, the "national" specificities that dominate border studies particularizes them and makes

regional and (geo)politics of whiteness invisible. To focus on the particularities of Bosnia and Kosovo today is to avoid the larger regional politics
of enclosure along the Balkan route where placement under international
supervision of both societies is not so much an attempt at postconflict
stability but rather regard for ostensibly "Muslim" communities along
the postnational borderland are suspected projects of whiteness. Roberto
Hernández's work has been particularly helpful in not only thinking
through the Balkan borderlands from decolonial and postnational perspectives but also in comparing the connections and continuities of Euro-
American geopolitical border points across continents. In *Coloniality of the
US/Mexico Border*, he points out that the "framework of coloniality aims
to transcend the naturalised claims to national sovereignty and border
security by historicizing and highlighting the simultaneous 'national' and
global colonial episteme that underpins violence on the border. When this
is done, violence and coloniality prove to be central and mutually constitutive features of the interstate system, embodied at national-territorial
borders. They are the underside of the modern nation-state and modernity rather than spaces of exceptionality in a thickening borderlands"
(2018, 20–21). From this perspective, taking decolonial routes in the Balkan context means not only unthinking national historiographies and the
ways in which racial realignment with whiteness converges in a regional
resurgence of racist politics but more importantly it means situating the
region in the broader histories of anticolonial resistance.

    With that in mind, moving from Bosnia to Kosovo and Albania,
chapter 3, "Enclosure Sovereignties: Saving Missions and Supervised
Self-Determination" opens with the organized resistance against the International Control Commission deployed by European powers to install
provisory independence in Albania in 1913 in the larger context of post-
Ottoman reconfiguration of European borderland territoriality in the
Balkans. Rather than thinking of these political processes as competing
imperial interests in the aftermath of the collapse of the Ottoman and
Habsburg empires, as narratives about the First Balkan War suggest, I
am interested in European powers in this period deploying joint international missions, like the one in Albania, as early Atlanticist attempts
to claim the Balkan borderlands by procuring and secularizing post-
Ottoman populations and places deemed ambiguously European through
provisional forms of sovereignty. By comparing this twentieth-century
deployment of deferred sovereignty to Albania with contemporary forms

of supervised sovereignty in Kosovo, I aim to illustrate how the refashioned post-Ottoman collaborative histories of Euro-American coloniality are redeployed in the postsocialist integration of the Balkans to reinvigorate old Atlanticist fantasies of white world supremacy. I argue that the Euro-American mission in Kosovo installed after 1999 was not meant to generate self-governing entities or sovereignty but a subordinate and dependent polity. Such interventions, constituted as they are by military corporatism, are less interested in creating self-determination or stability but, like the International Control Commission in Albania in 1913, secure and secularize suspect populations around its racial and religious b/orders.

The recursive and cumulative effects of these histories of coloniality propel particular kinds of racialized and gendered power relations that come to underwrite all aspects of life, but at their core they all are a "dichotomous hierarchy between the human and the non-human" (Lugones 2010, 743) that seeks to make and measure the colonized and racialized subject against the white wealthy heterosexual male. Indeed, such racialized Albanian embodiments of manhood through heterosexuality first emerged with the European International Control Commission and became historically reliant on the active post-Ottoman disarticulation of all previous ambiguous gender and sexual embodiments. As I discuss in chapter 4, "(Dis)Embodying Enclosure: Of Straightened Muslim Men and Secular Masculinities," these gendered subjectivities, imaginaries, and sensibilities that were set into motion during the colonial encounter require continuous straightening and whitening of the contradictions and complexities of the questionable whiteness and suspect sexuality of Albanians in the contact zone. In the first part of this chapter, I look at how the construction of the Albanian male heterosexual emerges not only as the patriarchal prototype in defense of his nation but also as the forgotten pre-Islamic medieval "giant" of the white race. If the reenactment of race and borders through gender during the International Control Commission functioned to create post-Ottoman orienting technology toward whiteness in the form of male/female heterosexual/homosexual binaries, in the postsocialist moment, sexuality and sexual rights discourses become the progenitors of Euro-Atlantic orientations. In the second half of the chapter, I examine the ways in which the geopolitical enclosure of borders along the Balkan route are constituted and mediated through the modernity/coloniality of gender (Lugones 2007), where sex and sexuality are deployed as secularism to create acceptable queer subjects along Euro-American homo and hetero norms but to also divide redeemable postsocialist white Europeans from the irredeemable colonial, religious, and racialized others. Indeed, control over queer desires—rather by repression or Euro-homoemancipation—becomes the tool through which contemporary racial and colonial regimes congeal their global political power through queer bodies, establishing a racialized distinction between bodies designated for desirability and bodies designated for destabilization and debilitation.

The second half of the book that starts with chapter 4 links the geopolitical to the body politic by looking at how racialized and sexualized subjects are produced as objects of threat to *geopolitical whiteness*, particularly at its borderlands. In order to move beyond the dominant discourse in the Balkans, which otherwise limits our comprehension of postsocialist politics to those of privileged men and mainstream politics, in the second half of the book, I focus on communities and experiences rendered marginal in postsocialist politics yet have been the main target of racist politics. With that in mind, in chapter 5, "Enclosure Demographics: Reproductive Racism, Displacement, and Resistance," I return to the racist undercurrents of the "demographic crisis" by looking at the collaborative projects of Roma displacement in Bulgaria following the racist rallies against "Roma aggression" in 2017. Most of the political commentary on the systemic violence and displacement of Roma communities is still read as electoral propaganda and a "punching bag for social and economic issues" (Hruby 2019), as one CNN piece noted in rendering the racist rampage of home burning that happened in Gabrovo, Bulgaria, in 2019, not as historical organization of violence against Roma communities but as momentary acts of racist raptures fueled by populist politics. This is where geopolitical Euro-Atlantic enclosures of Roma neighborhoods are localized and racialized along the peripheries of Balkan cities. In the first part of chapter 5, I look at how the "demographic" threat from being on the borderland of transatlantic whiteness mobilizes discursive forms of racism to control and contain bodies that trouble b/orders and fixe identifications. Here I look at how refashioning racism has become a violent validating tool for the installment of postsocialist racial and carceral capitalism through the selective privatization of public properties through evictions, expropriations, and demolition, as well as assaults on racialized communities and refugees as a way of making and marking Europe's geopolitical border zones. Specifically, I examine how racist rallies against

Roma aggression triangulate demographic threats from Islamization, migration, and Arabization to ratify evictions and the destruction of homes and communities while simultaneously monitoring and managing birth rates, desire, lives, damage, and death.

That these processes today are referenced in historical accounts of the post-Ottoman Bulgarian nationalist narratives of Western salvation from the clutches of "Ottoman oppression" only serve to reinforce Bulgaria as a historical site of struggle for white security and supremacy. Here, I look at how the political framing of these actions today as historical defenses of the West at its fringes have made the Bulgarian government a model for many fascist groups around Europe that have come to see Bulgaria, and the Balkan borderlands more broadly, as successful in unapologetically articulating white supremacy in relation to demography and border security. In the second half of this chapter, I look at music as a productive site of queer antiracist resistance. Here, I interpret Azis's music as an overlap and intersection of post-Ottoman and postsocialist pop that not only confronts heteroracist hate but unearths and curates restless spectral embodiments of buried pasts that, in refusing to retreat, challenge, and scathe the coherent racial classification of the spatial and temporal anchors of Bulgarian racism. Azis's interventions are not so much guided by a desire to deconstruct or reconstruct the world, a kind of world making that always extends and expands metropolitan coloniality even when it claims to unmake the world (Bhattacharyya 2019). Rather, his music and wit reach out for what is already there, celebrating Roma, queer, and refugee survival in the face of always-immediate borderland violence. Thinking through these new anatomies of antiracist politics that contest the material and epistemic violence of the enclosure may be just one of way of closing in on whiteness from its global peripheries just as undercommons expose the cracks and fissures in its metropoles.

A NOTE ON POSITIONALITY

I grew up in a Bektashi Albanian family in Lake Prespa, Macedonia (also known as Former Yugoslav Republic of Macedonia and more recently North Macedonia). In 1997, I moved from Macedonia to Michigan and enrolled at Henry Ford Community College while living with my extended family who had had immigrated to the city of Dearborn in the 1960s. Dearborn was predominantly white up to the late 1970s because of the outright segregationist commitments of its mayor Orville Hubbart to "keep Dearborn clean." With the arrival of displaced migrants from the 1991 Gulf War, Dearborn had a decent claim to be the Muslim capital of the United States. The real Muslim capital of the United States, however, remains Detroit, Michigan, which continues to be segregated from Dearborn spatially, politically, and economically. Once one reaches downtown Detroit from Michigan Avenue, the city unfolds itself *in the break*, to borrow from Fred Moten (2003). The impoverished outskirts of anti-Black violence are united at the Renaissance Center and encircle with the bizarre futurist People Mover—both neoliberal projects from the 1990s designed to attract white people downtown. Meanwhile, the Michigan Central Station, built between 1912 and 1913, looms in the background as a massive exemplar of modernist settler style, now a toxic testament to its failed industrialist aspirations. In the late 1990s, graffiti on Michigan Avenue near the rebuilt Tigers stadium read, "Detroit is black, or it ain't." Perhaps this was a response to the hipsters who had already laid eyes on the city for its cheap land and postindustrial ruins.

In Detroit, Islam was in the grip of what Sherman Abdul Hakim Jackson (2005) might call "the Third Resurrection," following the first and second resurrections ignited by the Nation of Islam—the movements that had produced Malcolm X and Muhammad Ali. For the first time, I heard *hutbes* (Friday teachings) on Palestine and attended *zikrs* (forms of Islamic prayer or meditation) at the Bektashi Tekke in Taylor with my relatives. Having grown up in Macedonia, I could not help seeing the similarities of spatial segregation in Detroit and Skopje as I moved in and around the city. It was in and through Detroit that I came to notice that the way race defines the increasingly cordoned-off enclosures of wealth and whiteness in American and European urban spaces is synonymous with the cordoning of the post–Cold War Euro-Atlantic geopolitical border regions and regimes.

When I arrived in Michigan, I enrolled in political science and international relations courses, landing in two fields that were flourishing in US academia at the time: postconflict peace-building and post–Cold War transatlantic integration. As I took humanities courses to fulfill my general educational requirements, I came across a different transatlantic history—that of the transatlantic slave trade, racism, and settler colonialism. The differentiation of the same transatlantic into two distinct and distant disciplines governed by separate spatial and temporal imaginaries and interests intrigued me. In the humanities, transatlantic studies were tracing the history of racial capitalism and coloniality that made possible the emergence of Euro-Atlantic modernity, if we understand modernity according to Walter Mignolo as "unfolding in the sixteenth century with capitalism and the emergence of the Atlantic commercial circuit" (2002, 58). In the social sciences, the transatlantic signified strategic policy studies concerned with the continuity of Euro-American global supremacy through the integration of postsocialist peripheries into the EU and NATO. The segmented and safely stored colonial and racist transatlantic histories in the past had seemingly nothing to do with the new post–Cold War color-blind and colonial-less politics of Euro-Atlantic integration. Never mind that President François Mitterrand saw the mass extermination of Muslims from the Balkans as a "painful, but realistic restoration of Christian Europe" (Branch 2010, 9–10). Euro-Atlantic integration and Christian European restoration that we were told had nothing to do with race or colonialism. Indeed, interethnic—and not racial and religious—violence was insisted upon as a way of leveling, localizing, and depoliticizing the genocide of Muslim and Roma people.

I was still in Detroit when the Kosovo war started in February 1998. In 1999, I volunteered and was employed by the International Committee of the Red Cross in Prishtina. In Kosovo, I had started socializing with queer activists organizing a community. As we had no offices, I had given out the Red Cross's office phone number so people could contact us. A couple of my friends had become regulars in the Red Cross office, sashaying through the "parachutist" foreigners, as we called them, teasing them about coming "here to help us." Shortly after, my Swiss boss told me I had to leave, because this was a neutral organization and I was getting too involved in local politics. In hindsight, getting fired from the Red Cross was the best thing that could have happened. Ann Marie Gayle, a Jamaican humanitarian lawyer from London and dear friend who had come to work in Kosovo, encouraged me to go into academia. I applied to whichever universities offered livable stipends, which, over the following ten years, led me to Strathclyde University in Glasgow, where I did my PhD, and City College of New York, where I completed my BA and MA in international relations. With the help of my Brazilian friend Antonio Da Silva, with whom I had done queer community organizing work in Prishtina, Kosovo, I moved to New York City. Along the way, thanks to my mentor at City College Marina Fernando and her daughter Mayanthi

Fernando, I read postcolonial theory, critiques of secularism, and anti-racist literature from Frantz Fanon and Audre Lorde to Ali Sheriati and Sara Ahmed. I later shared an apartment in Harlem with my friend Lisa Jemina Maria from West Papua, Indonesia. We were both enrolled in the international studies program at City College and were concerned with similar questions of sovereignty: Lisa through her studies on the West Papuan liberation movement and I through my studies of Kosovo. We had both been raised in countries that had positioned themselves as international leaders of the Bandung decolonization and nonaligned front with inconspicuous indifference to their internal colonial projects and struggles for sovereignty (West Papua in the case of Indonesia and Kosovo in the case of [former] Yugoslavia).

We found the Western canon and conversations dominating our curriculums, from Mark Fisher's blogs to Fredric Jameson's *Postmodernism, or, The Cultural Logic of Late Capitalism*, bleak. It was not that we didn't read them. We had to. But we did not find ourselves in them, as ours was an emerging world. We thought it was funny that in being assigned these works, we were being asked to immerse ourselves in nostalgic appreciation and mourning for the seriousness of Euro-American mid-twentieth-century social-democratic promise. We called them *first-world injuries*. I remember being assigned Nadezhda Mandelstam's *Hope against Hope* and Svetlana Boym's (2008) *The Future of Nostalgia* in one of my humanities courses at City College and found them ominous opuses on second-world modernity gone wrong. These we called *second-world shortcuts* or obscured histories and relations of power generally written to furnish Western academic curiosity for "progressive" reexaminations of Cold War "alternative" histories, where Yugoslav socialism figured prominently as the redeemer of the brighter side of modernity. In hindsight, they were not so much the funny funerary masses we considered them to be but canons of colonial knowledge that sought to reproduce in the reader a very Christian but ostensibly secular sense of righteousness by lamenting the loss of a modern white world as the end of the world itself. Belated as these afterthoughts came, in decade-long writings about socialist hangovers, decolonization takes work and time, especially when as a Muslim one has to sort through so much secular mythology and fiction particular to Euro-American academia. I like to think of this intervention as timely as once-racialized people in the Balkans are increasingly employed in the service of Euro-Atlantic enclosure with a tentative and tacit invitation to be integrated on the inside at the price of policing, containing, and blocking refugees along the Balkan route.

In thinking through Muslim positionality vis-à-vis white supremacy and coloniality, I have been deeply inspired by Salman Sayyid's (2016) call for *clearing* as a way for Muslims to think and act from a decolonial and autonomous position, as "Muslim autonomy requires not only Muslims to know their *deen* but also to know their history" without which he insists "any understanding of our *deen* will be stilted, and simply reproduce and reinforce Orientalism." Moreover, engaging with decolonial Islam with Sayyid is a process of both challenging "Eurocentric historiography and learning the history of Muslim agency" while also "changing the frame of reference bequeathed to us by the colonial order and internalized by the Westoxicated, and presented as the truth" (Sayyid 2016). Sayyid's invocation of Jalal Al-Ahmad's (2015) unfinished project of *gharbzadegi*, or "Westoxification," is in part rooted in a decolonial understanding of Islam that questions the binary Cold War "alternatives" for decolonization—socialism and capitalism—depicting them as two sides of the same "Occidentoxic" colonial paradigm.

Given that I am trained in international relations, it is inevitable that some of the ways in which I think of geopolitics are influenced by the absence of race in the field. Unsurprisingly, efforts to frame global politics as color blind refuse whiteness as a historically organizing geostrategic instrument by way of a "deep cognitive naturalization of Eurocentrism and whiteness," making the acknowledgment of racism as a "transnational *political* system" impermissible (Mills 2015, 222). In large part, this is due to the fact that "racism, capitalism and coloniality," as Olivia U. Rutazibwa points out, are "to varying degrees disavowed and erased in both IR as a discipline and public opinion" (2020, 222), but also because of what Charles W. Mills calls "an epistemology of ignorance" or "a particular pattern of localized and global cognitive dysfunctions [whereby] whites will in general be unable to understand the world they themselves have made." Mills's call for the interrogation of whiteness and white supremacy in both the global "assembly of white-dominated polities" and in "transnational patterns of cooperation, international legislation, common circulating racist ideologies, and norms of public policy" (Mills 2015, 223) has helped me conceptualize the instrumentality and history of racism in Euro-Atlantic collaborations. I was lucky enough to encounter people who helped me question, queer, decolonize, and acknowledge the complexity of my positionality as a queer Muslim cisgender man: when to speak and take up space, and when to step back and listen to the Indigenous people, to Black and brown people, to trans folks, to refugees and Roma people whose voices are the vanguard of what Catherine Walsh (2018, 34) calls *decolonial insurrection*. I am deeply influenced by Fatima El-Tayeb's and Houria Bouteldjas's work on the erasure of racism and coloniality from the European discourses of post–Cold War unification, especially in understanding the ways in which ongoing attention to far-right racist revanchism in Europe overshadows the systematic and structural racism that connects colonial and contemporary projects of European unification across the political spectrum.

Nonaligned Muslims
in the Margins of Socialism

The Islamic Revolution
in Yugoslavia

During the 1977 summer break from her studies in Paris, Melika Salihbegović (1945–2017) visited her brother, who at the time was working on a Yugoslav development project in Baghdad. Salihbegović had been a star student in Sarajevo, a poet, a member of the League of Communists of Yugoslavia and the Union of Writers of Yugoslavia, and a recipient of a state-sponsored study-abroad stipend for studying temporality in Paul Klee's paintings. In Paris, she grew close to Iranian and Arab students and exiles who introduced her to the ongoing decolonization debates across the Maghreb and the Middle East in what she would later recall as "those who read the Quran, those that read and thought in red and everything in between." As a communist and a Yugoslav, Salihbegović grew close to people who identified with socialist articulations of decolonization in the face of continued failures of the postcolonial pan-Arab nationalism that had failed to produce revolutionary breaks with the past. She saw Arab nationalism and postcolonial nation-states as Potemkin veneers of continued European and US dominance over the Muslim world. On the other hand, Islamic-informed decolonizing orientations and takes had seemed too invested in recovering some premodern and precolonial pure Islamic past that she found essentialist—not only because she had grown up in socialist Yugoslavia where religion was seen as perpetually reactionary but also, as she later came to believe, because she had come from a Muslim family that in their secularization process had tried to rid themselves of anything that would have rendered them less modern than the socialist society they lived in. Her meeting with Abdelkebir Khatibi, who introduced her to Ali Sheriati's *Red Shi'ism*, would have her reconsider Islam beyond what she had been taught to think of as "religion" confined to the Marxist reading of "religion." Sheriati's and Khatibi's work would inspire her to take the trip to Iraq, which she would later recall as her first *ziyarat*.

In her ziyarat in Iraq, she visited Najaf, Samarra, and Kadhimiya, but on a trip to Imam Hussein's shrine in Karbala, she resolved to embrace the wholeness of Islamic life. Upon her return to Yugoslavia, she decided to wear the chador and hand in her membership card to the League of Communists of Yugoslavia. This would result in a series of challenges for her, given that the veil had been banned in Yugoslavia in the 1950s and because, more importantly, she argued, "socialist authorities were afraid of intellectual women returning to Islam" (Melika Salihbegović, interviewed by Piro Rexhepi, July 20, 2015). As a consequence, she was persistently ordered by officials to remove her veil, threatened multiple times to be discharged from work, subjected to legal prosecution, and threatened daily for speaking out against the discrimination of Muslims in Yugoslavia. In the late 1970s, she grew close to a circle of Muslim activists around Alija Izetbegović whose *Islamic Declaration* had been circulating among Muslim activists in Yugoslavia and around the world for a decade. In 1980, resolved to join the Iranian Revolution, she wrote a letter to Ayatollah Khomeini asking for permission to move to Iran.

On March 23, 1983, Yugoslav security forces raided her apartment and found the personal letter she had written to Khomeini asking for permission to move to Iran. Her then six-year-old son who lived with her in her apartment on Albanska Street in Sarajevo remembers state security agents breaking into their apartment at 5 a.m.: "I [ran] to the door thinking it was my mother's friend, the poet Abdulla Sidran who would sometimes end up at our place drunk as he was from nights out, only to discover about ten people in civilian clothes arresting my mother and unfurling everything in the apartment" (Amir Knežević, interviewed by Piro Rexhepi,

July 31, 2017). In the letter to Khomeini, Salihbegović had written that "the Islamic Revolution came to restore my strength and my hope that it is still possible to live somewhere in this world in the wholeness of Islamic life." While under arrest, she was dismissed from work, expelled from the Union of Writers of Yugoslavia, and, along with twelve other activists, was arrested and tried on March 23, 1983, for having propagated the establishment of a global Islamic state and for having engaged in hostile activities against the state. Yugoslav and local media would cover the trial with headlines like "The Dark Refrains of an Enemy Group" (Oslobođenje 1983b) and "Ghosts of the Past in a Terrorist Coat" (Oslobođenje 1983a). In her deposition, in response to charges brought against her by the Socialist Federal Republic of Yugoslavia, she asked the court to consider why she would ask Khomeini if he would permit her to move to Iran if she intended hostility against the state (interview with author). Her sympathy for the conditions of fellow Muslims across the socialist and postcolonial world was also held against her as an attempt to destroy the brotherhood and unity of socialist Yugoslavia as well compromise Yugoslavia's standing in the Non-Aligned Movement. Sentenced to five years in prison, Salihbegović would be released in 1985 after a seventy-three-day hunger strike.

In 1988, under a general Yugoslav amnesty for political prisoners, the rest of the members of the Sarajevo Process were also released from prison. By this time, Muslims in Yugoslavia had gone from being treated as nonaligned tokens to being projected as traitors, constituting an internal threat to Yugoslavia. The anti-Muslim rhetoric in Yugoslavia was not detached from an emerging regional and global trend manifesting in both Cold War camps. In Bulgaria, as in Yugoslavia, these supposed threats would be characterized and historicized in terms of the long-standing threat of Islamic/Ottoman invasion. Meanwhile, Muslim activists saw themselves as part of a larger revival of decolonizing efforts across the Global South. Careful not to be associated with a dissident liberal movement that saw the resolution of the late socialist crisis in the integration of postsocialist spaces into the emerging European economic community with which Yugoslavia had entered into a cooperation in 1980, people like Salihbegović, particularly Alija Izetbegović, would draw attention to ongoing violence of Indigenous people and people of color who were frequently rendered invisible in the overall pro-European movements of the time. Izetbegović's universalization of the challenges Muslims faced in Yugoslavia was inspired by the Islamic intelligentsia that emerged in Iran in the 1960s, particularly Jalal Al-e Ahmad and Ali Shariati, the foundational thinkers of the Islamic Revolution, who saw the struggle for liberation not along national but international anti-imperialist lines. In his *Islamic Declaration* published in 1970 and translated into Arabic, Persian, Turkish, Albanian, and Russian, Izetbegović would argue that the postcolonial condition of Muslim people had been replaced by a new form of subjugation, where "capital on the one hand and ideology on the other have replaced the colonial armies, with the same goal of subjecting Muslims in spiritual infirmity and material and political dependency" (Izetbegović 1990, 49).

While most current debates foreground the ongoing proliferation of racism in Eastern Europe as a postsocialist phenomenon, this chapter explores how early twentieth-century racialized religious hierarchies in the Balkans informed and influenced the socialist geopolitics of race and religion. Problematizing putative socialist-era color blindness and examining their entailments in contemporary postsocialist politics in the first part of the chapter, I provide examples of the manifold ways in which socialist states subsumed racialized realities under class, frequently delinking early twentieth-century connectivities and continuities of coloniality and race within socialist states and societies. Here, I chronicle the complex conflicts and cooperation characterizing Yugoslav socialist Pan-Islamism and its role and influence in the larger decolonial debates in the Muslim world, from Alija Izetbegović's *Islamic Declaration* to the eventual arrest and trial of Muslim activists in what came to be known as the Sarajevo Process of 1983.

The chapter closes with an overview of how these debates converged with the early onset of larger global threats of Islamic fundamentalism and their disastrous effect on the wars in Bosnia and Kosovo. Looking at the emergence of the Islamic threat as a geopolitical constellation that would designate the Balkans as a potential gateway into Europe, the chapter illustrates how contemporary readings of late socialism elide the structural racism that informed post–Cold War Euro-Atlantic integration in the Balkans. In addition, the chapter interrogates the political itineraries of Yugoslav Muslim activists, situating them in the larger decolonial debates that defined the second half of the Cold War. Addressing the subject of an emerging Muslim International, one that was not part of the state-sanctioned, nonaligned conferences but was nonetheless made possible by bringing Islamic thought into decolonial praxis during the Cold War, thereby connecting the peripheries through concepts of solidarity shared by both Islamic and socialist teachings. Thus, the chapter examines both the oppression and resistance of marginalized communities in the 1970s and 1980s, highlighting the rich, complex, and multilayered connections and solidarities between the second and the third world beyond the official nonaligned lines.

FROM PEASANTS AND PROLETARIANS TO PAN-ISLAMISM

On a September afternoon in 1980, Melika Salihbegović arrived at a meeting of the of Communist Writers of Yugoslavia in Belgrade in her chador. In the Belgrade of the late 1970s and early 1980s, members of the Yugoslav Black Wave film crowd like Dušan Makavejev and Želimir Žilnik mixed with conceptual artists such as Neša Paripović and bands in the New Wave and post-punk scene such as Radnička Kontrola (Workers' Control) and Disciplina Kičme (Discipline of the Spine). Salihbegović's colleagues thought her wearing the chador was a performance piece. Yugoslavia was experiencing its most creative years just as the economic crisis was setting in. It was not just in Belgrade but throughout Yugoslavia that art, activism, and intellectual production skyrocketed. Salihbegović came from Sarajevo, where a neoprimitivist movement had appropriated Muslim urban slang and music from the city's neighborhoods for mass Yugoslav consumption. Yugoslav hippies had taken Muslim nicknames, at times mocking and trivializing the neoprimitivism of Sarajevo *mahalas* (neighborhoods), and jokes about silly Mujo, stupid Hasa, and naive Fata provided comic relief for the Yugoslav public from the economic crisis that had engulfed the country. Emir Kusturica made films, the rock band Zabranjeno Pusenje made songs, and the TV show *Nadrealista* would later consolidate the spirit of the movement into what became one of the most popular programs in Yugoslavia.

In magazines like *Naši Dani, Polet,* and *Ogledalo,* local intellectuals would consider, critique, and comment on the contours and aesthetics of the movement. For Yugoslav Muslim intellectuals, the movement "emulated what was being imported from the West under the cloak of seeming social and intellectual rebellion" (Džanko 1993), where Western new-age spirituality bizarrely merged with Yugoslavia's own stereotypes of lazy Muslim peasants who migrated into the city and refused to integrate.

Commenting on the Orientalist nature of the movement, the Bosnian philosopher Muhidin Džanko has pointed out how the movement targeted Sarajevo neighborhoods settled by Muslim peasants from Sandžak and eastern Bosnia, treating "the Muslim elements of these neighborhoods as a contamination of urban culture and obstructing all forms of cultural communication" (1993). The Muslim peasant was perceived as the carrier of Islam in contrast to urban Muslims who were considered secular, emancipated, and integrated but whose given Muslim names, which were not neoprimitivist sobriquets like the ones of the hippies, betrayed their coveted Yugoslav socialist modernity. Salihbegović's chador, however, was neither an act of neoprimitivism nor a rejection of it. In our conversations in her apartment in Sarajevo in the summer of 2015, she would note that she "wanted to draw attention to an intensified silencing and surveillance of Muslims just as non-Muslim socialist elites were picking up Islamic nicknames to both mock and trivialize our movement" (Melika Salihbegović, interviewed by Piro Rexhepi, July 20, 2015).

What Salihbegović considered the movement was not a coherent or specific organization that she belonged to, as the prosecutors of the Sarajevo trials of 1983 would suggest when associating her with the Mladi Muslimani organization and Izetbegović's followers. While she collaborated with members of the organization and maintained close comradeship with Izetbegović, Salihbegović believed that decolonization had to be personal and political, something that most of the members of the movement believed distracted attention from the larger political debates they wanted to bring attention to. Indeed, most of them saw her wearing the chador in public as a way of bringing unwanted attention by the authorities toward the movement. She would frequently confront members of the movement who were not paying enough attention to the classed and gendered hierarchies within Muslim communities, particularly Albanian and Roma Muslims who were considered not only second-class citizens in Yugoslavia but were also minoritized in the Muslim context. Bosnian-speaking, state-backed clergy dominated the dispensations of Islam and were frequently accused by Albanians of having a Slavicizing agenda (for more on this, see Blumi and Krasniqi 2014). Yet the differences within the movement were small, and the greater goal was to build solidarity and networks within Muslim communities, not only across the socialist bloc but among larger decolonization efforts across the second and third worlds. Part of this activism was simply visiting and establishing contacts with Muslim communities across the socialist camp but especially in Bulgaria where, by the early 1980s, reports about large-scale conversions and violence had been communicated.

From the mid-1970s to the late 1980s, nearly one million Bulgarian Muslim citizens were forced to take Bulgarian and Christian names. News of Muslim workers going on strikes brought enthusiasm to Salihbegović's circles, with Izetbegović asking her to pass around copies of the *Islamic Declaration* while on two trips she made to Bulgaria in 1981. She found Muslim resistance there organized around more direct forms of resistance, such as the agricultural workers spilling milk on the streets, workers putting broken glass in sugar at processing plants, and several arson and bomb attacks. In part, she believed the resistance in Bulgaria reflected harsh repressive measures as Muslims' adherence to their religious practices came to be interpreted, in the best-case scenario, as backward or, in the worst case, as a "sign of resistance" (Tahir 2017, 82). In both Bulgaria and Yugoslavia, Muslim repression led to the formations of small but strong underground movements. These movements were made further possible by the state-led exchanges between the second and third worlds. The presence of students from the Middle East, North Africa, and Latin America in Yugoslav universities in particular allowed Muslim activists to make connections and exchange experiences and literature. For Izetbegović, these connections were critical, as he would later recall in his deposition to the Sarajevo district court (Prguda 1990) during interrogations at the 1983 trial. Most of his reading material had come from his close friendships with Sudanese, Pakistani, Somali, and Palestinian students studying in Sarajevo, Zagreb, or Belgrade. Izetbegović wanted the Muslim activists in the Middle East and across the Sahel and the Maghreb to become familiar with the experiences of being Muslim in what was considered the better-implemented socialist project in Yugoslavia. One of the ways he did this was to always support his critique of both capitalism and socialism with examples from outside the Muslim world. Although his work was directed at mostly Muslim audiences, linking them to larger trajectories of colonialism not just in the Middle East but also in Africa, Asia, and Latin America, "he believed that most Cold War modernizing distinctions of developed and underdeveloped hierarchies were reproductions of the colonial processes that emerged with the colonization of the Americas and through the transatlantic slave trade" (Melika Salihbegović, interviewed by Piro Rexhepi, June 2016). This was also evident in his work *Islam between East and West*, where Izetbegović writes:

> History is being written by the civilized peoples and not by the "barbarians," and to this fact we should probably attribute the widespread prejudice that in barbarianism and civilization we see not only the extreme poles of social and technical development but also the opposites of good and evil. If somebody destroys a culture or performs genocide, we may call it a barbaric deed. On the other hand, if we ask for tolerance and humanity, we request the other side to behave "as a civilized nation." It is strange that these prejudices stubbornly live on in spite of so many facts that deny them completely. The history of the American continent alone could allow us to draw the opposite conclusion. Did not the civilized Spaniards (conquistador[s]) destroy in a most disgraceful and unheard-of way not only the culture of the Mayans and the Aztecs but also the very peoples of the region? Did not the white settlers (should we say from the civilized countries?) systematically destroy the native Indian tribes in a way unprecedented in modern history? Even in the first half of the nineteenth century, the American government paid a certain amount of money for each Indian scalp. During three hundred years, the shameful Atlantic trade of black slaves went on, together with the development of Euro-American civilization as its constituent part, ending not earlier than 1865. During that period, about 13 to 15 million free people (the exact number will never be known) were captured in a literal man hunt. Here again, civilized atrocity was faced with free and tame primitive man. In this context, we could also mention modern imperialism, meaning the encounter between European civilization and the so-called underdeveloped, uncivilized or less civilized people, but which has really manifested itself everywhere as violence, fraud, hypocrisy, enslavement, and the destruction of the material, cultural, and moral values of weaker, primitive peoples. (1980, 147–48)

Izetbegović, like Salihbegović, was keen on identifying the Cold War developmental discourses and practices in both camps as continuations of colonial projects that he believed required historical critique of what *human, civilization,* and *development* had come to mean in the modern world. In this sense, Izetbegović and Salihbegović were both influenced by Frantz Fanon's work, which, by the early 1970s, had been translated into Serbo-Croatian and circulated mainly through Yugoslav intellectuals who identified with the Praxis Group (for more on this, see Sabadoš, Gołuch, and Harding 2017). In the Yugoslav context, which is the position they spoke from, they questioned the centrality of Hegel in communist cadres without accounting for his contribution to racism and the justification of colonialism. Salihbegović remembers how

> infuriating it was to speak to Yugoslav communists, dissidents and "revolutionaries" who spent their time critiquing the red bourgeois, quoting Hegel and Marx but being entirely blind to their racism, which is why we had made a point of continuously remin[d]ing them of Hegel's racist views on China, Indians, Islam and Blacks. . . . I mean how could they read Hegel's views in the Philosophy of History that "there is nothing in the nature of the Blacks to resemble humanity" and yet rallied for socialism with a human face, we had to always ask them whose face? . . . how futile those efforts seem now as I am increasingly inclined to think that they were not so much unaware as they were and continue to be unapologetic about those views because their local and global political position of relative power were grounded in those same hierarchies of the human and Marxist humanism they proposed. (interview with author)

Exposing the links of colonialism and Cold War development, and the centrality of race and racism in it, was central in their critique of ongoing Yugoslav modernization in the nonaligned world that some of their close friends saw Yugoslavia as an anticolonial alternative to Soviet or US intervention. Salihbegović recalls:

> We wanted people in the Muslim world, and more broadly in the decolonizing world, who saw Tito and Yugoslavia as [allies] to not only know what was happening inside Yugoslavia itself, but also the Yugoslav approach and attitude to development [of] most of the non-aligned world was both racist and exploitative. Maybe some of those desires to "expose the enemy within" . . . we had learned from them themselves. Either way, our bigger concern was that while Yugoslavia was benefiting from cold war decolonization development projects, which some of my own family members were involved in, it was also contributing to silencing and stifling spirituality home and abroad. Not to mention Islam and Muslims remained a blind spot when they went abroad. Socialist states

were brilliant at propaganda in the third world. I remember meeting Bulgarian officials surveying their development projects in Libya and talking about solidarity with the Muslim people around the world just as [Muslim] villages in Bulgaria were besieged by the Bulgarian military with weapons coming from Vienna. The kind of anti-colonial nationalism that emerged between Tito, Nehru and Nasser became the secular stick with which Muslims were being beaten across the decolonizing world. In Yugoslavia, we were told that we weren't poor as Muslims because we were Muslims—since there was supposedly no such considerations in the worker's self-management structures—but because Islam kept us in the dark and we had to catch up. Time and again, this justification was served with two aims: to get Muslims to abandon Islam for socialist secular modernization but to also blame Muslims for the systematic racism of the state which was not so much formed as judgement but they really believed and saw the world through those developmental lenses . . . the parameters of this discourse ran deep to the point where we were ashamed of our own selves and we saw that shame among fellow Muslims across the decolonizing world. Just as we saw the racism of socialist Yugoslav officials a justification for our class subordination within a seemingly classless socialism, so we saw the racism of Yugoslav development projects in the world as reflecting the same dynamics. What drew me to Izetbegović's crowd, even though I never became fully a member nor am I sure that there was actual membership, was that they were not playing this game; they were resolutely speaking only to Muslims whereas a great deal of my youth was spent speaking to socialist cadres and being ashamed of who I was. (Melika Salihbegović, interviewed with author, June 2016)

Indeed, the feeling of shame was what Alija Izetbegović had set out to attack as an operating instrument of native promoters of modernity in the Muslim world who argued in the *Islamic Declaration* that the "self-styled reformers in present-day Muslim countries may be recognized by their pride in what they should rather be ashamed of and their shame in what they should be proud of" (Izetbegović 1990, 10–11). Part of the Islamization of knowledge and life that Izetbegović calls for in his *Islamic Declaration* was also meant to confront "the cold cynicism of modernizers whose short sightedness was keen on destroying real life, only to replaces with an imitation of it" (6). For Izetbegović, the *neoprimitivist* movement in Sarajevo

that shamed Muslim peasants was only the cultural logic of the structural subordination of Muslims. Instead of succumbing to its power, given the explosion of popular culture across the Muslim world, Izetbegović believed in embracing what he was being shamed for. The main priority of contemporary Pan-Islamism, he argued, had to be the "alignment of our reasoning with our emotions so that we remain true to who we are and what we want and not desire that which we are shamed to desire" (26). Most of this shame, he believed, was generated by postcolonial nationalism, which was misaligned from the folk-Pan-Islamist feelings across the Muslim world yet was not reflected in any practical measure of postcolonial Muslim nations. He writes, "What are these feelings never allowed to be uplifted for a common future? How can we explain the fact that news about the suffering of Muslims in Palestine, Crimea, Xinjiang, Kashmir or Ethiopia, trigger feelings of doom and condemnation in all of us, yet at the same time there is either no action or action is never in alignment with those feelings? The answer to this question is to be found in the fact that Western educated or Western influenced elites have promoted nationalism to the detriment of folk panislamism" (26).

The opportunity that many Muslim activists across the second and third world saw and sought in the emerging folk Pan-Islamism was largely inspired by the failure of Pan-Arabism and anticolonial nationalism in the 1960s. A failure that Izetbegović believed was a result of the immense socioeconomic division that postcolonial modernization had created, as well as the false debate of decolonization in the nonaligned world that centered on the false enlightenment of Eurocentrism where all futurity had to be debated in the conflict between socialist or capitalist development. Both Izetbegović and Salihbegović believed that one way to overcome this false but very powerful narrative was to appeal to and resonate with the affective dimension of Islam, believing that "Muslim people would never accept anything that is not aligned to Islam because Islam is not just an idea and law, but has transformed into love and feelings" (Izetbegović 1999, 10).

According to Izetbegović, a folk-led struggle for the genuine independence of Islam had to start anew and should organize around the love that people felt for Islam, among people in small gatherings, in mosques, in prayer rooms, in madrasas, and in all places where people came to find strength and inspiration from what he called the "indemnity of colonialism." Yet "the key, but not the sole, barrier to this project today is the conservative interpretation among the imams" who Izetbegović believed had not only monopolized the interpretation of Islam but had come under the direct authority of national governments. He saw the institutionalization of Islam across postcolonial nation states as a reproduction of religious structures articulated and assembled at the height of colonial knowledge-gathering practices deployed toward the governance of Muslim communities across the colonized world. This was particularly the case in Bosnia where the official Islamic religious community known as Islamska Zajednica Bosne i Hercegovine (the Islamic Community in Bosnia and Herzegovina), along with the ethnicization of Bosnian Islam, was a product of Austro-Hungarian attempts to detach its newly colonized Muslim subjects from the authority of the caliph. The critique of state intervention into the appointment and management of imams resonated deeply with Muslim communities across Yugoslavia, who increasingly saw and called out their imams for serving the state.

Yugoslav authorities denounced these politics as religious fundamentalism. On a visit to Bosnia and Herzegovina in 1979, Josip Broz Tito himself would alert the local communist cadres to pay close attention to their activities as well as the clerical circles and crush their networks "by taking severe measures if necessary" (*Borba* 1979). For the next several years, state surveillance closely followed several of the Muslim circles believed to be conspiring against the security of the state with counterrevolutionary activities. In March 1983, Yugoslav authorities arrested Alija Izetbegović, Melika Salihbegović, Omer Behmen, Hasan Čengić, Edhem Bičakčić, Džemaludin Latić, Ismet Kasumagić, Salih Behmen, Derviš Đurđević, Mustafa Spahić i Đula Bičakčić, and Rušid Prguda. Izetbegović's works, particularly his *Islamic Declaration*, trips taken to Iran by some of the arrested, and the various proclamations they had made in public and private about the conditions of Muslims in Yugoslavia and the world formed the basis of the trial and charges of counterrevolutionary activities.

In his defense against charges for hostile activities against the state, which the prosecution considered a call to overthrow the state and establish Islamic order based on his *Islamic Declaration*, Izetbegović spoke of his political work as transformation through Islam that moved beyond the state. The Islamic revolution, he said, was neither aimed at laws and states nor concerned with them—its main goal being to reach out to ordinary people (Prguda 1990, 57–65). In his defense, he reminded the authorities that the *Islamic Declaration* calls for Islamic renewal only when Muslims form a majority of the population and never when they are in the minority, which constitutes tyranny in Islamic law (59). Salihbegović's defense is significant, as it illustrates the broader political situation in which the trial takes place: "The last couple of years in Sarajevo [there was] a widespread craze of fear that 'one ghost is hunting the world, the ghost of Islam.' Islam is the milieu in which I awoke to my own intimate revolution. . . . I therefore warn the court that we speak . . . decidedly different languages here which you may not wish to acknowledge" (114–17). Unlike Izetbegović's somewhat evasive tone that sought to reassure the authorities that the revolution he had called for was not directed at Yugoslavia or states and laws, Salihbegović was less accommodating to the secular and socialist language and process of the court. Being the only member of the arrested group that refused any legal defense and renouncing the one that was assigned to her by the state, Salihbegović sought to expose the entire process as an abstraction of socialist approaches to justice while also attacking the court's and country's supposed right of religion. Discussing her expulsion from the Union of Writers and the state's custody over her son under the category of being "religious," she asked the court, "What is truly the right to practice religion? If I am prevented all religious attributes, is such religious practice to be enacted in some abstract private space but not in my creative undertakings? This division clearly does not exist but it is oddly the same one that my former husband calling on his communist and twentieth-century rights asking the court to take my son so as for him 'not to be raised religious.'" Salihbegović was keen on exposing the supposed public-private division in socialism by further asking the court what was private in Yugoslavia given that all her conversations, relationships, and records had been under state surveillance long before she had been charged with anything (115–16).

Particular attention was given to their national and international networks and activities, such as the attendance of some of the arrested at the Shiite-Sunnite unity congress in Iran in 1983 and various publications in the Arab press for "falsely representing the situations of Muslim people in Yugoslavia" (Salihbegović 1983). The court prosecutors seemed particularly sensitive to counterrevolutionary propaganda about the situation of Muslim people in Yugoslavia being published in Pan-Arabist publications. The charges brought against Omer Behmen, for instance, one of Izetbegović's close friends, included accusation of writing in the Pan-Arabist *Al-Arabi* in April 1978, with the help of a Sudanese student, in which he "questions the equality of all peoples of Yugoslavia and suggests that since WWII the state has attempted with all means possible towards the destruction of Muslim people" (Salihbegović 1983). Other members were accused of speaking openly about the oppression of Albanians in Kosovo and Macedonia and the overall impoverished condition of Muslims across the country.

Izetbegović would receive fourteen years imprisonment, the highest sentence of all the accused. From prison he would follow the unfolding of the Muslim question through emerging discourses that would stigmatize Muslim solidarity as a strategic security threat. Increased narration of acts of resistance across the Muslim world emerged as Islamic fundamentalism and Islamic radicalism. The increasingly hostile racism toward Muslim migrants across Western Europe in the 1980s, of assimilation and violence of Muslims in Bulgaria, and emerging reports of the beginning of sterilization of Roma people in Czechoslovakia would make him fear the worst. In a letter to Salihbegović, he writes, "We will find the world changed when we are released, and I fear, not the for the better. If we were once presented as comic creatures, now we are being depicted as criminals. You, myself and our friends know what this means on a personal level but I am worried that [it] is much larger than us or Yugoslavia, all of Europe seems to be engulfed in it . . . after the Holocaust, to many of them, we are seen as the last remaining thorn that needs to be torn, that needs to be ripped" (Salihbegović interview). Meanwhile, in his prison notebooks, he would note, "When we speak of European civilization, if exaggerated enthusiasm sometimes carries us away, let us remember that Nazism and Bolshevism were also products of this civilization. That memory cannot be avoided" (Izetbegović 2002, 58). Indeed, his prison notebooks reveal a turn toward the broader problems of colonialism and racism, especially how racism not only runs deep in Europe but reverberates across time. It was during this time that Izetbegović started to see the Muslim presence in Europe debated along much older anti-Semitic tropes.

In one of his many reflections on anti-Semitism in Europe, he writes, "Anti-Semitism in Germany is very old. Even at the beginning of the sixteenth century, renowned German humanists Reuchlin (1485–1522) and Urlich Kohn Guter (1488–1523) wrote piercing discussions and pamphlets against the Jews and advocated an imperial decree for the confiscation and destruction of all Jewish books. In this conflict, intellectual Germany was divided into two camps. The University of Cologne supported action against Jewish manuscripts, and the University of Erfurt put itself in defense of freedom and against any persecutions. This was more than 400 years before Hitler appeared" (Izetbegović 2002, 74–75). In many of my conversations with Salihbegović about Izetbegović's prison years and prison notebooks, one stands out the most: "When the push to get us out of here comes . . . by the mid-1980s we feared it might come to that, he believed that the only people that might attempt to stand up for us would be other colonized people but never Europe—Europe he thought would find it convenient that someone else would do the job that they've been wanting to do for a while . . . for him transnational solidary meant knowing as much as possible about the histories of colonized peoples and their ongoing challenges" (Melika Salihbegović, interviewed by Piro Rexhepi, July 2017). A daily practice was making entries into his prison notebooks about the history of other colonized and racialized people. In one of them Izetbegović notes, "Over 100 nations and ethnic groups live in the USSR, and they formally have their own national republics or autonomies. The Union contains fifteen federal and twenty autonomic republics, eight autonomic districts and ten national regions. In spite of this, Russian hegemony is felt throughout" (Izetbegović 2002, 63). In another, he writes, "Algerian poets are dissatisfied with the slow process of Arabization. They know what significance the act has of returning to their country a language that has been so cruelly taken away by French colonial politics" (65).

Having witnessed the mediatization of their own trial and the power of propaganda, both Salihbegović and Izetbegović were keen on being in touch with technology and how technology was rapidly racializing representation and resistance. From prison, Izetbegović would write, "First we had military-political colonialism, then economic, and now finally[] so-called technological colonialism, that is, the almost complete technological dependence of less developed countries on the most technologically developed ones. The gap is incessantly widening. The progress is so fast that particular technological solutions become antiquated in three to five years. Where are we?" (90). "By the time we came out of prison," recalls Salihbegović,

> we realized that a campaign against Muslim fundamentalists was being waged not just in our press, radios and televisions but those coming from the west [sic] as well like Voice of America and Radio Free Europe which we all listen to. When the siege, and later Srebrenica[,] came, we had already been circulating as a threat that had to be addressed. The entire

portrayal of the genocide on Muslim people as "inter-ethnic" violence that continues to dominate the narration of the wars in the West, emerged as we had no way of speaking, unless through those Western journalists who came here, not so much to save us as much as to save and promote themselves . . . my friend Baudrillard being perhaps the only exception. (90)

Indeed, Jean Baudrillard's commentaries on Bosnia during the war were so lucid that they require a reproduction in two long quotations for two reasons: (1) because they were so farsighted in their broader critique of the global racial regimes that emerged in the early 1990s, and (2) because they situate the wars in the larger geopolitical racialization of Muslims and Arabs, which is frequently overlooked as they predate the war on terror. Several months after the siege of Sarajevo in *Libération* on January 7, 1993, Baudrillard writes:

All the European countries are undergoing ethnic cleansing. This is the real Europe taking shape in the shadow of the Parliaments, and its spearhead is Serbia. It is no use talking about some sort of passivity or powerlessness to react, since what we have here is a program currently being carried out, a program in which Bosnia is merely the new frontier. Why do you think Le Pen has largely disappeared from the political stage? Because the substance of his ideas has everywhere filtered into the political class in the form of national opt-outs, cross-party unity, Euro-nationalist instincts and protectionism. There is no need now for Le Pen, since he has won, not politically, but virally—in mentalities. . . . It will end miraculously the day the extermination is complete , the day the demarcation line of "white" Europe has been drawn . It is as though Europe, irrespective of national distinctions and political differences, had "taken out a contract" with the Serbs, who have done the dirty deed for it . . . so far as the New European Order is concerned, the Bosnian operation seems set to succeed. The Bosnians know this. . . . They know they are doomed to be exterminated or banished or excluded. . . . The price to pay for modern Europe will be the eradication of Muslims and Arabs. (Baudrillard 1996, 136)

Two years into the siege, on July 3, 1995, and a week before the genocide in Srebrenica, his premonition of what was to come is probably the most significant account of its time:

No one dares, or wants, to take that step, which is to recognize, not simply that the Serbs are the aggressors (which is to state the obvious), but that they are our objective allies in a cleansing operation for a future Europe where there are no awkward minorities and for a New World Order where there is no radical opposition to its own values— the values of the democratic dictatorship of human rights and the transparency of markets. In all this, it is the question of the evil which is at issue. . . . We believe we have done all that is needful by point-ing to the Serbs as bad—but not as the enemy. And with good reason, since, on the world front, we Westerners and Europeans are fighting exactly the same enemy as they are: Islam, the Muslims. . . . In short, we may well bombard a few Serb positions with smoke bombs, but we will not really intervene against them since they are doing basically the same work as we are. (Baudrillard 1995)

A week later, between July 11 and 22, 1995, over eight thousand Mus-lims were killed under a supposedly UN-backed "safe zone." Baudrillard's accounts were an exception to the larger representation of the war in the media of the 1990s that increasingly labeled the conflict "intereth-nic" violence. Moreover, the arrival of fighters and aid from the Mus-lim world would merge the supposed Muslim migrant threat that had emerged inside Europe in the 1980s with an additional one emerging at its southeastern borderlands in the 1990s. A fictitious threat of a Muslim invasion, however, was not just a product of Huntingtonian clashes of civilizations, but socialist historiographies were replete with the Islamic threat. By the late 1970s and early 1980s, it reached its zenith of popular cultural production. In the 1980s in particular, films about the Islamic threat ranged from historical fiction to fictionalized histories that recov-ered Ottoman pasts as a way of reclaiming and reaffirming a new Chris-tian movement across the late socialist world. The most emblematic of these films remains Ludmil Staikov's *Време на насилие* (Time of vio-lence; Staikov 1988) . The film portrays the supposed forced conversion of Bulgarian Christians to Islam in the late seventeenth century, based on Anton Donchev's 1964 novel *Време разделно* (Time of parting), which relied on a falsified nineteenth-century chronicle of the violence Christians in the Rhodope Mountains endured during the Fifth Ottoman-Venetian war over Crete (1645–69). Released during the Bulgarian social-ist government's revival process discussed in the introduction, the film was meant to portray the forced conversion of Muslims into Bulgarians as a process of historical justice. Yugoslavia had developed an earlier, more advanced, and acrimonious approach to this cinematic genre.

Variola Vera, the 1982 Yugoslav film directed by Goran Marković, opens onto a street in an unknown casbah somewhere in the Middle East, where Halil Rexhepi, an Albanian *hajji* from Kosovo, buys a wooden flute from what seems to be a person infected with the variola vera virus.[1] In the next scene, Halil, along with other Yugoslavs returning from hajj, are showing their passports at the Yugoslav border with ominous music accompanying what the viewer already knows: one of them is bringing the variola vera virus into Yugoslavia. The story, along with a patient from Kosovo, then moves to a hospital in Belgrade where Halil reemerges, surrounded by a group of doctors who can't seem to diagnose his infection. Eventually it is confirmed that the patient has contracted the extremely contagious variola vera virus. The ensuing debates about the patient and the virus, delivered with subtle political undertones by some of the most noted actors of Yugoslav cinema, are replete with historical hints and national and geopolitical dilemmas of the time. An elderly doctor is invited into one of the meetings about the ensuing crisis, interjecting with authority what seems to be the indecisiveness of the younger staff who wonder if suspicion of the spread of the virus is enough to call a state of emergency. The doctor responds that "we must contain the region, with the army if necessary," stressing that "suspicion is enough to immediately occupy the entire region" (Marković 1982). The region, Kosovo, was being occupied just as the film was being shot.

Produced at the height of the Kosovo crisis, when the Yugoslav authorities sent thirty thousand troops to Kosovo to contain the April 1981 student uprising, the film assembles historical and aesthetic forces to create a politically relevant perception of the protests for the Yugoslav audience of the time. What made the film even more uncanny was that it was based on a real epidemic outbreak in 1972 brought on by an Albanian from Kosovo returning from hajj with the smallpox virus.[2] This modulation between fiction and facts allowed Marković to mediate multiple messages about that past, present, and future that are not only representative of how Albanians were mediated in late socialist Yugoslavia but became key features of fear, disgust, and pestilence. Marković's fabulation between the film and reality in Kosovo was conveyed through an ad hoc assembled central committee in charge of containing the spread of the virus, and its chair, who, in listing the tasks facing them, stresses "the second, and more important question" after containment, declaring "an embargo on all kind of information to prevent disinformation that could create panic and tension among the residents which can be used by the enemies of our country and our self-governing system" (Marković 1982). In the background, a corrupt hospital administration, incompetent staff, and deteriorating professional standards and divisions among them were all meant to depict a general Yugoslav political and financial crisis of the early 1980s. In the end, the virus is brought under control. Or is it? In the closing scene, the chair of the committee reads an award letter received from the World Health Organization congratulating Yugoslavia "for preventing a catastrophe of immense proportions at the gates of Europe"; yet even after the statement has been delivered, journalists stay around in a prolonged and uncomfortable scene as if waiting for more baleful news. The last scene of the film portrays the larger geopolitical position of socialist Yugoslavia—not of a nostalgic Yugoslavia wanting to be remembered as a bridge between the Cold War worlds but as a guardian of the gates of Europe in the midst of security threats about an Islamic *zelena transverzala* (green transversal). The green transversal, which would become a national obsession in Yugoslavia, culminating in Miroljub Jevtić's *Contemporary Jihad as War* as the national best seller in 1989, was understood as the Muslim-populated territory along the Balkans that today constitutes one part of the Balkan refugee route.

INSTEAD OF REPAIR: RACIAL AND RELIGIOUS
ENCLOSURES ALONG THE BALKAN REFUGEE ROUTE

Amid celebrations of the thirty-year anniversary of the fall of the Berlin Wall in November 2019, a video emerged on Bosnian social media of refugees being rounded up with police dogs in the courtyard of the former Bira factory turned refugee camp in the city of Bihać in northwestern Bosnia near the border with Croatia/EU. Encircled by large fences, the refugees ran in panic and were then force-marched as the police closed in on them at the gates, pushing them toward the empty buses waiting to load them up and send them to the refugee camp Vučjak. Vučjak is an old landfill surrounded by land mines from the siege of Bihać during the war and named by the migrants' "jungle camp." Around the camp, posters alerting refugees of land mines are meant to further limit their movement.

The video was reminiscent of similar scenes less than two decades ago of similar encampments that gathered the mostly Muslim population in busses toward the now infamous extermination camps. The Feminist Antimilitarist Movement (Feministički antimilitaristički kolektiv, 2019) condemned EU-sponsored "migration management" through the remilitarization of the Bosnian police by the EU. While EU representatives denied any direct involvement, police dogs and the training of Bosnian officers, along with new tactics to round up people, were part of larger EU externalization of borders and illegal pushbacks supervised by the European Border and Coast Guard Agency. The operation was a result of an agreement between the EU and the Bosnian government, signed earlier in February 2019, as part of the larger legal and political Euro-Atlantic integration reforms meant to "address counter-terrorism and radicalisation, but also transnational organised crime and border security, in line with the new Integrative Internal Security Governance model and in cooperation with the relevant EU agencies" (Council of the European Union 2017). The geopolitical imaginaries that have come to inform such policies rely on colonial and racial Cold War cartographies such as the green transversal, depicting Muslim-populated areas in the Balkans as a threat to Euro-Atlantic security and stability. Yet the new language has sought to conflate and associate refugees and the Balkan route with what the EU and NATO have termed the "crime-terror nexus." As Sohail Daulatzai and Junaid Rana point out, "'terror' talk" is becoming "the new race talk—the 'terrorist' (or the 'militant' or the 'radical') is the twenty-first-century way of saying 'savage'" (2015, 39).

Serbia and Croatia have used the refugee panic around Europe to launch similar attacks as those propagated in the late 1980s and early 1990s, projecting Bosnia as a safe zone for militant Islamists on their way to Europe. In July 2019, the *Jerusalem Post* reported that during her visit in Israel, the Croatian president Kolinda Grabar-Kitarović claimed that refugees were bringing Bosnia under the control of "militant Islam," with connections to Iran and terrorist organizations, arguing that although "nearly all claim to be Syrian refugees, most are actually African or Pakistani migrants who try to break through the border from Bosnia-Herzegovina" (Cashman 2019). Similar concerns had been iterated the previous year by the Serbian foreign minister Ivica Dačić on the occasion of discussing the new Belgrade-Sarajevo highway, claiming that the project would revive the green transversal, which continued to pose a security threat to the region and Europe as it spatially connected Muslim-populated areas from the Bosporus to Bihać. These debates are similar to those that Madina Tlostanova describes in Russia during the "migrant crisis" of 2015, where the "recurrent argument was that Europe should let in and venerate the civilized white Christian migrants (i.e., racialized post-Soviet groups) instead of 'Muslim savages'" (Tlostanova 2018, 34). Similar racialized refugee categorizations followed the exodus of Ukrainians following the Russian invasion in February 2022, where many Eastern European countries who until then had waged war on refugees at their borders, opened welcome centers to take in Ukrainian refugees while simultaneously singling out and preventing refugees of color from the Global South and East from entering their countries (Limbong 2022).

On the occasion of another rejection for EU membership for Albania, Macedonia, and Bosnia-Herzegovina in 2019, the French president Emmanuel Macron declared that it was neither Albania nor Macedonia that posed a real problem in the EU enlargement but that Bosnia was the problem. Bosnia, argued Macron, was a "time-bomb that's ticking right next to Croatia, and which faced the problem of returning jihadists" (*Economist* 2019). The projection of Bosnia as a threat to Euro-Atlantic security echoed the early 1990s when another French president, François Mitterrand, had objected to the idea of an independent Bosnia as "unnatural," being the only Muslim nation in Europe where British officials saw the genocide of Muslim populations in Bosnia as a "painful but realistic restoration of Christian Europe" (Branch 2010).

For nearly a decade now, the EU has sought various ways to block the Balkan refugee route, with Dimitris Avramopoulos, the European commissioner for migration, home affairs, and citizenship, authorizing the deployment of Europol in the Western Balkans in non-EU countries to "to strengthen the cooperation and information exchange on migrant smuggling and counter-terrorism investigations and activities" (Avramopoulos 2017). In addition, countries of the region were expected to uphold the Western Balkan Counter-Terrorism Initiative established by the Council of the European Union in 2015 to centralize information gathering and border security through the Regional Cooperation Council that would act as a governing body between local authorities and the EU (General Secretariat of European Council 2015). Yet refugees are only part of this security concern, as the "Arab" presence in Bosnia is considered a security threat. A 2016 report published by the Regional Cooperation Council, a member of the EU initiative, discusses the Arab presence in Bosnia-Herzegovina as a security problem, raising concerns over the "increases in investment and tourism relationships with investors of conservative styles of faith and dress (particularly from the Gulf states) [that] have recently increased visible signs of the new conservative Islam in many communities" (Regional Cooperation Council 2016, 27). The report recommends that the EU and local governments should "support scholarship programs aimed at confirming to questioning Muslims that democracy and liberalism do work for them, and that democracy, constitutional liberalism and Islam are compatible" (33).

Most of these efforts go above and beyond to project Bosnian Islam as a different kind of Islam than a supposedly Arab one, one that is not only racially and spatially divided from the "Arab world" but one that is also thoroughly secularized through socialist modernization. Under these broader b/order reforms, while attempts are made to suggest Bosnia and Bosnians are historically European, the local Muslim population is considered suspect and tainted, a population whose assimilation into Euro-Atlantic security structures is presented as simultaneously desirable but equally impossible. Indeed, the racial iteration of Bosnians as potentially white and European but not quite is concurrent with the arrival of other racialized migrants along with investment in the recovery of a European past in Bosnia has been given prominence in the political and legal processes that have accompanied border enforcement. Considerable attention on Bosnia's past as a colonial province of Austria-Hungary has been mounted to corroborate its present Europeanness. The EU has granted Austria, its (former) colonial power, a central role in the management of Bosnia, both in its ongoing civilian and military missions that were installed after the genocide. The current head of the EU military deployment Operation Althea (formally the European Union Force Bosnia and Herzegovina) Reinhard Trischak and the previous head Martin Dorfer are Austrians. The high representative for Bosnia and Herzegovina Valentin Inzko is also Austrian. Austria's colonial-era knowledge of Bosnia and Bosnians is understood as superior and relevant to its contemporary control, a knowledge system that has sought to portray Bosnians as racially white and European despite their *Islamization* during the Ottoman Empire. It is this colonial knowledge and racial realignment that Bosnian institutions iterate today to distinguish themselves from Black and brown migrants and Muslims passing through the Balkan route.

Building on Aníbal Quijano's (2000) coloniality of power, Encarnación Gutiérrez Rodríguez (2018) points out how new Euro-American migration regimes rely on colonial-racial hierarchies whereby "it conceives the Other as radically inassimilable, oscillating between the positions of strangeness and similarity" with "migration policies . . . [reiterating] such racialized objectification reminiscent of colonial times" (24). Central to this differentiation, she argues, is what María Lugones (2007) terms the "coloniality of gender," where "gender plays a significant role in the interplay of racialization and global capitalism, fundamentally shaping the coloniality of power within asylum and migration policies" (Rodríguez 2018, 20). The targeting of Muslim women's bodies in Bosnia, and the Balkans more broadly, has become a central focus of the racially configured Euro-American geopolitical b/ordering strategies toward the control and closure of the Balkan refugee route. These strategies have been operationalized through a diffused coordination of institutional and discursive practices that facilitate a gendered racial and religious differentiation anchored on the premise and production of Muslim women as susceptible agents of Islamist radicalization.

Attending the UN General Assembly in September 2016, for instance, the Austrian foreign minister Sebastian Kurz hosted a small gathering for Western Balkan leaders at the Permanent Mission of Austria to the United Nations in New York City. Reiterating his support for the integration of the Western Balkans into Euro-Atlantic structures, Kurz warned his colleagues from Albania, Bosnia and Herzegovina, Macedonia, Montenegro, Serbia, and Kosovo about Islamic radicalization in their countries emanating from Middle Eastern Islamic organizations. These organizations, argued Kurz, were spreading "religious-ideological influence" among their Muslim populations, paying women "to go out in [the] streets completely covered" (MIA 2016). Yet concerns over the hijacking of Muslim women's bodies by Middle Eastern Islamic organizations that prey on their (post)socialist poverty are part of long-standing gender-race tropes deployed within the logic of Euro-American securitization of the Balkans. Such concerns are only one aspect of a larger discourse that has narrated the troubling Middle Eastern Muslim and migrant presence in the Balkans as a radical penetration of Islamic fundamentalism into the Indigenous white European and secularized Muslim communities of the Balkans. Here, the gendered "rhetoric of salvation" (Abu-Lughod 2002) deployed in the legitimization of "humanitarian violence" in Bosnia and Kosovo (Atanasoski 2013) serves to secure a different post–Cold War global strategy: that of race making through the saving of gendered and sexed bodies. For the Austrian foreign minister, the fact that Muslim women in the Balkans "go out in [the] streets completely covered" represents a covering of otherwise visibly and viably white and therefore savable European bodies in the face of abject and unsavable refugee bodies.

It is important to note here that efforts to incorporate Balkan Muslims into the EU do not simply project the racially suspect marker of the European Muslim onto the new racialized refugee Muslim. Rather, racialized modalities of exclusion continuously shift. Although Balkan populations labeled "Muslim" do not meet the unspoken but essential criteria of European "normalized, Christian(ized, secular) whiteness" (El-Tayeb 2016), migrant movements into Europe render Balkan Muslims potentially recoverable Europeans imagined and claimed in contrast to raced migrant Muslim bodies. The mixing of local Balkan Muslims with newly arrived migrant others shores up security anxieties over definitions of who is white and European and can therefore be provided security and who can be left to die or be actively pursued for death at Europe's border. These tactics also play out in pitting white Balkan Muslims against migrants within EU borders as well, where the whitening of the Balkan Muslim is exemplified as a model Muslim compared to the rest of the migrant Muslim communities that come from nonwhite spaces. Statements by Doris Pack, the EU Parliament rapporteur for Bosnia and Herzegovina, are relevant here because they illustrate the kind of colonial imaginaries that inform such tactics: "When I came to Sarajevo, I saw fewer scarves than in some municipality around Berlin. We have opened the door for such an Islamization. This Islam is a European one, these Muslims are European ones as well as Orthodox and Catholic people here. They were never a threat to us and they are not a threat today" (*Sarajevo Times* 2017).

Played out in broader geopolitical tensions, these debates have been layered with counterterrorist, counterradicalization, and border security language that continuously creates and reinforces a clear georacial distinction between Arab Muslims and the white local European Muslims. Examining Islamic radicalism in the Balkans, the EU Institute for Security Studies suggested that "radical interpretations of Islam are somewhat alien to Muslim communities in the Balkans" whereby "50 years of communist rule in the region instilled a sense of secularism in Balkan Muslim communities, and gave rise to an Islamic tradition that is markedly different in its interpretations and practices to its more conservative counterparts in the Arabian Peninsula" (Missiroli et al. 2016, 1). The more recent racialization of refugees through religious practices is not just a product of the corroboration of whiteness by Muslims in the Balkans entangled in postgenocidal trauma and failed attempts to repair and re-exist without having to apologize for their existence but is also part of a more protracted colonial epistemic infrastructure reinforced through (post–)Cold War ethnographic studies. Indeed, ethnographies of Muslims in Bulgaria, Bosnia, Kosovo, and Albania coming under threat by "Eastern aid" became the central lens through which post–Cold War Euro-American academics approached Muslims in the Balkans.

Couched in a larger crossover between postconflict democratic peace-building and postsocialist transition studies undertaken in the midst of the war on terror, Muslim communities in the Balkans appear innocent victims of Islamization by their radical coreligionists from the Arab world. With knowledge production reviving, the resurgence or return of Islam in the Balkans and the danger of Islamist networks spreading into Europe through the Muslim belt in the Balkans appeared both as an academic pursuit and Euro-Atlantic policy concern. Arab presence in the Balkans was rendered a geopolitical threat. These processes on the ground, which manifested themselves through raids of Islamic relief agencies and closure of Islamic schools and "illegal" mosques—a term that had not existed before the 2000s—went hand in hand with the knowledge infrastructures of European and American academics who problematized Islamic aid as the cause of interethnic conflict.

The intersection of second- and third-world Muslim resistance and solidarity did not limit the imagination of Muslims in the Balkans—only struggles in the Muslim world—but allowed them to see themselves as members of the larger third-world movement for liberation. The Algerian War of Independence and the Israeli-Palestinian conflict would resonate deeply with Muslims in the Balkans. A year after the massacre of refugees at Tal al-Zaatar, a Palestinian refugee camp during the Lebanese Civil War in 1977 (Al-Bahloly 2013), a Muslim poet from Kosovo would write, "You are the first and the last surah of a new Qur'an" (Mufaku

2009, 178). Invoking solidarity through common Islamic legacies, the poet replaces the Qur'an with the pain and suffering of Palestinians as the new reference point among Muslims. Similarly, the Albanian poet Adelina Mamaqi, in solidarity with the Algerian revolutionaries, wrote, "We have been murdered in the past and we are still being murdered, under these dark clouds! You can't murder an entire nation with bullets! We Algerians have fire in our blood, such offspring has Africa, it has Lumumbas" (2009, 174). More than any event, however, the Iranian Revolution influenced Muslims, particularly in Yugoslavia, to think more critically of their position in the country and their historical othering during socialist modernization. In this context, the request of Melika Salihbegović to leave Yugoslavia and move "somewhere in this world in the wholeness of Islamic life" (Salihbegović 1983) needs to be understood as a transnational and transtemporal search for meaning and belonging pursued by Muslims around the world since the onset of colonialism and particularly with the decline of the last sovereign Muslim entity, the Ottoman caliphate. The transnational solidarity of Muslims in the socialist bloc with those in the nonaligned world is also an illustration of decolonial Muslim resistance to the continuities of a racialized global order of (post)modernity/coloniality.

The fear of mixing, however, was not invented by the post–Cold War clash of civilization geopolitics. Its prehistories of socialism were no less imaginative in their conceptualization of the unstable Muslim subject crossing the second and third Cold War borders and, within them, the racial and religious ones. Migrants are no longer just passing by in the Balkans; they are returning and staying. Migrants change infrastructures of the empire at its borderlands, where new landscapes, affective economies, and solidarity emerge both out of necessity and nostalgia for lost pasts and developing futures but also because economies along refugee routes are subterranean and subversive. In exchange, common languages and political process generate new subjectivities that may not invest in being saved by the empire, as the previous generation was.

The orientation toward whiteness, wealth, and the West traverses colonial archives of ethnicization. In the case of Bosnia, contemporary orientations toward the West through re-Westernization and whiteness are a product of (post)genocidal politics of Euro-Atlantic integration through Habsburg colonial heritage. The formation of colonial ontologies and arbitrary markers of identities on Muslim subjects in the Balkans emerge during the advancement of the Austro-Hungarian empire in Ottoman territories. In seeking to incorporate these populations into the Austro-Hungarian empire, colonial agents sought to produce them as proto-Europeans tainted by Islam. With that in mind, the following chapter examines the ways in which the excavations of colonial sites and institutions in Bosnia today seek to facilitate and fuse Bosnian history with colonial temporalities while reiterating and renewing its morality and salvation in the face of racialized enclosures and historical erasures.

Historicizing Enclosure

Refashioned Colonial Continuities as European Cultural Legacy

....

European enclosures rely on the recovery of colonial relics of modernization, museums, buildings, and boulevards by laying historical claims to territories and people whose colonial pasts are repurposed to fit the shift from "old" colonial Europe to the new (post)colonial European Union (El-Tayeb 2008). The "'vestiges' of colonial constructions," as Stoler calls them, are now "outfitted with new agents; the segregated divisions of colonial urban planning may be demolished but still mark the social geography of where upscale housing clusters and where dense settlements of privation remain. While many of the roads, railways, bridges, and canals built under colonial engineering projects with forced local labor may be in disrepair or bombed out, elsewhere they have been refurbished to move people and produce to service new profit-sharing ventures between national elites and foreign multinationals" (2016, 4). This chapter examines the ongoing recovery of Habsburg colonial sites and knowledge institutions in Bosnia the tutelage of the European Union (EU). It covers the ways in which the EU curates and preserves Habsburg colonial sites as cultural heritage (all the while renouncing any links to colonialism) as well as emerging movements that seek to confront their appropriation, enclosure, and privatization.

The first part of the chapter looks at the rebuilding and repurposing of Vijećnica in Sarajevo, the colonial seat of Austrian-Hungarian authority in the city and the site of the assassination of Archduke Franz Ferdinand, and contestations around its use by Austria and the EU during the commemoration of the centennial of World War I. Looking at the various collective efforts to confront the neutralization of the commemoration, the erasure of the anticolonial resistance to the Habsburg empire, and the simultaneous privatization of these sites, I draw attention to new forms of contestation of co-optation of colonial landscapes and ruins. Yet questioning the coloniality of built environments, or the "hardened, tenacious qualities of colonial effects," to quote Ann Laura Stoler (2016, 7), and the movements they propel leaves the sedimented genealogies of knowledge they forward and sustain frequently unchallenged. Focusing on the Islamic Community of Bosnia and Herzegovina as the longest-serving Austria-Hungarian-funded institution in the country, in the second part of this chapter, I look at the continuing critical significance of colonial-funded institutions and their newfound contemporary claims of Habsburg roots as a modern model for moderate "Islam" as a preemption to the radical Islam that could take root in Bosnia.

The EU-sponsored deployment of these colonial sites and speculations in Bosnia are happening at a time of intensification of European panic around refugees and the closure of the Balkan refugee route. The strategic importance of Balkan Muslims integrating into the geopolitical enclosure of Europe while delinking them from the racialized Arab others projected as a continuous threat at its border requires the historical harnessing of liminal Muslim whiteness. As Nicholas De Genova aptly points out, "It is precisely the southeastern European countries that previously found themselves within the Ottoman Empire, where many Europeans themselves are Muslim, that the borders of Europe become riddled with ambiguity, whereby cultural essentialisms can be readily converted into effective racialized ones," where "European-ness comes to encompass a variegated and contradictory nexus of racialized formations of whiteness that extend toward a series of 'off-white' or 'not-quite-white' borderland identities" (2017, 19–20). It is in these domains of coloniality that the rhetoric of "Europeanization" through the salvation of colonial sites as cultural heritage and the iteration of colonial Islamic institutions as white, nativist, and autochthonous European institutions of Islam occur and are curated under a broader umbrella of the mission of the EU, with Bosnia and the Balkans becoming outposts against the ongoing "threat" of refugees on the interiority of whiteness. Whiteness and belonging to its interiority are thus the desired goal of the postconflict and (post)genocidal condition of Bosnia, which requires not only a bonded relation of power but also artificially induced affective and *artif/ictive* attachments to whiteness. By *artif/ictive* I mean the convergence of colonial, conscripted artifacts that today merge with fictive renditions of history to produce a Bosnian imaginary in alignment with Euro-Atlantic temporal trajectories and territories. Thus the curation of whiteness in the Balkan borderlands is not just about bodies and borders but also artifacts, architecture, and spiritual and historical knowledge-producing institutions that labor in producing racialized hierarchies of belonging where the EU comes to the aid of the locals to epistemically and historically re-Westernize and reconstitute themselves as white.

My goal then is to delink local histories from whiteness and Eurocentrism as a way of decolonizing our present pasts and thereby reclaiming the decolonial struggles of negation by those who refuse this insidious invitation to whiteness. In this respect, I am deeply influenced by Madina Tlostanova's counsel that "local communities and individuals must do crucial work on memory, on historical traumas and restless ghosts that continue to consume us and erase our futures" (2018, 119–20). This is particularly important for Muslims, Roma, and migrants living in, or passing through, the Balkans since they have had to continuously confront erasure and silencing on two fronts: first through the secular submissive servitude required by and rendered to Euro-American security structures in the Balkans and second from the postsocialist nostalgia appropriating postcolonial approaches that anesthetize or directly disavow the socialist-era structural racism addressed in the previous chapter. In this sense, this chapter is a modest effort that seeks to unimagine geopolitical whiteness in the Balkans as a praxis of confronting global white enclosures at their borders, creating spatial and temporal openings that can lead to the abolition of Euro-Atlantic racist imaginaries through solidarities and flights toward fugitive futurities.

Narodna čitaonica (People's reading room) read the banner on the staircase of the Sarajevo city hall Vijećnica, where a group of Sarajlis sat reading books and newspapers in a cold December day in 2016.[1] The event had been called out on social media through the hashtag #VijećnicajeNaša (Vijećnica is ours). The organizers, Jedan Grad Jedna Borba (One City, One Struggle) and Dobre Kote (Good Spots), sought to bring attention to the privatization of common spaces and the increasing commercialization of former public gathering sites. In one of their bulletins written in partisan pamphlet font, they declared that "Vijećnica after World War II belonged to all of us. Making it a library in 1949, the authorities of the time gave the building to all BiH society," drawing attention to the historical significance of the building. One of the organizers from Jedan Grad Jedna Borba, Svjetlana Nedimović, told me it was important to remember that the designation of these sites as public spaces after the World War II liberation of Sarajevo by socialist authorities was not accidental but was guided by a broader attempt to undress them from the illegitimate powers that had built and utilized them during and prior to the war. This transformation of colonial and fascist sites by socialist authorities was not unique to socialist Yugoslavia. Colonial sites and institutions in the Balkans after World War II were frequently transformed into public libraries and universities as a way of absolving them of their colonial and fascist vestiges and reappropriating and redeeming them for socialism. The Casa del Fascio and the Home of Fascist Youth in Tirana, for instance, which were designed by Gherardo Bosio who was involved in designing similar buildings in Italian-occupied East Africa, were transformed into university and library centers.

Discussing the colonial nature of the building, Nedimović pointed out that "the historicization and commercialization of Vijećnica is not so much about the past as much as it had to do with solidifying present social relations of power in a city not only under international administration but also under neoliberal destitution, segregation and object poverty and unemployment" (Svjetlana Nedimović, interviewed by Piro Rexhepi, July 2017). Jedan Grad Jedna Borba had been a vocal critic of EU policies in Bosnia, particularly in regards to the ongoing "refugee crisis." Commenting on the EU enlargement in the Balkans characterized by external border strengthening, one of their bulletins was titled

"Don't shoot at each other—attack the refugees running away from Euro-American wars." Jedan Grad Jedna Borba noted that the "EU is keen that we are well equipped and ready to defend their privileges at their borders from people who are running from their destroyed homes by western [sic] imperialism." The statement echoed multiple EU, NATO, and US calls to utilize the refugee crisis as an impetus for the integration of the western Balkans into the transatlantic security structures.

From 2013 to 2019, I had made multiple visits to Sarajevo to work in the city and federal archives on the Sarajevo Process and continue my interviews in the city. Like many people in the Balkans, I followed the plenum protests of 2014 closely as the first postconflict movements that sought to confront the internationally imposed ethnic tripartheid established by the General Framework Agreement for Peace in Bosnia and Herzegovina, also called the Dayton Agreement. The High Representative for Bosnia and Herzegovina Valentin Inzko stated that "Austria will increase its troops" in response to the protests and that "if it comes to escalation we would have to consider the intervention of EU forces" (Kirn 2014). He had sent a clear message to the people that the current configuration of power was not to be challenged. Yet the solidarity that emerged out of the plenums continued to reverberate across Bosnia. This was particularly visible in June 2014 during the discussions around the co-optation of the World War I centennial by Austria and the EU and the erasure and neutralization of the war where spectacle characterized most conversations. Most activists in the city were concerned the events could impact the momentum of transformation. At the time, the assassin of the archduke Gavrilo Princip was being co-opted by Serb nationalists in Republika Serbska with a bizarre real-life enactment of the assassination organized by the film director Emir Kusturica in his Disney-style town called Andrićgrad. Meanwhile, the Austrian-dominated EU mission in Sarajevo had sought to make the assassination and mourning of the archduke the central event of the centennial. Most people believed that the revisionist histories were dangerous because they deepened the already institutionalized shift between Bosnian Serbs and Bosnian Muslims created by the Dayton Agreement.

On June 28, 2014, commemorating one hundred years since the assassination of Archduke Franz Ferdinand, the Vienna Philharmonic held a memorial concert in Vjećnica. Paying tribute to the dead emperor in Sarajevo, the concert opened with Joseph Haydn's "Emperor." The chairman of the Vienna Philharmonic, Dr. Clemens Hellsberg, noted that this event was "more than just a concert which brings us together in the magnificent Vijećnica, the symbol of the City of Sarajevo, a city which itself can be considered a symbol of Europe, having always been a place of meeting between east and west, between Orient and Occident" (Hellsberg 2014). Hellsberg closed his remarks by highlighting the idea of a united Europe as the most visionary project of the continent, hoping that "God would save peaceful and European Bosnian and Herzegovina."

Destroyed during the war, the building had just reopened in May that year with funding from Austria and the EU under the patronage of the current high representative, a position that many locals believed exceeded the powers of colonial-era governing authorities. The Austrian president Heinz Fischer hosted the event as a successor to the Habsburg colonial administration. The High Representative Inzko, also an Austrian, called the building and its reconstruction "a gift of the citizens of the EU to the people of Sarajevo." The irony of a Habsburg colonial building that was now being reconstructed and regifted to the people of Sarajevo was lost on no one. One of the activists of Dobre Kote noted that "Sarajevo is convenient to Europeans to commemorate all those inconvenient truths about their histories that they can't seem to have in their own capitals but have to externalize them and rebrand them abroad" (Dobre Kote, interviewed by Piro Rexhepi, Sarajevo, July 2017).

Multiple EU initiatives to center the centennial of World War I in Sarajevo had been ongoing for several years. At the plenary session of the European Parliament in 2011, the Christian Democratic Union of Germany MP in the EU and former rapporteur for the EU parliament on Bosnia, Doris Pack, asked her colleagues to support naming Sarajevo a European capital of culture for 2014, arguing that "Sarajevo has a special place in European history and culture," and that with this act of recognition, "we could send an important signal for the multi-ethnic character of the city and the state of Bosnia and Herzegovina, which could also give the political class in that country cause to rethink their ideas" (Pack 2011). The framing of the local citizens of Sarajevo as the core problem has been a common feature of Pack's and other postwar European high representatives' commentary, where the attempts of EU missions to civilize the natives were continuously subverted by stubborn locals. More recently, the rise of imperial nostalgia has generated parallels between the EU and the Habsburgs that erase colonial and neocolonial formations in the name of European stability. Note, for instance, a recent account by the Carnegie Endowment for International Peace where the journalist Caroline de Gruyter provided the following accessible narrative: "Most Habsburg emperors loathed warfare, just like the Europeans who, traumatized by two world wars, set up the European Economic Community in the 1950s. The emperors preferred to acquire territories peacefully by marrying off family members all over Europe. And like in the EU, small nations felt relatively safe and protected in the empire: being part of it meant being protected from invasion by bigger neighbors. All nations were granted equal rights under the Crown" (De Gruyter 2016).

On opening day, as local and international officials gathered for a concert, a group of citizens outside the building wore Gavrilo Pricip masques. Seeking to confront the erasure of the anticolonial nature of Mlada Bosna—the underground organization that Pricip belonged to—they wore banners that read, "We are occupied again by imperialism, by [the] EU and international community, by fascism, by MMF, by capitalism, by nationalism" (see figure 2.1). "We are not here to just protest the neocolonial power of the EU and the 'international community,'" said one of the protestors to the crowd, "but also the local pawns and power brokers—they mutually sustain each other—when we protest they like to blame each other which only reinforces and legitimized their power" (personal conversation). Others pointed out how their protests were not just

FIGURE 2.1. Protests in Sarajevo, June 28, 2014. Photo by Adla Isanović.

directed at official representatives of the EU and the local authorities but also civil society organizations that did not support the plenums, "all of those on the payroll of internationals or benefiting from their rule here from NGOs to religious leaders and the media." Further away from the protesters with their slogans stood a group of citizens who had also come out to protest but were not part of what they called the "anti-imperialist" crowd. I spoke to a couple of them. Most were retired citizens who had come out to express their grievances about low pensions and high prices. When I asked an older man in his seventies why he chose this particular day of the reopening of Vijećnica, he responded, "We are being told this is a gift to us, thank you but we don't need gifts—we need living pensions and wages." He was interrupted by one of his friends, who was listening in, and said, "What gift? We built this building with our own sweat."

These protests "have become public weeping gatherings," said a woman in her late forties who noticed that I was talking to people about the protests: "They are our last refuge from the *lopovi* [thieves]." I moved with the crowd in various directions as cordoned by the police. Some of whom were people I had met on my earlier visits. Rushed as I was by my neoliberal academic record keeping at the time, I made the mistake of asking too many questions, and most of the people saw this as a moment to gather and connect. I asked a young woman who was handing out pamphlets if she thought Bosnia was in a colonial condition. Somewhat annoyed, she responded, "What do you think?" Pointing to some of the protest signs, she asked, "Can you not read? The Office of the High Representative has unlimited power here and is not only their over dictation of politics that concerns us but their support for a corrupt governing coalition that serves their single aim in this country—stability at all cost."

As the high representative and local Bosnian governing officials arrived for the Vienna Philharmonic concert at Vijećnica, the crowd booed and jeered the officials with "lopovi." Signs unfolded on the Miljacka quay read, "Defiant Balkans Unite" and "Europe you owe us: remember 92 + 95." In the evening that same day, the EU had sponsored a lavish program called A Century of Peace after the Century of Wars. I had managed to convince Salihbegović, who rarely left her apartment at that time, to join me for the event. At my insistence that we find a place to sit at one of the cafes across Vijećnica, we walked there through streets full of people. As we approached the building, Salihbegović said, "Call me morbid, but I wished they would never fix it up. I preferred it when it smelled like urine after the war; it was a monumental reminder of the war that refused to remind you otherwise. Now they've managed to take it over and turn it into a theater for their imperialism." After a grotesque rendition of the German nationalist folk song "Wenn die Soldaten," accompanied by a group of Sarajevo children dressed as soldiers with rifles, she asked that we leave. On the way back, we passed by Inat Kuća, which can be loosely translated as the "stubborn house." An urban legend in Sarajevo is that the owner of a house where the Austro-Hungarian administration had meant to build Vijećnica refused to let his building be destroyed and so he moved it "stone by stone" across the river Mljacka—the house came to be known as Inat Kuća, or the stubborn house. "I love this place," said Salihbegović: "This should be celebrated as a testimony to the stubbornness of the people of this city to give up or give in."

In addition to Vijećnica, the EU had also sponsored the reopening of Zemaljski muzej Bosne i Hercegovine (the National Museum of Bosnia and Herzegovina). Established by the Habsburg colonial administration in 1888, the museum sought to forge a post-Ottoman project of *bošnjaštvo* on the excavation expeditions sponsored by Vienna to assert the pre-Ottoman ethnic and racial whiteness of Bosnians. Most of these projects took pains to imagine a pre-Ottoman Bosnian kingdom as an ally of the Habsburgs and Hungarian kingdoms in their struggle against Ottoman occupation. The establishment of the museum and various ethnographic, linguistic, and historical research enterprises were also central to late nineteenth- and early twentieth-century Habsburg expansionist ambitions into Ottoman Albania, Kosovo, and Macedonia (Kapidžić 1973, 437). In Vienna, Sarajevo was primed as the seat of Habsburg southern expansion. Knowledge produced and circulated by Habsburg ethnographers would become central to both Bosnian and Albanian nationalism, discussed in the following chapter. These projects in particular were carried out concurrently with other biopolitical forms of governance that the Austro-Hungarian scientific establishment used to both test the newly acquired population and territory and to civilize the locals toward an emerging eugenic and Eurocentric scientific approach to life (Fuchs 2011, 58). The Habsburgs' attempt at an overarching classification of Bosnians through their project of bošnjaštvo countered both lingering Ottoman sympathies of the local population after the Austro-Hungarian occupation (Amzi-Erdogdular 2013) and the post-Ottoman Serb and Croat nationalist claims on Bosnia (Hajdarpasic 2015).

In the summer of 2016, Salihbegović informed me that she had been diagnosed with cancer. Without going into details, she said, "I am afraid that I will not speak fluently and what I would want to convey might no longer have coherence or chronology." If she was born in this age, she said, and not in the mid-twentieth century, her narratives would have made her a hip-hop star, better than Sassja.[2] I amusingly warned that she was starting a rap rivalry between Tuzla (where Sassja came from) and Sarajevo. That summer we spent time together talking; I didn't ask questions about politics, Sarajevo, or the war in her past that I would want to utilize for my research, as I felt that I had to be present for her. I had shown her the performance of the Bosnian Roma artist Selma Selman's "You have no idea" (Momentum Worldwide 2016) and she loved it. We would play it on Vimeo; "Piro," she would say, repeating Selman's performance, "you Have No Idea!" There was something in Selman's voice, her strength and sovereignty, that Salihbegović loved and could relate to. I tried to keep her entertained by putting on the 2011 *Wild Wild East* album by the local band Dubioza Kolektiv, especially the song "Dubioza kolektiv" (Euro song): "Auf Wiedersehen [see you again] Miss Merkel / You are not my friend / When I tell you merhaba / You don't understand. . . . All around the Europe / Right wing taking power / They want to kick me out / So I live undercover." She particularly loved their *Absurdistand* album (2013), which included a song that was widely played during the 2014 protests: "Op, op, opa / Dolazi Evropa / Sa'će da nas biju sile / Svjetske milicije" (Op, op, opa / The arrival of Europa / Now we'll get the stick / By the powers of the world police).

Her thinking had become so lucid, and she seemed in a better mood than I had ever seen her before and yet everyone around her knew that she was dying. I had never brought up the subject, except for when she first told me about her diagnosis. When I once asked her how she felt toward the end of the summer, she responded that "Muslims accept fate." Having lived her life in alignment with her convictions, she showed no signs of regret. Hers, she frequently said, for better or worse, was not a life unlived. On the last day of our meetings that summer, we performed "Ya H'afeez" dhikr together for what seemed like an hour. Thinking that we might not see each other again—though we would meet later in the summer of 2017—she had prepared a small gift box for me at the tail end of that summer, a small archive that included several books, pictures, a framed poster of Šejla Kamerić's artwork titled *Bosnian Girl* that used to hang in her bathroom, and Bosnian artists Kurt & Plasto's *Greetings for Europe* postcard series, which I had told her I couldn't find in Sarajevo since the series had gone out of print in 2007. "I know you will make good use of them," she said, and so I am here. The last two items were very dear to both of us; we both thought they formed the most significant artistic archive that defined the (post)war racialization of Bosnians. Kamerić's *Bosnian Girl* was a black-and-white art piece consisting of postcards, posters, and billboards with denigrating phrases superimposed over a female figure: "No teeth? A mustache? Smell like shit? Bosnian girl!" It was originally written in the village of Potočari, in the municipality of Srebrenica, by Dutch soldiers stationed there under a UN mandate to protect civilians. Šejla Kamerić then placed the words over a picture of herself as a commentary on the intersection of gender and racism that characterizes the racialization of Bosnian women.

In *Greetings for Europe*, Sarajevo artists Kurt & Plasto present a series of postcards by ironically replicating the EU verbiage in postwar Bosnia: "All the greetings we are sending are deeply rooted in the rich European historical heritage, from ancient Greece to today—from the first cities, states and democracies to the development of civil society. The labor in the 'Greetings for Europe' contain our stance and thoughts on Europe, how it has always been, how it is and it should be—but is not" (Kurt & Plasto 2005). Two of the postcards became particularly popular: "nEUrosis," where the artists pose with EU flags as hijabs, and "Prince EUgen," which drew a parallel between the Habsburg colonial and EU treatment of Bosnians as children with diapers but was also a reference to the Habsburg prince Eugene of Savoy who, under Habsburg patronage, sacked and burned Sarajevo in 1697. The artists' goal was to address the "prejudice of Christian Europe towards other cultures and regions and the imperial nature of Europe" (Kurt & Plasto 2005). Kurt & Plasto were among the first to critique the emergence of the Habsburg colonial pasts as proof of their capacity to be integrated into Euro-Atlantic structures, a discourse that gained prominence in the early 2000s. Note, for instance, Sven Alkalaj's speech in 2007, then minister of foreign affairs of Bosnia and Herzegovina, delivered at the Austrian Diplomatic Academy of Vienna conference, titled "Islam in Europe: Thirteen Centuries of Common History":

Bosnian Muslims are indigenous European people with their origin, their culture, their religion. . . . It should be emphasized that Bosnian

Muslims have educated themselves throughout Europe, especially during the Austro-Hungarian Empire. Thus, they have enriched their Ottoman heritage with new values and teachings of west Europe. Now, I would like to point out the fact that right here, in Vienna, and in other European and world cultures and educational centers, Bosnian Muslims, as well as members of other religious communities, citizens of BIH, have successfully studied for decades. Enriched with new knowledge they came back to their country and contributed to its development. Today, they still do the same thing and thus facilitate the process of association of BIH into Euro-Atlantic integrations. (Alkalaj 2007)

In *The Colonial Harem*, Malek Alloula points out that the postcard "is the comic strip of colonial morality" (1986, 4). In their interpretation, Kurt & Plasto seem to subvert and mock the processes of othering that travels through the visuality of the postcards as a colonial-less and color-blind postulate of "nostalgic wonderment and tearful archeology (Oh! those colonial days!)." The postcards also encompass "the motivations and the effects of this vast operation of systematic distortion" that return in a "new guise: a racism and a xenophobia titillated by the nostalgia of the colonial empire" (Alloula 1986, 4). Indeed, these works best illustrate the kind of racist and colonial tensions embedded in the larger Euro-American mission in Bosnia, whereby, on the one hand, it demands Bosnian Muslims to corroborate their whiteness; on the other hand, it continuously questions their alliance to Europe by pointing out the danger of their association and alignment with "Arab" Muslims, as discussed in the introduction and chapter 1. In this sense, the attention given to Habsburg colonial sites and institutions today is illustrative of how the EU has come to claim these colonial landscapes as part of European cultural heritage, but these persisting colonial narratives also travel through their ties to the former colonial capital, Vienna. "Even quite well-informed people here in the United States and in Europe," wrote Susan Sontag from Sarajevo while under siege in 1994, "seem genuinely surprised when I mention that, until the siege began, a middle-class Sarajevan was far more likely to go to Vienna than to go down the street to a mosque" (1994, 93). Sontag pleads with her audience that Muslims in Sarajevo are not like the devout Muslims of "Teheran or Baghdad or Damascus," that they "are physiologically identical with their southern

Slav neighbors, spouses, and compatriots, since they are, in fact, the descendants of Christian southern Slavs" (93–94). A year before, in 1993, John Kifner wrote in the *New York Times*, "Islam has a distinct cast in the mountains, valleys and cities of Bosnia, shaped by a history and culture far removed from the fundamentalism the Western world has come to fear from Iran, Afghanistan, Lebanon or Saudi Arabia" (1993). Accounts like these became ubiquitous in Western writing about Bosnia and frequently relied on colonial and Cold War racialized imaginaries that saw the first, second, and third world through a locked-in, georacial lens whereby geographic proximity to Europe, phenotypical and physiological whiteness, and secularism denoted redeemable humanity that deserved salvation.

The Austrian presence in Sarajevo today is ubiquitous—from historical preservation projects of the Austro-Hungarian period to the high representative Valentin Inzko. Cultural funding for Bosnia by the EU is also filtered through Vienna. The bigger ambition of the far-right government of Austria under Sebastian Kurz has been to utilize both its current and colonial links to Bosnia toward the establishment of a governing framework for its own Muslim population. Indeed, Kurtz's rise to power was in no small measure part of his projection of radical Islam as a geopolitical threat to the Balkans and therefore to Europe and his ability to control the borders as well as regulate Muslims inside Austria.

IMPERIAL INVENTORIES AND ISLAMIC INSTITUTIONS

In September 2016, Kurz Skyped into a conference in Sarajevo organized by the Federal Minister for European and International Affairs, the Austrian embassy, and the Austrian Cultural Forum, along with the Islamic Community of Bosnia and Herzegovina. The conference was in Sarajevo and called "State and Religion in Bosnia and Herzegovina and Austria: A Legal Framework for Islam in a European Context." The conference was one of the many activities organized by Austria in Sarajevo based on 2016 being declared the year of cultural relations among Bosnia, Herzegovina, and Austria. Earlier in the year, on a visit to Sarajevo in February, Kurz had announced the year of cultural relations among Bosnia, Herzegovina, and Austria open by noting, "Austria and Bosnia-Herzegovina are united by a bond of long-standing partnership and friendship. Now we have to seize the opportunity of getting to know each other even better"

(European Western Balkans 2016). The conference was organized months after ratified amendments to the already controversial Islam Law in Austria to "prevent parallel societies" that had gone into effect on March 1. In the face of criticism by the Muslim communities of Austria, the government wanted a "European model of Islam for Austria." The Bosnian Islamic Community was happy to oblige. Indeed, for many years, one of the key branding campaigns of the Bosnian Islamic Community has been the Europeanness of Bosnian Islam and its potential use for the development of "Balkan" and "European" Islam rooted in the coloniality of the institution of the Islamic Community itself. As mentioned in the previous chapter, in 2016, the Islamic Community of Bosnia and Herzegovina established an EU representative office in Brussels. In the promotional booklet published for the opening of this office, the Grand Mufti of Bosnia, Husein Kavazović, reassured the EU that "Bosniaks and the Islamic Community were recognized as the most loyal citizens and a factor of stability while Austria-Hungary ruled over Bosnia and Herzegovina" (2016a, 21).

Like Zemaljski muzej and Vijećnica, the Islamic Community of Bosnia and Herzegovina was established by the Habsburg colonial administration in 1882 to separate the newly acquired Muslim population from their spiritual orientation toward Istanbul and the Khalif (Amzi-Erdoğdular 2013). The institutionalization of Islam by colonial powers was not specific to Bosnia. Most European colonial powers established complex governing structures on Islam that relied on, and were reinforced by, various ethnographic and anthropological knowledge production such as the invention of "national" Islams.[3] The Islamic Community of Bosnia and Herzegovina was organized and regulated by several subsequent laws and regulations, including the Islam Law, known as *Islamgesetz*, which was promulgated in 1912 (Amzi-Erdoğdular 2013; Rexhepi 2019). Similar to the purpose of the museum, the legal measures were part of a larger Habsburg ambition to create a more permanent framework for governing Muslim subjects, resulting in an interpretation of Islam that incorporated more Ottoman Muslim populations and territories farther south. Like the centennial celebrations of World War I, the centennial celebrations of the Islam Law of Austria in 2012 were also layered with reverence toward the visionary approach to multiculturalism of the Habsburg empire and its similarities to the EU. In his speech, Sebastian Kurz, then state secretary in the Ministry of the Interior, praised the Habsburg legal framework for Islam in Bosnia as a model for Austria today.

Kurz was a rising star in "integration" debates in Austria in the early 2010s, promoting the idea of integration ambassadors and speaking of the importance of dialogue with religious communities as key to integration. Integration through dialogue had emerged throughout the EU as a problem-solution imperative to the migrant and Muslim problem. Schirin Amir-Moazami's work on Germany illustrates how in the larger "intertwined processes of securitization and integration, 'dialogue' with Muslims has become salient . . . [and] a tool for integration and social cohesion" (2011, 11). Kurtz's implementation of the 2011 Zusammen: Österreich (Together: Austria) project gave him visibility as a rising star of the right that was seen as someone who was serious about tackling radicalism and refugee influx—issues that in Austrian public debates were discussed interchangeably. Following the 2013 elections, he became the minister of integration and foreign affairs, making the integration of the Balkans into the EU his main foreign policy goal. He framed the questions of integration as security measures around the control of migration along the Balkan route and positioned Austria as a key player in curbing and controlling migration at its geopolitical gateways. At the same time, as a minister of integration at the height of the crisis in 2015, Kurz would reform the 1912 Habsburg law to counter extremism and "reduce the political influence and control from abroad and we want to give Islam the chance to develop freely within our society and in line with our common European values" (BBC 2015).

In his visits to Bosnia, warning against radical Islamic influences coming from the Middle East that could endanger the Euro-Atlantic integration of the country, Kurz urged Bosnian leaders to "confront the radicalization of Islam" since "Europe needs the kind of moderate practice of Islam that exists in Bosnia and Herzegovina" (USKINFO 2015). Meanwhile, congratulating Kurz on his 2015 reforms of the 1912 law, the grand mufti of Bosnia, Husein Kavazović, commented on how the "Austria-Hungarian empire, and Austria and Bosnia and Herzegovina today, with their Muslims in their Islamic communities can offer Europe a possible alternative" (Kavazović 2016a). Earlier in February, Kurz had invited Balkan ministers of foreign affairs and the ministers of interiors to Vienna for the "Managing Migration Together" conference, where EU integration called for the swift implementation of the Vienna declaration "Tackling Jihadism Together" (a declaration that Kurz also developed) in response to "the increasingly visible connections between illegal migration and extremism"

(Managing Migration Together 2016). In the 2017 electoral campaign, he would frame himself as the responsible person capable of closing the Balkan route, in the hope his popularity would bring him the Austrian chancellorship. Indeed, the EU-Turkey deal of 2016 that has closed the Balkan refugee route was in no small part a product of Kurz's lobbying. Heading the EU presidency in 2016, he would make "protecting Europe" from migrants his main priority and would succeed in securing an EU-wide deal (General Secretariat 2018), taking what Kurz has called an "Australian approach" to stopping and containing migrants outside EU borders by coordinating their containment in third-world regions such as North Africa, the Balkans, and Turkey. Implementing the 2015 amendments to the Islam Law, which included banning foreign funding of religious communities, by June 2018, Austria also closed down seven mosques, six of which belonged to the Arab community. In Bosnia, these politics would engender processes of surveillance, securitization, and criminalization of local *džamats* (Muslim communities) that were not under the control of the official Islamic Community of Bosnia and Herzegovina.

In January 2016, Bakir Izetbegović, the Bosniak member of the tripartite presidency of Bosnia and Herzegovina, warned that the illegal džamats, or *paradžamats*, could "bring about chaos and trouble for Muslims in BiH and the European Union," directing the Islamic Community of Bosnia and Herzegovina to close down all illegal mosques by April 2016. Accordingly, between January and March 2016, the Islamic Community undertook a series of meetings with all the paradžamats. In its annual report, it announced the establishment of a working group that would seek to discipline the various illegal mosques, whose interpretations and practice of Islam were imported from imams who had studied in the Middle East, questioning the legitimacy and image of the traditional domestic Islam (Kavazovic 2016b). It so happens that these mosques haves been the most active in assisting and hosting refugees traveling through Bosnia.

That same year, I visited two such supposed illegal džamats, one in the village of Stijena and the other one in Podgredina, both near the city of Cazin in northwestern Bosnia. In both instances, upon entering the villages I was stopped by what seemed to be permanent police patrols controlling the axes of entry into the villages. At Stijena, I was questioned by the police officers for over two hours, and when I was eventually allowed to enter the village, I was warned by the police officers that I was going into the village at my own risk. In both villages, members of the community complained of surveillance and policing, which was coming both from the local police force as well as the Islamic Community to force people to register within the framework of the institution and acknowledge the authority of the grand mufti of Bosnia. In conversation, one of the members of the community in Stijena said, "They call us illegal or parallel mosques because they argue that we are obliged to join the Islamic Community as the only legal institutions under which Islam can be practiced in Bosnia. How can Islam be turned into an institution? If we don't join, we are called Wahabis and Salafists, but we reject those names because they are all indented to make us seem dangerous, we are just Muslims committed to practicing Islam through our own reading of the Qur-an" (interview with Piro Rexhepi, 2016). People in Podgredina expressed similar concerns over the monopolization of faith by the Islamic Community of Bosnia and Herzegovina. One of the elders there pointed out that instead of the Islamic Community protecting all Muslim mosques,

> to practice Islam as they choose, [they] want to predicate only one type
> of Islam that serves politics and ideology which we are not interested
> in . . . every time we have met with their representatives, we've asked
> them to show us where is it written that we must come under their
> authority and their only explanation is that all religious communities
> in the country must come under religious hierarchy trying to con-
> vince us by examples of the Catholic or the Orthodox Church, but we
> are not Christians and have nothing against them but Islam does not
> recognize that kind of authority. (interview with Piro Rexhepi, 2016)

In conversations, I asked several members of the community if they thought that the institutionalization of Islam in Bosnia had to do with its colonial past since they were established by the Austro-Hungarian empire. Their responses were mixed, with most arguing that the current attitude of the Islamic Community was mostly a product of the socialist period where all religious communities had to come under one umbrella of centralized religious authority, which allowed for easier control of religious communities. Colonial history was something that the current administration of the Islamic Community was promoting for the "West." In Stijena, a man in his thirties who accompanied me during my visit there added an interesting point as we discussed in more detail the various historical claims of the Islamic Community: "The way we see Islam[] is not just the Austrians that tried to institutionalize Islam but the Ottomans did the same thing too—so [it] is not like the institutions that claim [a] monopoly on Islam today are just Austrian they are Ottoman too. The Hanafi school also monopolized Islam in Ottoman times" (interview with Piro Rexhepi, 2016).

On my return to Sarajevo, I discussed the issue with Ahmed Alibašić, a professor of Islamic studies in the Faculty of Islamic Studies at the University of Sarajevo, and Dževada Šuško who runs the Institute for the Islamic Tradition of Bosnians (Institut za islamsku tradiciju Bošnjaka). Both confirmed that the institutionalization of Islam through the Hanafi school had started with the *Tanzimat* reforms in the mid-nineteenth century when the Ottoman Empire sought to "catch up" with the European empire and rushed to consolidate political institutions in the modern European fashion. Islam and Islamic religious practices, according to Alibašić and Šuško, were not exceptions to these larger Europeanization reforms. Indeed, according to Šuško, the Institute for the Islamic Tradition of Bosnians, funded by the Islamic Community of Bosnia and Herzegovina, is meant to work toward the further Europeanization of Islam.

The readiness of the Islamic Community of Bosnia and Herzegovina to become a "representative participant in the process of developing European forms of credible representation for Muslims" (Kavazović 2016a, 6) is prompted by both the EU and the Islamic Community to increase their political leverage in the EU integration bargaining processes. What is interesting is that the selling point of the Islamic Community as a model for the institutionalization of Islam in Europe is frequently its "modern structural form known to this day" (10), which of course dates back to its establishment during the colonial occupation of the Habsburgs. In the context of my argument here, the extent to which there is a viable possibility for the Islamic Community to become a template for the institutionalization of Islam in the EU is less significant than the deployment of Bosnian Muslims from the periphery to police migrant Muslims in the metropole. One of the most unsettling features of this strategy is the zeal with which the Islamic Community has attempted to prove its qualifications. Its representative to the EU, Senaid Kobilica (2016), points out that its fellow migrant Muslims in Europe should be more concerned with their responsibilities than their freedoms and that "thanks to centuries of European experience, understanding, and open-mindedness, our Bosnian imams" guide them toward dialogue and cooperation (23). Though this seems to be one of the more attractive features of the Islamic Community of Bosnia and Herzegovina for Austria (and arguably the EU as well), the ability of the Islamic Community to monopolize the interpretation and practice of Islam remains questionable at best. The Islamic Community of Bosnia and Herzegovina has become a site on which the tensions of postcolonial and (post)socialist histories are continuously contested by various movements but also emboldened by increased recognition and support by both Austria and the EU in developing a "European Islam." In the case of Bosnia, it is particularly important because it illustrates how the politics of privileging moderate and modern Islam converges with European colonial entailments and EU racialized bordering regimes.

Re-Westernization and whiteness through colonial landscapes and spectacles of remembrance, such as the one in Bosnia, needs little commentary. Yet that commentary is nearly entirely absent from the vocabulary of the city as it frequently goes by other names, such as Europeanization, postconflict development, and Euro-Atlantic integration. What does it mean that the celebrations of the centennial of World War I are held in a colonial site, organized by the former colonial power, and neutralized as a memorial of sadness and grieving for the assassinated Archduke Franz Ferdinand? The arrival of the Vienna Philharmonic to middle-class Sarajevans who, as Sontag supposes, are "far more likely to go to Vienna to the opera than to go down the street to a mosque" (Sontag 1994, 93) means very little to those crowds gathered to protest poverty, privatization, nationalism, and thievery. Yet the dominance and persistence of these narratives and their repeated resuscitation leave lasting marks on the collective memory of the city—reminding and remaking people into a present-past not their own. Re-Westernization here is tantamount to the Habsburg attempts to reintegrate post-Ottoman Bosnia into the "West," inasmuch as the post-socialist Euro-Atlantic integration project relies on and seeks to solidify what was started by Habsburg colonial expansion.

These modes of controlling and shaping of the past through multiple mediums are too many to cover here. Suffice to say that in addition to recovered colonial buildings, narratives, and museums, the colonization of faith and fate through the institutionalization of Islamic practices is perhaps the more concerning measure of coloniality, especially since any alternative narrations of the history of Islam in Bosnia are frequently radical and "illegal" by Muslim clerics and Muslim institutions in the political pursuits of Euro-Atlantic integration. In small towns and villages across Bosnia and the Balkans, being called a "radical" or attending an illegal mosque have grave social and security consequences as they are all too easily lumped together with the war on terror. As an Albanian Muslim in Bosnia, I sensed the same sensitivity in talking to, being with, and relating to others—engagements require a great deal of being evasive—both because we are never sure how to talk about what happened and what is happening without looking over our shoulders, but also because there is still existential angst hanging in the air about the proper posturing and positioning to avoid falling prey to the narratives that position us as fundamentalists and radicals, deserving of everything that happened to us. In our desire to meet the acceptable criteria of good and acceptable Muslims allowed to live in "Europe," we continuously police ourselves and each other with almost existential anxiety, performing the kind of loyal and loving subjecthood that coloniality/modernity relies on. This feeling of anxiety produces a kind distancing from our own selves and communities and compensates the need for love and support through affective attachments and adulations toward the West and whiteness. But this love for the West and whiteness also serves to renew its appeal and authority in the postsocialist borderlands, just as racialized refugee bodies shoring up on the Balkan refugee route are also a way of maintaining a racial differentiation in indifferent times and porous spaces. With that in mind, in the following chapter I turn to the aesthetics of love as debt for our saving and the structured feelings for the West and whiteness in Albanian cultural productions that traverse ongoing colonial/modern saving missions.

Enclosure Sovereignties

Saving Missions
and Supervised
Self-Determination

....

Since the Euro-Atlantic intervention in the Kosovo war, Albanian appreciation for the West has proven to be an enduring reference for the liberal
audiences in the United States who, in the face of Donald Trump's election to the presidency, sought to redeem some of their supposedly more
enlightened transatlantic legacies. Amid the 2016 election and Trump's
declaration that he would ban Muslims from entering the United States
if elected, US media rushed to Kosovo to provide proof that despite globalization of Islamophobia, not all Muslims hate the United States. In
one such CNN rendition, "A Muslim Country That Loves America," the
journalist Frida Ghitis wrote, "In this time of dispiriting headlines—
when Islamist terrorists target Christian children and their mothers
on an Easter Sunday outing in Lahore, Pakistan; when an American
presidential candidate advocates stopping Muslims from coming to the
United States; when ISIS terrorists have just killed dozens in Brussels;
when the very possibility of peaceful coexistence sometimes seems re-
mote, there is a place that may just restore our faith in the future: Welcome to Albania" (2016). Ghitis reminded the US public that "Albanians

fell in love with the United States in 1919, when world leaders, gathered at the Paris Peace Conference to redesign the world after World War I, dismantled the empires that had held sway over much of the planet" and "President Woodrow Wilson stood up for Albania." These absurd attempts to rebrand US history as essentially anti-imperialist—through Wilson nonetheless, whose contribution to white world supremacy cannot be overstated—that traverse through the enactment of Albanians as Muslims who loved America, intensified after the election of Trump. In February 2018, NPR ran a special, "Welcome to the Country with the Biggest Crush on America," reminding US audiences that despite Trump, Albanians were still dedicating love songs to the United States, with some natives even giving relocation advice to Americans who wanted to move to Kosovo, called "Kosovo If Trump Wins," its motto, "Love your country as much as Kosovars love America" (Kakissis 2018). Meanwhile, the *Guardian* ran a photo-essay titled, "51st State: Kosovo's Bond to the US," noting their "emotional, political and economic bonds" and some of the highest approval ratings of US leadership in the world (Dezfuli 2018) at the same time the Kosovar prime minister Ramush Haradinaj named Kosovo a "Euro-Atlantic nation" (Reinl 2018).

This kind of affective adulation to both the West and whiteness in Albanian spaces does not just come at the price of enduring genocidal trauma where appreciation is attached to the desperation that comes from the experience of violence but also fear of what might happen should the United States change course and abandon Albanians. Indeed, since the Euro-American intervention, Albanians are routinely reminded that their very existence hangs on the thread of Western support. Consider, for instance, a speech delivered by Joe Biden in 2002 (Albanian American Civic League 2013), addressing the Albanian American Civic League, in which he reminded officials from Albanian and Kosovar migrant communities that they were

> at the hinge of history, that [the] door will either slam shut and you and the ethnic heritage you represent will remain in the backwaters of Western civilization for another hundred years or the door will be open to the painful process of full and total integration into Europe and the Western world. For you all know your heritage is long, deep and noble. But the fact of the matter is, you have been used as pawns for four hundred years, arguably seven hundred years, and people have benefited

from your divisions, now you've arrived at a moment where we have to decide or more accurately, you have to decide where you will go. (2013)

Like Bosnians, Albanians are kept under a state of suspension of sovereignty through frameworks of statehood that are never finished and require not only continuous Euro-American civilian and military presence but also affective manifestations for the conditional guardianship the West. The improvised affective adulations among Albanians today directed at the United States and Europe may not just be showing gratitude but also reconciling the replacement of Serbian structural violence with situational safety and fear, the fear that the Albanian right to exist can only be secured by the Euro-Atlantic alliance. This chapter looks at what Ann Laura Stoler calls "states of deferral" and arrested developments of coloniality such as "imperial guardianship, trusteeship, delayed autonomy, temporary intervention, [and] conditional tutelage" not as the exception but the rule of colonial formations (2013, 8). I am less interested here in how these states of deferral function through state building structured "by and through a contemporary global colonial matrix of power," as Meera Sabaratnam argues. They are not meant to "work in producing or contributing to the production of autonomous and coherent self-governing political entities" (2017, 137). Rather, I am interested in how residual and unfinished post-Ottoman mapping of racial and religious borders of Europe is reactivated in the post–Cold War moment to reinvigorate Euro-Atlantic collaborations toward enclosure.

From a historical standpoint, there are two sedimented trajectories of being saved by the West that dominate contemporary Albanian historiography and public discourse—one at the beginning of the twentieth century, and the other at its end. The similarities between the International Control Commission established by the European powers at a London conference in 1913 and the one installed in Albania to facilitate its partition from the Ottoman Empire with the mandate to build a European state and citizens with the United Nations Mission in Kosovo (UNMIK) established in 1999 are striking not only in their organizational and political characteristics but also in the geopolitics that engendered them. In both instances, the mandates and materialization of the missions were designed and deployed to ostensibly save and Europeanize Muslim Albanians but to also redraw global racial borders. I am interested in what the histories of these interventions can illustrate about early geopolitical mapping and the making of race in the post-Ottoman moment that are contingent on, yet occluded from, contemporary epistemic and political infrastructures of Euro-Atlantic enclosures along the Balkan route. In attending to the contiguities of the past and present through occluded histories, I am not only interested in illustrating how those "occlusions," to quote Stoler again (2016, 10), help conceal or insulate the coloniality and collaboration of Euro-American geopolitical enclosures but also trace and bring attention to alternative imaginaries, insurrections, and international solidarity.

POST-OTTOMAN RACE MAKING AND RESISTANCE IN ALBANIA

In June 1914, Sheikh Haxhi Qamili led a Muslim uprising, challenging the legitimacy of the newly established Albanian state and its partition from the Ottoman Empire. The insurgents demanded the removal of the German prince, Wilhelm zu Wied, installed by European powers through the International Control Commission.[1] Since the European powers behind the commission forbade the appointment of a Muslim prince, they installed a new Christian prince, and the uprising gathered momentum. The insurgents demanded that Albania be returned to the sovereignty of the *khalīfah* (the Ottoman sultan), as an autonomous province governed by a Muslim prince, and that the Arabic alphabet be restored (Armstrong 1995). Qamili, a sheikh of the Melâmî Sufi *tarqia* (school) that practiced intentional poverty,[2] also demanded the abrogation of land privileges that the Albanian aristocracy had acquired though the so-called organic statute. The statute, which served as a provisional constitution for the new Albanian state, transformed all Arazi Mirie, which were Ottoman-owned public property (bestowed for use to loyal subjects), to Arazi Memluke, or privately owned land.[3] Since the beneficiaries of these reforms were the small group of landowning Albanian aristocracy who supported Prince Wied, Sheikh Qamili demanded the abrogation of their land titles and the subsequent redistribution of the land to the peasants (Puto 1978). In less than two months, the insurgents seized most of the territory of the Albanian state, and Durres, the capital, remained the only territory controlled by Prince Wied, his provisional Albanian government, and the International Control Commission. It should be noted that Prince Wied's recruits, who served as a provisional army, refused to fight their "Muslim brothers" when sent to extinguish the insurgency.[4] In a letter to the foreign ministry in Vienna, written in response to the prince being forced to leave the country, the Austrian-Hungarian ambassador to Rome, Kajetan Mérey von Kapos-Mére, stressed that unless there was a collective intervention on behalf of European powers to suppress the uprising, the "credibility of European prestige" was at stake (Verli 2014). In addition to the requirement that it should explicitly call for the protection of the prince and his family, the intervention was supposed to "teach Albanian rebels a lesson on European unity" (*Times* [London] 1914). But by September 5, 1914, the rebels had taken over Durres, entered the royal palace, and replaced the Albanian flag with the Ottoman one and would proceed to govern Albania for the following eight months. However, by May 1915, the Serbian state had organized the "Albanian expedition," invading Albania and ending the short-lived return to the khalīfah. Qamili was tried and hanged on August 16 of that year (Pearson 2004; see figure 3.1). The Serbian expedition is not only significant to note here because of its role in ending the first organized Muslim resistance to European incursions into Ottoman lands but also because it is emblematic of how newly

FIGURE 3.1. Haxhi Qamili on trial, Marubi, August 1915.

established Christian states in the Balkans attempted to colonize Muslim lands, employing European colonial practices along with the logic of "freeing" Europe from the last remaining Muslims.

Despite its failure, this short-lived resistance to European intervention in the Ottoman Empire resonated deeply with Muslims throughout the colonized world. In an article titled "A Pan-Islamic Movement in Albania," the *Tribune* in Lahore wrote that the rebels' demands for reinstating the Arabic alphabet were unreasonable and could harm an otherwise "justifiable movement" (*Tribune* 1914). The All-India Muslim League also protested the ill-treatment of Muslims in the conflict and warned against such an international intervention. Then, two thousand volunteers responded to an appeal to fight alongside the rebels in Albania (*Tribune* 1914). In Singapore, the newspaper *Majalah al-Islam* condemned the intervention of Western powers into what it considered the internal affairs of the Ottoman Empire ("Kuasa Sunia" 1914). In addition, the *Times of India* wrote "In Praise of the Rebels" that "Moslems are apprehensive that they will be persecuted by the Christian government of Albania as they are in Montenegro and Serbia, where hundreds of families are being forced into exile because they are Albanian Mohammedans" (*Times of India* 1914).

American Christian missionaries believed that the failure of the European-led International Control Commission to make Europeans out of Albanians was in their lack of bottom-up movement. Christian missionaries saw an evangelical mission in Albania that could be expanded throughout the Muslim world. Writing in April 1914, just as the peasant rebellion in Albania had reached its peak, Charles Telford Erickson, one of the most influential proponents of Protestant missions to convert Albanians back to their Christian faith in "Albania, the key to the Moslem world," advised that Albanians be considered "the Children of Israel [who] were trained and disciplined in Egypt and the wilderness to become the moral teachers and guides of the ages, . . . God has had this people under the same rigorous discipline, and, as I believe, for the same divine purpose, to lead a conquest against the last unyielding fortress that opposes the world-wide dominion of our Lord" (1914, 115–19). Erickson believed that Albanian networks in the Ottoman Empire could incite a larger evangelical mission while their conversion to Christianity would secure the geopolitical borders of Europe in the Balkans. Erickson developed a close collaboration with British Orientalists whose knowledge of the population and contacts with the Albanian independence movement were critical in seizing this opportunity. Among them were Aubrey Herbert and Edith Durham who had become key interlocutors between the Albanian independence movement and the Congress of London in 1913. By 1915, Erickson had become an honorary member of the largest Albanian diaspora organization in the United States, the Pan-Albanian Federation of America, or Vatra.

Most of the Protestant activists proposed Albania to an increasingly interested US government, forming foreign policy in Europe under Woodrow Wilson's missionary zeal. Played right, Albania could become an agent of stability; if ignored, its large Muslim population and its connections to the larger Muslim world under European colonial regimes could be a destabilizing force. The president of the Pan-Albanian Federation of America, Kristo Dako, would also echo Erickson. In *Albania, the Master Key to the Near East*, published for the Paris Peace Conference in 1919, Dako argued that "Albania can be a powerful ally for peace, but neglect it at the world's peril" (1919, xii). Dako and Erickson maintained close friendships with influential figures such as Charles Crane who had met Dako on his visit to Albania in 1911 and through whom he had met key figures of the Albanian independence movement (Hosaflook 2019). A wealthy Arabist and a Slavicist, Crane donated generously to Wilson's presidential campaign and would later become one of the most influential foreign policy advisors to the Wilson administration, serving in the 1917 Special Diplomatic Commission to Russia and the Paris Peace Conference.

The Albanian diaspora was quick to sense the rise in the new Wilsonian world order where race, racial purity, and local and global racial segregation became cornerstones of domestic and foreign policy. With Crane's support, the spiritual and political head of an influential Albanian community in Boston, Fan Noli, would meet Wilson in July 1918 and plead the case for Albanian independence. Noli was a polyglot and a larger-than-life figure who had translated Shakespeare into Albanian, declared independence of the Albanian Autocephalous Orthodox Church from the Greek Ecumenical Orthodox Patriarchate, and later in 1924 became a short-lived prime minister of Albania after mounting a democratic revolution against the post-Ottoman landed governing Albania since its split from the Ottoman Empire. In Boston, Massachusetts, he oversaw two important publications, *Dielli* and the *Adriatic Review*, the former a newspaper informing the Albanian diaspora about opinions on the politics of the great powers on Albania, the latter meant to inform US and European policy makers about the autochthones of the Albanian people and their right to be permitted to stay in Europe given the imminent collapse of the Ottoman Empire, which secured inside status for Albanians in the new georacial frontiers set forth at the Paris Peace Conference.[5]

The *Adriatic Review* would also publish selected works on the "Albanian question" by European and American Orientalists advocating Albanian independence as a geostrategic, necessary node for the West. For instance, in "The Future of the Albanian State," published in October 1918, J. S. Barnes would write that Albania "occupies an enviable geographical position with the making of good harbors on the narrowest portion of one of the most important waterways in the world; and she lies across the path of what will one day be the quickest mail route from London to Suez via Brindisi, Vlore, Janina, Kalabaka and the Pireus" (1918, 78). In November 1918, the *Adriatic Review* published a memorandum on Albania sent to President Wilson and his team before leaving for the Peace Conference, pointing out the many contributions to civilization the Albanian race had made. The authors trace the racial purity of Albanians in the "Illyrians, Macedonians and Epirotes," with their language being "the only living specimen of the tongues spoken by the aboriginal Aryan settler of Southeastern Europe," in the hopes that the United States and Europe would "do justice to the ancient Illyrian race which survived the tyranny of the Turk" (Barnes 1918, 97–100). By the end of World War I, the Albanian diaspora was both supported and inspired by the American Christian Atlanticism that emerged, and it was organized around influential American journalists and academics like Carlton Hayes, Ross Hoffman, and Walter Lippmann—all of whom believed that a global alliance between Europe and the United States was the only way of preserving Western hegemony by securing and sealing its territoriality (Alessandri 2010).

The Japanese victory over Russia in 1905 had raised fears in white intellectual circles across the Atlantic over race wars. Anxieties over race mixing were both local and global (Mishra 2012). Wilson, who came out of this school of thinking, believed that the rise of the colonized and colored people within settler colonies and across the colonized world required a buffer zone of independent countries around Euro-Atlantic territories that was populated by white and off-white majorities, an idea that gave birth to the "national self-determination movement" that dominated the Paris Peace Conference in 1919 and from which mostly eastern European and some peripheral Mediterranean countries benefited in securing semisovereignty. Albania's geopolitical position and claims to racial purity seem to have convinced the Wilson administration enough to press the case for, and secure, some self-determination for Albania at the Paris Peace Conference and a seat at the League of Nations in 1920.

The reemergence of this racialized geopolitical cartography after the Cold War was common, as were references to them in the immediate aftermath of the fall of the Berlin Wall. Visiting Albania in 1993, the US secretary of state James Baker would remind Albanians, as the communist regime was collapsing, that the United States "will stand with you as we stood with you early in this century, when President Woodrow Wilson championed your cause," and that "every part of this continent, just as every citizen of this country, must be part of what President Bush calls 'a Europe whole and free'" (US Embassy Tirana 2016). Baker had been a key figure in discussions around a new Euro-Atlantic architecture, offsetting customary European suspicion but also confronting fears of an emerging isolationist movement in the United States by pointing out that "America is a European power and will remain one" (Office of Public Communication 1989).

The Albanian question became symbolic of how the Balkans reemerged as cartography in the geopolitical imagination of the American and European public and policy makers who saw the Albanian- and Bosnian-populated territories as holes in the geographical wholeness of their new Euro-Atlantic club. Kosovo in particular, and its status, was perceived with both peril and opportunity after the collapse of the Cold War. The emergence of the Third Way (or competitive socialism) in the last decade of the twentieth century, like Wilsonianism (derived from liberal internationalism) at its beginning, was concerned about and centered on Euro-American geopolitical interests that sought to solidify the EU-US alliance through NATO shifting its representation from Cold War to post–World War II united narratives of the victory of fascism. Commenting on NATO'S defining moment in Kosovo, its secretary general Javier Solana would argue that Kosovo was "a challenge for all countries in the EuroAtlantic area," and that the support received for Kosovo by all partner countries cemented a "fundamental truth: the countries of Europe and North America share not only a common heritage, but a common destiny" (NATO 1999). The framing of the NATO war in Kosovo was a "restaging of World War II," producing a continued reference to what Fatima El-Tayeb calls the "West uniting to save the world from fascism"

(SBSCMES 2013). It was also a means of structuring the internal cohesion of the Euro-Atlantic alliance along late nineteenth- and early twentieth-century racial imaginaries.

CONVENIENT MUSLIMS
AND RECURSIVE COLONIAL HISTORIES

Writing in the *Georgetown Journal of International Affairs* less than a year after the 1999 NATO intervention in Kosovo, John Esposito and Vali Nasr, two of the most prominent scholars of Islam during the Clinton administration, argued that US intervention in Kosovo provided a "foreign policy break-through" (2000, 22). Kosovo, they proposed, belied many of the assumptions about the clash of civilizations that dominated US foreign policy after the Cold War and now provided an opportunity for the United States to rebrand its relations with the Muslim world by projecting itself as the guardian of mainstream moderate Muslims, similar to the ones believed to reside in Bosnia and Kosovo. The United States, they claimed, had not only saved Muslims from extinction in Eastern Europe but was also "the only Western power that accepted Bosnian and Albanian claims to be Europeans and to have a right to exist in Europe" (Esposito and Nasr 2000, 21).

In what sounds like rebranding, Esposito and Nasr point out the multiple benefits the United States could capitalize on if they were to save Muslims in the Balkans. The foreign policy breakthrough from US intervention in Kosovo, they argued, would project the United States as a benevolent universal humanitarian power, allowing it to forge stronger ties with liberal-minded Muslims and, at the same time, prevent possible ties with radical Islam. Much like Charles Telford Erickson (1914) proposing the assimilation of Albanians as "the key to the Moslem world," Esposito and Nasr suggested that Balkan Muslims could serve as model Muslims for the rest of the world as a way of forestalling radical-Islamist alternatives by showcasing the salvation the United States reserved for well-behaving Muslims. After September 11, 2001, however, American foreign-policy circles routinely warned Albanians that their saving hinged upon their commitment to the West. The criminalization of "Albanians" in Western Europe, the US, and the Balkans as notorious mafia cartels became a prominent feature of Euro-American security structures. Repeatedly issued warnings to the EU and NATO that Albanian organized crime penetrating the EU and the Balkans was also becoming involved in radical Islamism turned into a serious threat to the Euro-Atlantic border in the Balkans. Yet this depiction of Albanians as viral agents or sleeper cells that could—though seemingly white, secularized, and attached to Euro-American ideals—wake up to Islam and reactivate their links to the Arab world at any given time. In this sense, it is not their racial otherness that makes Albanians suspects but their similarity and proximity to whiteness, people who, once inside the Euro-Atlantic enclosure, can move seamlessly and pass the policing gaze. This passing of white Balkan Muslims has been an ongoing predicament in Euro-American security structures because people are not primed to read a white body as suspect.

Meanwhile, the international civilian administration and the NATO military presence in Kosovo was status quo. A growing economic crisis and political blockade by Serbia erupted in the Kosovo-wide riots of 2004. Former Italian prime minister Giuliano Amato, now the EU vice president of the Convention on the Future of the European Union, noted that "the real choice the EU is facing in the Balkans is: Enlargement or Empire" and that "if Europe's neo-colonial rule becomes further entrenched, it will encourage economic discontent; it will become a political embarrassment for the European project" (Amato et al. 2005, 11). The echoes of the Austro-Hungarian ambassador to Rome, Kajetan Mérey von Kapos-Mére, that the failure of the International Control Commission in Albania was questioning the "credibility of European prestige" could not have been more poignant. In the first decade of the twenty-first century, a movement for self-determination emerged, calling for an unapologetic decolonization from both Serbia and the international administration. Vetëvendosje, or the self-determination movement, sought to confront the depoliticization of the Kosovar people after the establishment of the international administration by asking poor and working-class citizens to participate in decision-making processes. Its critique of the indefinite deferral of independence coupled with postintervention privatization that resulted in mass unemployment, poverty, and corruption would strike a chord with Kosovars. In the meantime, a new generation of Albanian writers, artists, and poets were confronting the historical erasure of Islam in the Albanian public sphere. Enis Sulstarova's *Arratisja nga Lindja* (Escaping East; 2006) brilliantly captured the internalized Islamophobia and Orientalism framing the Albanian public since their modern inception in both Kosovo and Albania as an ongoing "escape from the East." Responding to increased criticism in Kosovo and the rise of the self-determination movement, the Albanian establishment sought to confront what it saw as "Ottoman nostalgia," with noted Albanian author Ismail Kadare remarking how Haxhi Qamili's ghost had returned to haunt Albanian territories. Drawing parallels between the Qamili rebellion in 1914 with new calls to revisit Albanian historiography, Kadare described these tendencies as Islamic infantility and the inability of Albanians to grasp the geopolitical moment and to identify as white. The Albanian, he wrote in a much-publicized and controversial debate between him and the Kosovar academic Rexhep Qosja in 2006, "like the European continent is white," and the Albanian language in "the most favorable case is inherited from Illyrians . . . in the most unfavorable case [it] is from Traecho—Illyrians" (Kadare 2006). Kadare was also responding to emerging trends in literary and artist circles to reappropriate Ottoman-era slang and style, like Ervin Hatibi, who mocked both the standardized modernist-socialist-realist Albanian language rooted in the Tosk dialect and the formal bureaucratic Gheg dialect that influenced the postindependent orthographic form. In addition to the supposed unquestionable whiteness, the Albanian language was the second-most significant proof that Albanians could use to prove their Aryan origins, and Kadare, long recognized as an unquestionable national master, saw himself as its most ardent protector. He regarded the emergence of *tallava* music in the 1990s as a bastardization of the Albanian language for its reclaiming of not only the Ottoman maqam style of rendition but also its Ashkali and Romani roots, which I will return to in the next chapter. Awarded the Man Booker International Prize for his novel *The Siege*, Kadare was admired across Europe and the United States for his metaphor of Albania as a Christian fortress vis-à-vis Ottoman invasion because it spoke to converging racist, xenophobic, and Islamophobic panic.

As Kosovo declared independence in 2008, Albanian imperial debt peaked. Within a decade after the Kosovo War, former secretaries of state, ambassadors, and special envoys who had contributed to Kosovo's liberation came to collect their dues. Madeleine Albright's company Albright Capital Management issued a general bid to buy Kosovo's public telecommunications network, while Wesley Clark, now chairman of the company Envidity, sought to privatize its mines. Christopher Dell, whom Albanians remember as the US ambassador who texted the name of the next president of Kosovo to its assembly members minutes before they voted on the next head of state, managed to push the Bechtel Corporation as the prime bidder for the construction of a national-unification highway between Albania and Kosovo. The Bechtel Corporation finished the 77-kilometer (47.8-mile) highway in Kosovo for a total of $1.13 billion, paid for by the taxes of the Balkans' poorest semicountry. The exchange of love and leverage produced an odd Albanian affective attachment to the empire, especially under the optimistic promise that with Kosovo's independence, the Albanian question in the Balkans would be resolved once and for all under the Euro-Atlantic umbrella. Indeed, a year after independence, Kosovo was ranked the most optimistic country in the entire world just as it plunged into becoming Europe's poorest (BIRN 2008). As Kodwo Eshun brilliantly put it, "You see the dark side of a political context through its relentless focus on its optimism" (HKW 2013).

Albanians became a melancholic accessory to the shambling Euro-Atlantic transatlantic coloniality, the last bit of the empire that could redeem and speak of its height in the immediate aftermath of the Cold War. Unsurprisingly, they were primed for the same role at the end of the first World War, where they became the poster child for Wilson's "national self-determination" of nations that depicted Albania as an example of the new international system guided by American politics while most of the world's people, including Indigenous people in the United States, continued to live under (settler) colonial rule. Albanians built statues to Woodrow Wilson, Bill Clinton, and George W. Bush as Bush and the UK prime minister Tony Blair were particularly keen on utilizing this affective capital to save their own legacies. Having used Albania as a US rendition site during the war on terror, as a destination for former Guantanamo Bay prisoners, and as resettlement location of the People's Mujahedin of Iran, in 2013 the United States requested Albania to also take on the destruction of Syrian chemical weapons. The last request reached the limit of affective Albanian solvency for the Euro-Atlantic alliance. Since the mid-2000s, Albania had become a destination for European toxic metal residue and radioactive waste. The Alliance against the Import of Waste (Aleanca Kundër Importit të Plehrave) became one of the most widespread and popular resistance organizations since the collapse of socialism. Their calls to prevent the transformation of Albania into Europe's dumping ground resonated deeply with people and resulted in spontaneous mass protests. The larger underlining factor, however, was the near-total collapse of the economies of both Albania and Kosovo. In

2015, as the refugees from the Middle East passed through the Balkan refugee route, a massive wave of Albanians from Kosovo joined them in their journey to Europe.

DEFERRED SELF-DETERMINATION

In October 2019, Vetëvendosje won the national elections in Kosovo. In its brief tenure from October 2019 to June 2020, the government, headed by Albin Kurti, tried to do what no government had done in Kosovo or the region: it set a bold task to dismantle a sedimented network of cronyism and corruption established through postwar privatization, the acquisition of public wealth, and the institutionalization of client-capitalist relations. It started from the ground up with the removal of unqualified civil servants and board directors who had handled lucrative privatization schemes coordinated after the conflict with UNMIK, the EU, and the United States Agency for International Development (USAID). The reforms were far-reaching and ranged from annulling judicial appointments and notary exams that had become notoriously nepotistic to investigating various enrichment schemes by previous governing coalitions, mainly headed by Hashim Thaçi in various positions because of standard postsocialist power switching from prime minister to president. During this time, the government faced the COVID pandemic and endemic pressure from the United States to lift the reciprocity measures. Vetëvendosje set out for Serbia, who had continued an exploitative economic arrangement after the war. It was a symbolic gesture, but what reflected its transformative politics was the demolition of the fences that enclosed government buildings installed by the international administration that Vetëvendosje had seen as a colonial regime that replaced the Serbian one. As the 2020 US presidential election neared, however, Trump's special presidential envoy for Serbia and Kosovo peace negotiations Richard Grenell aggressively pursued a Kosovo-Serbia deal and came to see Vetëndosje as an impediment. Grenell did what previous US envoys and ambassadors before him had done when reaching whatever deal was necessary to produce US foreign-policy "breakthroughs" for the election. Between April and June 2020, Grenell, in collaboration with President Thaçi, pressured Vetëvendosje's ruling partners to quit the coalition and install a puppet government that would be willing to travel to Washington, DC, and sign a deal with Serbia in the presence of President Trump.

Like previous US administrations before, Trump also sought to capitalize on the convenience of good Albanian Muslims who could be recruited once again to engineer a preelectoral "foreign-policy breakthrough" while also seeking to capture the votes of the Albanian American diaspora in Michigan with media sound bites. On September 4, 2020, Trump tweeted, "Another great day for peace with Middle East—Muslim-majority Kosovo and Israel have agreed to normalize ties and establish diplomatic relations. Well-done! More Islamic and Arab nations will follow soon!"[6] Israeli prime minister Benjamin Netanyahu followed with a statement announcing that "Kosovo will be the first Muslim-majority nation to open an embassy in Jerusalem" (*Times of Israel* 2020). The tweets were followed by a spectacle in the White House where Trump announced before the press, the Serbian president Aleksandar Vučić, and the Kosovo prime minister Avdulla Hoti, seated in front of Trump, that

> Serbia and Kosovo have tremendous numbers of people in the United States. They're—they love your country. They love your country so much. They love your country so much. . . . We've also made additional progress on reaching peace in the Middle East. I will say that Kosovo and Israel have agreed to normalization of ties and the establishment of diplomatic relations. The agreement we made with UAE has been incredible, the—what it's represented, what's it's meant. And we have other countries in the Middle East coming very much to us and saying, like, "When do we go? When can we sign?" I think we're going to have great peace in the Middle East. And nobody has been able to say that for a long time. (Hoti 2020)

Israeli and American media lauded Kosovo by quoting Kosovo President Thaçi's various statements of love toward Israel: "I love Israel. What a great country. Kosovo is a friend of Israel. I met so many great leaders when I was there—Netanyahu, Sharon—I really admire them" (Spritzer 2007). In turn, Kosovo committed to opening an embassy in Jerusalem and adopting the controversial definition of anti-Semitism promoted by the International Holocaust Remembrance Alliance, which considers critique of the settler-colonial state of Israel as an act of anti-Semitism. But the more interesting aspect of this agreement was the identification of Kosovo as an "Islamic" and "Muslim majority" country in the Middle East, conveniently serving both Trump's claims that he could get Muslims to recognize Israel while promoting himself as a deal maker among

Muslims. Having been pressured to provide secular assurances in order to be saved, Albanians were perplexed by their sudden association with Islam and the Middle East. Objections were swift and visceral, as they usually are in such instances where Albanians are "mistaken" for Muslims. A varied set of arguments emerged, from claims that not all Albanians were Muslims to Kosovo and Albania being in Europe and Albanians being an Aryan race. Indeed, claims to the Aryan race were corroborated in opposition to being referred to as Muslims or Middle Easterners. But the false Serbian history and propaganda, which has sought to present Albanians as nonnative to the Balkans to justify their expulsion and alignment of its colonial objectives with the European ones, was confronted. This cursory secularism has not only sedimented a particular kind of white Albanian objecthood through internalized Islamophobia but also mandates that Albanians secure and structure the (geo)politics of race through religious difference. Islam thus prevents Albanians from being acknowledged as fully and unquestionably white, a predicament that requires relentless affirmation of racial purity to secure sovereignty.

In *The Wretched of the Earth*, Frantz Fanon argues that "colonialism forces the dominated people to constantly ask itself: who am I in reality?" (1963, 124). This argument is made not because he assumes a fixed political position from which the colonized can announce themselves but rather he suggests the contradictions that colonial powers deploy to continuously shift the signifiers of race situated in particular relations of power within a specific time and place. Ghassan Hage makes a brilliant point about the vagueness of race in relation to Islamophobia, arguing that "racists have always managed to be exceptionally efficient by being vague. It could even be said that vagueness, empirical 'all-over-the-placeness,' contradiction, blocking-of-the-obvious, and even sometimes a totally surrealist grasp of reality, are the very conditions of possibility of the maximal efficiency of racist practices" (2017, 9). But race, according to Achille Mbembe, is also a "complex of microdeterminations, an internalized effect of the Other's gaze and a manifestation of secret, unfulfilled beliefs and desires" (2017, 31). We can read Mbembe's unfulfilled beliefs and desires in this context as the deferral of sovereignty that puts the local into a constant state of anxiety due to their failed aspirations to become, once and for all, white. Needless to say, such processes are underwritten with shame, overcompensation, self-hate, fear, and trauma—all of which function to sustain the state of deferral and, by extension, maintain colonial relations of power while engineering whiteness through the re-inforcement of inferiority. These racial substructures that inform the transatlantic spatiotemporality are rooted in colonial epistemologies that either "center futurity in the white subject and disqualify non-human subjects from full humanity and thus from a forward-oriented agency, or confines these subjects to zones of death and sacrifice in service to white futurity" (Smith and Vasudevan 2017, 211).

Vetëvendosje's removal from power illustrates that the Euro-American mission in Kosovo was less of an intention to forge a self-governing entity but, like the International Control Commission in Albania in 1913, per-manently put, under deferred sovereignty, suspect populations around the fringes of the Euro-Atlantic enclosure. But to focus on the larger politics of sovereignty and coloniality, as I have done in this chapter, is to not only elide what Ann Laura Stoler (2016) calls the more hardened and tenacious durabilities of colonial missions stored in the substructure of our sub-jectivities but also to overlook how sexuality was central in securing the more intimate affiliations with whiteness and coloniality. The mandates of modernizing post-Ottoman Muslim populations in the Balkans, like the International Control Commission in Albania, were not just guided by the geopolitical racial reconfigurations of the world at the end of the nine-teenth and beginning of the twentieth century. They were also invested in ordering, sanitizing, and secularizing the locals through the moderniza-tion of (post-)Ottoman social, medical, and educational codes that sought to engender a distinction between normative and deviant national subject-hood. These were not top-down processes of local elites but were deeply in-vested mediators of coloniality/modernity. For Albanian nationalist elites who understood their geographic position in Europe as incompatible with the religion of the majority of its population, disavowing Islam became im-perative to their racial and national alignment with Europe. The tackling of gender and sexual deviance as Ottoman or Islamic remnants came to inform nationalist progress whereby the Albanian male escapes the ho-moerotic past as an Islamic affliction and embraces heterosexuality as a racial affirmation toward Europeanness. With that in mind, the follow-ing chapter traces how the saving, straightening, and secularization of the Albanian male in the post-Ottoman period returns to reinforce racial b/ordering regimes through sexuality.

(Dis)Embodying Enclosure

Of Straightened
Muslim Men and
Secular Masculinities

Pietro Marubi was an Italian revolutionary who, after the Risorgimento (unification of Italy), sought political exile in the Ottoman Empire and became Pjetër Marubi, the founder of the first photographic studio in Albania. Along with Kel Marubi, his adoptive son, and his grandson, Gegë Marubi, he documented the most significant events in Albanian and Balkan politics, leaving a largely unexplored archive of everyday life in the Balkans from the late Ottoman period to the mid-twentieth century. The image of Haxhi Qamili on trial in 1915 in chapter 3 was taken by Kel Marubi and illustrates, both in terms of significance of the event and the angle from which it is shot, a photographer that is conscious of witnessing the collapse of the Ottoman caliphate amid the Albanian national independence movement. There are seven images from the Marubi archive that I want to draw attention to as a way of introduction into this chapter. In the first one (figure 4.1) Pjetër Marubi himself is seated as sumptuously as a *bejtexhi* (poet) on a divan as if interrupted by the camera while playing the lute.[1] Two *dylbers* (admirers of the poet) posing over his shoulders are meditating in stillness, seemingly taken by his art of

aheng (poetic gathering).[2] The image is meant to emulate what was already becoming a dying art in Albania: a poet and his two lovers indulging in poise through music, *meze*, and *raki*. The dylbers are identified as Emilio Simoni and Oso Faltorija. Faltorija is most likely a sobriquet for a fortune-teller in the feminine form. Men in homoerotic poses but not necessarily in a relationship (see figures 4.2 and 4.3) are the subject matter of several of Marubi's works, through which he seems to have wanted to extend the tradition in the face of the Europeanizing gender and sexual dynamics of late nineteenth-century Ottoman attempts at modernization.

In particular, in figure 4.3 we see one of the men dressed in traditional costume wearing an Ottoman fez, while his partner is outfitted *ala franga*, or in Western-style clothing, mediating the body and geopolitical transformations of the time. The figure of the bejtexhi, like that of the central Asian steppe's *ashik* (singer-poet) immortalized in Sergei Parajanov's *Ashik Kerib* (1988), is a queer one, not only because the bejtexhi's relation with his dylbers was an erotic and poetic one, but also because in the context of late nineteenth-century Albania, when the picture was taken, the bejtexhi tradition was a dying art and was slowly transforming into

FIGURE 4.1. Rapsodi, by Pietro Marubi, 1887.

FIGURE 4.2. Two men with fezzes holding hands, Marubi, year unknown.

FIGURE 4.3. Two men holding hands, Marubi, year unknown.

an Orientalist fantasy. The fourth image (figure 4.4) depicts the encounter of an Albanian *köçek* (cross-dressing or cross-gender dancer) offering a flower to what seems to be the arrival of European clientele, with two men kneeling in attendance with plates as if to contemplate and welcome the arrival of the European admirers into a world still untouched by the hetero-homo regime.

In the fifth image (figure 4.5), we witness two soldiers of the International Control Commission (discussed in the previous chapter) around 1914–1915, seeming to be admiring or acquiring a seated köçek with an Albanian man, possibly posing as his/her lover or pimp, standing and looking at the camera in approval. The last, and perhaps most insightful, staging of the erotic politics of the time (figure 4.6) is two soldiers of the International Control Commission, one pulling an Albanian man by the ear while the other is assaulting his köçek partner with a sword.

In both images, the weapon carried by the militia of the International Control Commission intersects the intimacy of the staging. In figure 4.5, the firearm rests on the köçek's body while in figure 4.6 it is held by the soldier pulling the Albanian man's ear, as if to discipline his desire with

FIGURE 4.4. Mati Kodheli and Giovanni Canale with friends, Marubi, 1860.

the long, tilted weapon. Marubi, who, judging from the amount of ho-moerotic images one finds in his archive was probably *queer* himself, sought to capture the multilayered civilizing mission of the European International Control Commission in Albania, photographing military and civilian parades, battlefields, the prince and his entourage, and their interactions with natives. All of the images center on bodies that elude categorization and had not yet come under the radar of Ottoman modernization in Istanbul, where the Young Turk Revolution sought

FIGURE 4.5. Italian soldiers of the International Control Comission in Albania stationed in Shkodra, Marubi, 1914.

FIGURE 4.6. Italian soldiers of the International Control Comission in Albania stationed in Shkodra, Marubi, 1914.

to Europeanize the empire. At its edges, this modernizing came with other European and American colonizing objectives, such as US protestant missionaries and the installment of the International Control Commission in Albania or the Habsburg mission discussed in chapter 2. The socialist period in between (if we can call it that) heterohistoricized the histories of post-Ottoman projects of modernization and colonization in the historical-materialist fashion that defined the national historiographies of the socialist world. Their reemergence from archives after socialism—as Haxhi Qamili's ghosts—came to haunt the seemingly finished Euro-Atlanticization of the Muslims in the Balkans, possibly because, as Shawn Michelle Smith argues, photography "is emblematic of the way a past continues to inhabit and punctuate a present" and "encapsulates a temporal oscillation, always signifying in relation to a past and a present, and anticipating a future" (2020, 1, 5).

The encounter of civilian and military members of the International Control Commission with native sexual and gender "deviants," as depicted in the images in this chapter, would come to transform the ways in which Albanians came to imagine their gender and sexual embodiments in their encounters with Western missionaries. The bejtexhi poets, who mainly wrote in Ottoman Albanian using the Arabic, Persian, or Ottoman alphabet, addressed homoerotic themes that were not compatible with the homo-hetero regime emerging in late nineteenth-century Albania. They adopted cross-gendered metaphors for themselves and their lovers while frequently equating their love for their dylbers with their love for Islam.[3] The term *dylber* has been the most common term used in Albanian public discourse today to both discredit and defy genealogies of same-sex desire and nonbinary gender embodiments. Indeed, the bejetexhi poets, their works, and their dylbers became the central repertoire from which Albanian nationalists drew their material for the heterosexualization and Europeanization of Albanian gender and desire in the late-socialist and postsocialist period. I draw on these images and imaginaries of nonnormative Albanian bodies to think of their heteronormalization as a his/torical process, as both body and geo-orienting methods, not only as imagined and enacted under the colonial mission of control in the early twentieth century but whose reverberations are still present today as Albanian aspirations of and orientations toward whiteness traverse through sexual orientations and continue to trouble the seemingly stable whiteness and heterosexuality of Albanians.

In 2018, the Horizontal Facility for the Western Balkans and Turkey, a body of the European Union and the Council of Europe, launched the project "Fighting Bullying and Extremism in the Education System in Albania," implemented jointly by the Council of Europe's Education Department, the Council of Europe's office in Tirana, and the Albanian Ministry of Education and Sports. The project was implemented by local Albanian LGBTQI+ organizations that conducted trainings on antibullying and homo/transphobia. A homophobic panic ensued over homosexual "propaganda" in schools, generating a host of conspiracy theories about the "gay agenda" being pushed in an attempt to weaken, destabilize, and eventually destroy the Albanian family. The noted Albanian publicist and curator Artan Lame, who had previously been chastised for his homophobia in Albanian media and who was seeking to somewhat redeem himself, launched an attack by claiming that Albania had been a paradise of homosensuality, illustrated in the numerous bejtexhi songs: "We all sang them until the communist regime did away with them in the [']50s" (BalkanWeb 2015). In Kosovo, the mainstream *Kosovarja* argued that the "songs of the ashiks and dylbers, which we are all familiar with, were not only not hated, they were welcomed" (*Kosovarja* 2018). The Kosovar television station T7 produced a short segment called "Our Rhapsodes Also Sang to Same-Sex Desire." The video includes clips of the last known and widely admired bejtexhi Riza Bllaca (1919–88) singing "Walking the *kaldrma* like a *Shah* / with your coat thrown on one shoulder / o man for the love of God / gift your dandy one sunrise," concluding with, "Don't buy a *qefin* for me / bury me in my *dylber[']s* shirt / in the grave do not submit me / near my *dylber* leave me."[4] Bllaca is heard between songs bursting in joyful laughter and telling his present dylbers, "May I eat your mustache!" (T7 2018). Seeking to protect the bejtexhi tradition from its association with homosexuality, literary critics came out in defense of the bejtexhi poets being projected as "homosexuals," frequently clarifying that the bejetexhi poets were not homosexuals and that most of their poems where they compare their lovers to the face of Imam Ali or the palm of the prophet were actually spiritual metaphors of the time.

In this chapter, I look at how anxieties over the hetero-European orientations of Albanians are at times constructed against the queer Muslim as a renegade of the Ottoman past that continues to haunt the Albanian orientation toward Europe, and at other times, sympathetic narratives toward homosexuality are employed to advance Albanian's European progress and emancipation. The goal here is not only to expose the ways in which the mobilization of Orientalist categories of sexuality and Islam in the Albanian public are deployed toward the (dis)embodiment of white heteronormative masculinities but to also think about how nonhetero-sexual bodies re-exist outside the mandates of desire bequeathed by coloniality/modernity. To do this, in the second half of the chapter, I engage with queer interventions that disrupt and negate Euro-gay-oriented subject formation by calling into visibility the violence embedded in such liberatory strategies.

This chapter is situated in a broader critique of the instrumentalization of gender/sex rights in the in Euro-American colonial and postcolonial projects of national modernization in the Muslim world (Mahmood 2004; Najmabadi 2005; Massad 2008; Abdou 2019; Salaymeh 2020; Thobani 2020; Mitra 2020) and the ways in which Muslim and migrant populations in Euro-American spaces have been racialized through sexual rights discourses (Puar 2007; El-Tayeb 2011; Scott 2019; Haritaworn 2015). While my work has been deeply influenced by this scholarship, Muslims in the Balkans are generally an anomaly in literature in that they are neither located in the former first or former third worlds. Situated in a trajectory of "unconventional imperial-colonial histories," I think through the intersections of Islam and sexuality in this chapter through the decolonial option, as the "decolonial option does not accentuate the historical description of (neo)colonialist strategies but rather the long-lasting ontological, epistemic, and axiological traces left after any colonialism seems to be a matter of the past" (Tlostanova 2019b, 165). In this sense, I problematize the sex/gender binaries, imaginaries, and embodiments not as derivatives of colonial/capitalism but as structurally coconstitutive parts of coloniality/modernity based on one single Eurocentric conceptualization of humanity (Lugones, 2008, 2010; Miñoso, Correal, and Muñoz 2014; Tlostanova, 2013; Kancler 2016). This allows me to attend to what Rahul Rao calls the "messy critical task of determining how responsibility for ongoing oppressions must be apportioned between colonial and postcolonial regimes . . . including those that enable formerly colonised states to become colonial in their own right" (2020, 9). In this sense, the legacies of colonially imposed models of sexuality and subjectivization that were instrumental in the ongoing attempts of the Albanian man to meet the expectations of European orientation—be it the demand to become straight in the post-Ottoman moment or queer in the postsocialist one. While I argue here that these are not just discursive practices but also embodied realities, where sexuality legitimizes the racialized mappings of space and time along the Euro-Atlantic enclosure as measures of masculinity and modernity, I also wonder how sexual moments and movements can gesture and generate new social and spatial relations.

THE INTRICATE WEB OF "ISLAMIC SEXUALITIES"

In an interview in 2009, Ismail Kadare, who had just received the Prince of Asturias Award, speaking from his position as a dissident writer in communist Albania, argued that "what excited suspicion [by the Albanian communist regime] was, 'why does the western bourgeoisie hold a writer from a Stalinist country in high esteem'?" (Flood 2009). Yet the communist regime not only allowed the Albanian writer to travel to France—a rare privilege reserved only for those close to the regime— but engaged in promoting his rise to prominence in European literary circles. For the communist regime, Kadare crafted historical fiction that, as Peter Morgan argues, "represented Albanian identity as something native and authentic against Ottoman, Soviet or, later, Maoist, influences," mirroring the regime's desire to situate Albania not only as a constitutive part of Europe but as a guardian of the frontier between Europe and its eastern Others (2011, 18). For the Europeans, Kadare presented an opportunity to gaze inside what was considered one of the most isolated communist regimes, providing semifictionalized Orientalist narratives of oppression and violence that Albanians endured under the Ottoman Empire, which he later argued was a metaphor for communism.

First published in 1986, *Viti i Mbrapshtë* (A vicious year) is considered one of the most accomplished novels by Ismail Kadare (2009). Set in 1913 Albania, a year after partition from the Ottoman Empire, the novel fictionalizes the installment of the International Commission for Control to guarantee the reign of German-born Prince Wilhelm zu Wied. In the background, a Muslim uprising seeks to overthrow the foreign Christian prince in favor of an Ottoman Muslim one. The Muslim uprising is led by one of the main characters, Kuz Baba, a fictionalized representation of Haxhi Qamili, presented as a ruthless, uncontrolled, hypersexualized Muslim who, in fighting to preserve Islam in Albania, is actually fighting to preserve his privilege to have access to beautiful men. In the midst of a war that will decide the faith and future of Albania, Kuz Baba can't be bothered with politics but is instead consumed by grief for his murdered lover and a fresh desire for the Dutch soldiers of the new German prince: "So taken he is by thinking about boys that since he seeing the Dutch, he is obsessed with fetching one as a slave" (Kadare 2009, 469). Kuz Baba's violent, vulgar, irrational, and uncontrolled sexuality throughout the novel is constructed against the backdrop of a character named Shestan, a beautiful, rational, heterosexual, naïve soldier who, along with his friends, decides to fight in favor of the German prince and therefore for the European future of Albania. Shestan's early lack of determination matures when he reads his first newspaper in Albanian and comes across a picture of Albania depicted as a "girl or a young woman laying on a hospital bed, surrounded by masked surgeons with knives and scissors in their hands" (Kadare 2009, 476). Amid chaos and ambivalence, Shestan's deepfelt sympathy toward the representation of Albania as a fragile woman under threat by masked surgeons representing both the encroachments of neighboring states makes him the ideal male citizen. Kadare projects the chaos of an infantile state with the infantile Shestan who then matures through his rejection of Kuz Baba's advancements. For Shestan's sexuality to mature, Kuz Baba's unsublimated and unsacrificial sexuality cannot be oriented toward the advancement of the nation and, as such, cannot represent the future, but only a failed past. Shestan's coming of age is employed to imply and register Albania's coming of age into modernity and Euro-hetero order, equated with returning to, or rediscovering, Europe.

In order to establish a semblance of order in an ambivalent time and space, Kadare has to work against multiple sexual subjectivities that don't always align with the Euro-homo-hetero binaries that he wants to introduce as a hetero ordering device. Kuz Baba is not simply a homosexual but represents an entire homoerotic culture modeled after the bejtexhi tradition that escapes homo-hetero binaries as well as the gendered male-female order. In this context, Kadare's depiction of the queerness of bejtexhi homoerotics is not reductive, albeit he does mock its sentimentalities. For instance, Kuz Baba claims that he was told by a certain dervish that "dylbers must be covered in hijabs as women to avoid scenes, wherever it appears, the knife is not far" (Kadare 2009, 436). Kadare discrediting the bejtexhi tradition in the production of homo-hetero binaries is manifold. While Kadare exploits the bejtexhi tradition to legitimize his historical fiction, he uses irony to banalize its homoerotic aesthetics.

This is not accidental, as it appears at a critical juncture of orientation, both sexual and geopolitical. In *The European Identity of Albanians* (2006), for instance, Kadare explicitly states that the bejtexhi poetry had "a hidden agenda to unman and morally weaken" the Albanian man, as "it needed no more than a few 'boys' and 'fags' of that sort for not freedom, but the very idea of freedom to disappear forever" (2006, 6). Albanian anxieties around these queer sexualities, which Kadare frequently places in various Islamic settings such as a Bektashi Tekke or a dervish, are not specific only to his writings. Contemporary Albanian literary works have frequently engaged with Islamic sexualities to construct the hetero-male character as a way of saving him from potential queer and Islamic orientations by valorizing his ability to overcome such temptations and re-orient himself toward Europe.

The contemporary, cursory employment of Islamic sexualities in different modalities to locate the ideal Albanian heterosexual in relation to Europe emerges at a time when old anxieties around fractured and unfinished European orientations became subsumed in debates about contemporary European expansion. These debates, reflected in the literary taste for "belonging to Europe," expose old and new contradictions of historical narratives in Albanian literature. For example, in *Otello, Arapi i Vlorës* (Otello, the moor of Vlora) Ben Blushi (2009), one of the most popular authors in Albania in the last two decades, employs the queer "foreign" Muslim to reinforce a narrative of heteronormative European masculinity to tell the story of Albania before the arrival of the Ottomans. Set between 1300 and 1400, in pre-Ottoman Albania, *Otello, Arapi i Vlorës* recounts the fall of Vlora to the Ottomans through the personal story of Otello. Otello, an African slave, ends up in Albania after he is purchased by a Venetian family whose patriarch takes him on a trip to Vlora to visit his relatives. The family ties between a Venetian family and the ruling family of Vlora reinforce Albania's historical relations with Europe before the Ottoman invasion. In Vlora, coming under suspicion for murder, Otello ends up in prison where he meets Hamit, a sly Muslim queer who seduces Otello and introduces him to homoerotic love. When Otello tries to seduce Andrea, a new Albanian prisoner, Andrea resists engaging in anything more than just touching and pretending to be sleeping while Otello admires his body. Sexuality here is attributed to both the racial and religious other. While both Otello and Hamit are presented as feeble men who fall prey to their uncontrolled desires,

Andrea resists this urge by deciding to join the army and save Vlora from the arriving Ottoman armies, which is equated with sacrifice and resistance to sexually deviant behaviors and the preservation of heterosexual integrity. In the end, the Ottomans defeat the Albanians. Hamit, who has now joined the Ottoman forces, takes Andrea hostage and out of resentment for Otello's love toward Andrea cuts Andrea's head off and paints it in oils and perfumes. This corporal disfigurement of Andrea's head serves to remind the reader of failed Albanian heterosexuality in the face of Ottoman conquest and that only through the disintegration of his body could Hamit subdue Andrea's heterosexual masculinity. The fall of Albania to Ottomans registered in the disembodiment of Andrea's body suggests that Albania's temporary misalignment from Europe during the Ottoman Empire did not and could not convert Albanians into Ottomans, as this could have only been attained through death.

Similarly, in 2008's, *Të Jetosh ne Ishull* (To live on an island), the character of Ali Tepelena, a semirealistic depiction of Ali Pasha of Tepelena (an Ottoman Albanian ruler from 1740 to 1822), is styled as a queer despot who seduces young Christian men for his harem. His homoerotic sexuality is equated with Islam, a foreign infliction in the body of the nation that cannot be purged but only assimilated. The main character, Arianit Komneni, reflects on how "Islam has been pushed onto our beds, our homes and our souls," and "now we can't kill this foreign beast as we will hurt ourselves . . . if we want to live in peace with it, we have to tame the wildness of the beast, feeding it with our Christian body and soul" (Blushi 2008, 403). The foundational narrative of Albanian identity here emerges as a diluted, damaged, and compromised hybrid of wild Islam penetrating loving Christianity. Blushi, while destabilizing the boundaries of "us" and "them," employs Christian ethics of victimhood and sacrifice to suggest that, as Christ carries the burden of sin in being reborn free, the Albanian man in being reborn as European must tame and bring under control Islam. While Blushi operates through Christianity to establish the Europeanness of Albanians, Kadare uses northern Albanian Catholicism and classical Greek mythology as an orienting device toward the Balkans and Europe. In his works of both literature and literary criticism, the catholic Albanian North represents a space not fully contaminated by the Ottoman Empire and is fanatically engaged in preserving "Albanianness" in the ancient Greek tradition that is therefore proto-European.

It is important to note here that the dialectical tensions around Islam, sexuality, whiteness, and belonging to Europe are not framed in opposition to homosexuality, per se, but specifically Islamic "queer" sexualities. In Kadare's *Konkurs Bukurie për Burrat në Bjeshkët e Namuna* (Beauty pageant for men in the Accursed Mountains, 1999), unlike Islamic sexualities, the Catholic Albanian homosexual is ontologized through ancient Greek mythology and rendered a victim-hero rather than a villain. This desire to save the Catholic, and by extension ancient Greek and European Albanian homosexuality, from the Queer Muslim one is to introduce homo-hetero binaries as protection from uncategorizable abjection. Situating the narrative in northern Catholic Albania, the hero of the novel, Gaspër Cara, is portrayed as a kind, emancipated citizen from the capital who suffers his homosexuality in silence. Cara's love for Prenk Curri, a confident highlander and suffering-in-silence desired heterosexual, is committed, stable, and exclusive. In contrast to Kadare's licentious queer Muslim characters who have multiple lovers and frequently abuse them, Cara's love for Curri, while homosexual and tragic, is still depicted as an acceptable love within the realm of possibility. It is also interesting to note that the construction of Carra as a modern European homosexual is enacted through his state-of-the art dress and as a reader of Oscar Wilde's *The Ballad of Reading Gaol*. The civilized look and behavior enables him to engage with the rest of the local Europeanized intelligentsia who not only understand him but sympathize with his predicament (Kadare 1999, 117–55). The difference in the portrayal of Muslim and northern Albanian Catholic sexualities is therefore related to European belonging. The latter is not projected as a threat, as his European homosexuality keeps heterosexuality intact and stable. Muslim sexualities on the other hand are projected as destabilizing and impossible failures.

Indeed, in an interview after his reception of the Man Booker International Prize (now the International Booker Prize), when asked what he made of Lord Byron's account of "Greek love" among Albanians in the court of Ali Pasha of Tepelena, Kadare replied that "what Byron saw had nothing to do with Ancient Greece, . . . It came with the Ottoman occupation and was pedophile, little boys" (Fallowell 2006). The desire to pathologize and discredit Ottoman Albania, and by extension Islamic sexualities as failed and perverse, serves as a reminder of the continued Albanian anxiety around the desired integrity of their European orientation. On the other hand, the introduction of the Catholic homosexual as a victim, at a time when certain homosexual bodies are integrated into European citizenship, suggests that while Islamic sexualities cannot be fully expelled they can be stabilized and assimilated into homo-hetero binaries. Europe then presents the possibility of redemption and escape of past failed sexualities, straightening and administering their permission as a testament to tolerance and diversity. This coincides with European integration discourses built around "returning to Europe" as an escape from violent non-European pasts.

HOMOEMANCIPATION
AND THE QUEER POLITICS OF TIME

In an interview given for *Stigma* (European Union External Action 2014), a documentary funded by the EU project "Challenging Homophobia in Kosovo," the European Parliament rapporteur for Kosovo, Ulrike Lunacek, appears at a press conference and explains to Kosovar viewers that homosexuality is not a disease. In another segment, Lunacek suggests that she is "sure that there are artists in this country who are quite popular who are also lesbian and gay, but are afraid to say so," stressing the importance that some of these people "show their faces," closing her remarks with, "I have said here in Kosovo that I am a lesbian myself, [it] is part of my life, so what?" The documentary renders the queer community in Kosovo almost entirely invisible. Kosovar society is pathologized as pervasively patriarchal and ignorant with an almost irreconcilable difference between queers and the rest of their communities. These statements are not just located in mediated discourses; they also advance EU-funded projects geared toward saving the LGBTQI+ community in Kosovo from homophobia and transphobia through the promotion of normative LGBTQI+ rights that rely on Western and white homoemancipation concepts of coming out, visibility, and top-down institutional approaches devoid of other factors of marginalization.

The debate around in/visibility is an important one to question as it registers those subjects whose sexuality can be understood in Euro-American sexual politics. As Jasbir Puar reminds us, "Coming out as a normative queer (secular) practice is thus scripted as religious confession, which accrues the force of what Foucault terms 'the speaker's benefit'— those who can speak about sex are thus seen as free, having transgressed its (religious) confinement" (2017, 235). Thus when Lunacek argues that there is no visibility, she not only ignores the visibility of queer individuals and formations in Kosovo who do not identify with the dominant LG-BTQI+ discourse but also fails to acknowledge those who reject visibility as a categorical need to label and classify their sexuality through specific categories and arbitrary markers over more complex subjectivities and realities that can't always fit the neatly defined Euro-American politics of LGBTQI+ rights. Moreover, problematizing coming-out as a Western and cisgender narrative, Saffo Papantonopoulou, for instance, asks, "[What] does it mean for a transgender person to *not* be 'out'[?]" (2014, 283). In other words, the projects that invest in "saving" the LG BTQI+ community in the Balkans not only seek to project the EU as the defender of these communities, even in instances when these communities reject its patronage, but also legitimize Euro-American coloniality through homoemancipation.

In a promotional video made by the US Embassy in Kosovo called "Judge Ted Weathers and Family Discuss LGBTQI+ Issues in Kosovo," we are introduced to the honorable Theodore Weathers, his husband, Terry McEachern, and their daughter, Elizabeth. McEachern, a financier from San Diego, reminds the viewers that "gay people have been born into every culture and every religion since the beginning of the world" (US Embassy Pristina Kosovo 2014). During a series of images of the US ambassador surrounded by LGBTQI+ activists during Pristina Pride, the video features Weathers commending Kosovo for its new constitution, drafted primarily by USAID lawyers, that protects LGBTQI+ rights. In another interview given for the magazine and media outlet *Kosovo 2.0*, Weathers argues, "The folks here and the LGBT community, they are fearful. They are not out to their families or co-workers. It reminds me of where we were 30 years ago, personally and also in the USA, when it was a much more fearful thing to be openly gay. . . . Things have changed so much in the last 20–30 years in the USA, and I suspect, and I hope that it will be the same in Kosovo" (Marí 2014).

Neda Atanasoski points out that since the 1990s, one crucial task of US liberal multiculturalism was to distinguish normative modes of inhabiting and representing diversity from aberrant ones, which could lead to "tribalism" and separatism of the kind witnessed in former Yugoslavia, Chechnya, and Rwanda (Atanasoski 2013, 34). While projecting post–Cold War Balkan countries as premodern societies stuck in ethnic and religious hatred and rooted in the failures of the socialist experiment, multiculturalism emerged as an emblem of national unity and liberal democracy and as a sign of the end of racial and racist history in the West. Alongside this portrait of integration, "ethno-religious nationalism and conflict in post-socialist Eastern Europe portrayed the region as an anachronistic reflection of a pre–civil rights era U.S. racist past" (36). This myth of US racial progress, argues Atanasoski, which had, since the 1950s, been narrated as *domestic* racial advancement, was resignified following the demise of state socialism as an *evolutionary model* for the former Eastern Bloc nations (36).

Visiting Albania on a homoemancipation tour to attend the first official US-sponsored conference held outside the country, prominent gay US author Kevin Sessums wrote, "As I look out at so many young people in the audience today who have come to Tirana from all over Eastern Europe and the Balkans for this conference on LGBT rights, I am reminded of those brave young people half a century ago who came to Mississippi during Freedom Summer, at great risk to themselves, in order to organize and demonstrate and strategize not only for the advancement of the rights of African Americans but, in so doing, the advancement of society as a whole" (2016). He proceeds to situate the civil rights struggle in the postracial registry by comparing the number of Mississippi's white residents back then to the number of the residents of Eastern Europe and the Balkans now, deeply resenting any attempt by young activists to change their society.

Echoing the "it gets better" narrative that was popularized in the United States to address LGBTQI+ bullying and suicide, Sessums here projects the United States as a postracial society no longer haunted by racism yet still animated by anxiety over which racist past gets permission to be visible in the struggle for LGBTQI+ communities in the postsocialist and culturally backward Balkans. Rahul Rao points out how the internationalization of "it gets better" narratives "evoke central tropes of homonationalism, deploying queer tolerance to reproduce extant geopolitical hierarchies" (2020, 144). Moreover, such narratives not only reinforce the myth of postsocialist, (neo)liberal capitalist progress in Eastern Europe but, more importantly, they entirely ignore the structural violence, criminalization, poverty, incarceration, and death regularly administered on Black and brown transgender and queer bodies in the United States. As Bassichis and Spade write:

The fantasy of life "getting better" imagines violence as individual acts that bad people do to good people who need protection and retribution from state protectors . . . rather than situating bodily terror as an everyday aspect of a larger regime of structural racialized and gendered violence congealed within practices of criminalization, immigration enforcement, poverty, and medicalization targeted at black people at the *population* level—from before birth until after death—and most frequently exercised by government employees. (Bassichis and Spade 2014, 196)

The time and timing of humanitarian, and now queer, interventions in the Balkans have continued to be read in the registry of the United States coming to the aid of societies stuck in time and in socialist projects gone awry. If the early 1990s politics of assertive humanitarianism were defined by missions to save Muslims in the Balkans, today similar saving projects target LGBTQI+ populations to save them from radical Muslims. These narratives converge with histories of post-Ottoman coloniality of secular states and subjectivities and are braided through the invention of the post-Ottoman Muslim citizen at the borderlands of Europe, discussed in chapter 2 and 3, at both the end of the Ottoman Empire and their revitalized lives after socialism. If Europe in the twentieth century, a secular and socialist nation-state coloniality, has constituted itself against fictitious *Islamic sexualities* in the Balkans, today LGBTQI+ politics are employed in the service of Euro-American enclosures.[5] The intersection of sexuality and Islam as orientation points to the construction of European identity for the Muslims in the Balkans, guided by a desire to whitewash them from their Islamic pasts in favor of histories that support totalizing narratives of Europeanness. In this context, the confluence of sexual orientation and European orientation in Albanian and Bosnian literature and film have been complex, contradictory, and corrective. By corrective I mean that the destabilizing subjectivities and lived experiences that fail to conform to European-oriented politics of local elites are, at times, rendered invisible or attacked as Oriental renegades of Ottomanism and Islam.

As questions around Muslim integration inside the EU are framed around *coexistence*, in Bosnia and Kosovo they have been framed in terms of *orientations* toward Europe, both concepts suggesting incompatibility, distance, failure, and perhaps impossibility. While coexistence suggests that Muslims are "external to the essence of Europe" so that "'coexistence' can be envisaged between 'us' and 'them'" (Asad 2003, 165), orientation toward the EU raises the question of alternative orientations. Reinforcing the idea of a European orientation suggests that there is an alternative, a possibility, a desire among these populations against which European orientation is enforced. In other words, against which other futures are the Muslims in the Balkans being directed toward the European future? While the Euro-Atlantic enclosure presents itself as an unmarked category, as the self-evident and only possible orientation for the Balkans, the queer Muslim is employed to stabilize Balkan anxieties about belonging to Europe and discipline its disoriented bodies. Islamic sexualities are not only traded in the postcolonial marketplace, always in need for new others that can be co-opted and incorporated; they also allegorize the anxieties of the Islamic self as an unfinished queer self that fails to follow Euro-American orientations.

I want to return to the question of visibility and Lunacek's assumption that there are no queer artists in Kosovo who "show their faces." This is an important discourse that needs to be exposed, for it not only hides the important work that queer artists and activists in Kosovo have engaged in in the last decade but also legitimizes as permissible the EU discourse on LGBTQI+ rights denying queer Kosovars the ability to tell their stories by controlling their narratives. Looking at queer Kosovar artist Astrit Ismaili's work, however, may provide some insights as to why certain queer artists in Kosovo are made invisible to the EU.

In the performance piece *Trashformations* (Ismaili 2014), the Kosovar queer artist Astrit Ismaili appears with a swimming cap, swimsuit, and one shoe on, with what seems to be a garbage bag over his shoulder. Resembling both a swimmer and a body washed offshore, Ismaili opens the garbage bag asking those present to throw whatever trash they have with them in the bag. Leaving the bag aside, he then proceeds to question the limits of defined and codified subjects and rights by opening the possibility of trashforming those rights in the context and circumstances in which subjectivity is situated and where bodies can take different shapes and forms. To illustrate the limits of confined rights, he wraps himself in adhesive tape, symbolizing the restricting nature of codified rights, their impossibility, and the borders they create between bodies, communities, genders, classes, and temporalities. The taping of his body to the walls of the studio also suggests the binding nature of these rights to certain material and discursive realities that limit our ability to physically move, see, and be beyond them. He points out during his performance that one needs a visa to pass through these borders and "if you don't have one, you go to jail," further illustrating how these borders also sustain the biopolitics of who lives and dies, who passes and doesn't. He then starts to throw money at the audience, as a way of bringing attention to the various economies that sustain and profit from drawing and maintaining borders. Reminding the audience that he does not want to be a victim and that he is not one, he questions the "war is over" discourse in Kosovo, suggesting it is fictitious since his war is still ongoing. Finally, pulling out an EU flag as a symbol of the ultimate blinding and binding ideology that the EU has come to represent in postwar Kosovo, Ismaili remarks that while looking at the EU flag, he doesn't see the stars and the sky. Questioning the promise and premise of what the EU is, he shoves the EU flag in his mouth as a way of using things we don't like to simply get by. Throwing up the EU flag into the garbage bag, he symbolically thrashes it in a hope of trashforming EU borders and the violence that sustains them that had started to emerge in the Balkans in the early 2010s. Like Pajtim Statovci in *Crossings* (2019), Ismaili tries to convey both the privilege of Albanians' position to pass—not just with gender and race but across borders—all the while acknowledging the alienation it takes to get there, because while their skin may not betray them, their walking, their staring, and their desires may.

Ismaili became a much-talked-about figure in the Albanian queer scene. In 2016, he produced Era Istrefi's video for "E dehun jam" (2014). In the video, Istrefi appears in a traditional Albanian gold-plated *jelek* with her face painted in temporary tattoo lines after the Gorani women of southern Kosovo. The opening traditional Albanian aesthetics and styles—which have defined Kosovar popular-culture defiance to Serbia—are a prelude to a shifting scene of queer punk youth dancing in the new Serbian Orthodox cathedral of Pristina built by the Serbian regime on the university grounds as a way of marking the territory as "sacred Serbian land." In the background, Nexhmije Pagarusha, the icon of Kosovo music, is heard singing, "I am drunk / my feet no longer hold," with Era adding, "Shots of tequila and beer work / to remove the pain / a little bit of Bob Marley too / so when I roll / I no longer stop at the patrol . . . and even if there isn't love there is always enough raki / Doesn't matter what you gonna say about me / Doesn't matter what you gonna say about me / Doesn't matter what you gonna say about me / Doesn't matter what you gonna say about me" (Istrefi 2014). But despite the carried-away carelessness that has come to dominate Albanian Kosovar postwar pop and publics, Albanians, argues the Kosovo Roma Artist Bajram Kafu Kinolli, "not only care how the West sees them but is central to all their cultural productions," so much so that the rejection of *tallava* has to do with Albanian racist anxieties over their whiteness given its Romani roots (Kika 2018). And yet, "all their bellies start to vibrate," agues Kinolla, once tallava is on, activating stored sensibilities that betray their performances of modernity. With his band *Gipsy Groove*, Kafu, as he is known in the Kosovo music scene, has made significant antiracist interventions by building solidarity that has gravitated toward communal repair, but he also takes Albanian and Balkan artists and audiences to task about the striking appropriation of Roma culture, which most of the Albanian music scene is entrenched in today. He believes that what Albanians find threatening about tallava, just like what Bulgarians find threatening about challaga, is not only the Islamic Roma roots of the music but also its perceived femininity as mournful music in a time when Albanian heteronormality is increasingly seeking to replicate the Euro-hetero model.

Questions of gender and sexuality are mobilized in postsocialist societies, both by states and NGOs (nongovernmental organizations), to mediate projects and ideals of sexual rights aligned with recognizable Euro-American models of sexuality. The deployment of LGBTQI+ issues in the service of Euro-Atlantic integration propels new forms of (homo) nationalist activism dominated by wealthy, urban, cisgender success stories of postsocialist neoliberal reforms, generally disconnected and depoliticized from broader questions of social and economic justice. The politics of visibility, marriage, and pride has erased racialized, disabled, and impoverished queer and trans folks and fails to address the intricacies and assemblages of sexuality in postsocialist contexts. This body- and geopolitical bordering through queerness results in racialized desires and dreams that establish distinction between bodies designated for desirability and the destabilized, debilitated, and damaged others. It is in this context that postsocialist queers are called to rehabilitate the ailing, misaligned, postsocialist patient and deliver it toward progress. In this Eurocentric worldview, the road to the EU and NATO is mapped out through the affirmation of queer bodies, with resistance to such a road leading to political itineraries that violate queers. In postsocialist geographies, queer bodies thus become the battleground of geopolitical realignment of Cold War 2.0. With that in mind, the following chapter looks at the intersections of Roma and Muslim racism in Bulgaria and the ways in which *queer* responses have sought to destabilize its seemingly inevitable straightening of bodies and sealing of borders.

Enclosure Demographics

Reproductive Racism,
Displacement, and Resistance

....

The day after the Bulgarian-Roma Muslim fight described in the book's introduction, local Bulgarians were joined in a spontaneous protest by biker clubs and racist groups from other parts of the country. Some of those marching through Asenovgrad tried to enter the Roma neighborhood, but the police blocked them. Following the protest, the mayor of Asenovgrad, the general secretary for the Ministry of Interior, and the deputy prime minister, Valeri Simeonov, also the leader of the far-right political party the National Front for the Salvation of Bulgaria, met and announced a plan to conduct regular and thorough background checks on everyone in the Roma quarter, with the intention of expelling all unregistered inhabitants, demolishing all "illegal homes,'" and closing down an "illegal mosque." Thirty houses were demolished in the Roma quarter throughout July and August 2017. The imam of the neighborhood mosque had been taken into custody although he had not been part of the fight that had resulted in several arrests around town. Two orphans in their late teens had been residing in the mosque under the care of the community, and the police closure of the building had left them sleeping outside in its yard.

The racist rallies grew in size and continued throughout July. Biker groups put on motorcycle shows accompanied by neo-Nazi chants of "Циганите на сапун, турците на нож" (Soap out of gypsies, Turks under the knife). The sole violent incident was an attack by the infamous migrant hunter Petar Nizamov on the cameraman for a popular TV channel. Nizamov, a vigilante star in Bulgaria who had come to prominence when YouTube videos surfaced of him and his border patrol torturing migrants at the Bulgaria-Turkey border in 2015, spoke to the gathered crowds that he had come to Asenovgrad because his patriotic duty was not just to defend "our national borders" but also the "borders of our towns and villages." Locals from Asenovgrad's Roma quarter, located at the outskirts of the town, claimed that the scandal was provoked by politicians. On behalf of the Asenovgrad Roma, the Movement for Rights and Freedoms party condemned the violence, and its leader, Mustafa Karadayi, related it to aggressive rhetoric and policy emanating from the governing parties of the Bulgarian nationalist alliance, the Patriotic Front: the National Front for the Salvation of Bulgaria, the Bulgarian National Movement, and Ataka. Karadayi explicitly mentioned Deputy Prime Minister Simeonov, who had instigated a new wave of violence on minorities when he used force against an elderly Bulgarian Turk trying to cross the Bulgarian-Turkish border during local elections in March the same year.[1] In the aftermath, the government made use of the racist rallies as a pretext to initiate the creation of a new police department in the Roma neighborhood from which the police could control the quarter's entrances and exits. Some locals believed that the rallies were instigated intentionally to create police checkpoints around Roma and Muslim neighborhoods.

The following month, August, Simeonov returned to Asenovgrad with the Minister of Interior Valentin Radev to attend the ceremony for the opening of a police station in Loznitsa he had promised to build. Neighborhood Roma and Muslim representatives rejected the invitation to participate in the opening celebrations. Meanwhile, under the European Union (EU) and Bulgarian flags, local and central government representatives, Bulgarian Orthodox priests, and teenage girls dressed in traditional Bulgarian outfits held two large trays with bread, salt, and candles as the priests blessed the new police station. In the interior of the neighborhood, community members danced and played loud *challga* music to annoy the official opening of the police station. The entire city was under tension.

Earlier in the day, Simeonov had met with racist groups protesting "Roma aggression." The gathered groups pressed Simeonov to resolve the question of Roma aggression, not just in their "ghettos of Asenovgrad" but in the city centers around the country. In the meeting, he promised the crowd to expel eight hundred people without residence permits, to demolish all remaining illegal homes, and to enclose Loznitsa with twenty-four-hour police surveillance. Most people were surprised to hear that residence permits were required to move around the country, knowing police registration for moving had been lifted since the collapse of socialism. This increased the tension in Loznitsa as most people were not sure what the city and police authorities meant by residence permits. Some rushed to get identification cards from the municipality, yet most were denied when they failed to provide a residence address that could be identified in the official urban map. Nearly half of the neighborhood could not obtain identification documents due to lack of supporting documents, with almost all of them being born and raised in the city. Within a week, the police made rounds around the neighborhood, knocking on peoples' doors and dragging people out of their homes in scenes that were terrifying to witness. Later that week, Simeonov announced on his Facebook page that in a matter of one week, "we have expelled 843 unregistered Gypsies from Asenovgrad, demolished 15 illegal buildings with local institutions working on more" (Karagozov 2017). Following the evictions, the municipal authorities were also engaged in starting a process of expropriation. One proposal that made the rounds in the city was that the municipality was searching for presocialist owners of lands where Loznitsa was built to return those properties to the rightful owners. Within weeks, several dubious contenders had emerged, claiming the expropriated parcels in the neighborhood through the eviction of Roma residents.

By October 2017, Asenovgrad mayor Emil Karaivanov announced in a press conference that the axis in and out of Loznitsa had been placed under camera and police surveillance, including the main arteries within the neighborhood. The enclosure of Loznitsa in Asenovgrad was a project that Simeonov had been propagating for years for Roma neighborhoods around Bulgaria through the establishment of "Gypsy ghettos," where the isolated Roma communities could also serve, according to him, as tourist attractions that should be modeled after Indigenous reservations in the United States and Australia. Addressing the crowd in Asenovgrad, Simeonov argued that the new police station in Loznitsa would be the first of its kind, but not the last one, and that Asenovgrad would become the model of a clean city. Simeonov had used the term *clean city* on several occasions to appeal to racist undercurrents in Bulgarian and wider Balkan society that considers Roma communities full of urban and racial contamination.

Drawing on fieldwork, political debates, music, and mass media, in this chapter, I argue that these processes of racialization are tied to and constitutive of the demographic panic that has resulted in the systematic enclosure of Roma and Muslim communities parallel to the larger Euro-Atlantic enclosures of whiteness in the Balkan borderlands. Here, the threats of sexual, racial, and religious difference are historicized and geopoliticized through the enfolding of racialized bodies into bordering debates and practices reliant on recovered Islamic threat situated in Bulgarian post-Ottoman national narratives as guardians of the "frontier" of whiteness and Europe.

Throughout my visits to Asenovgrad, there was open expression of contempt for the Roma in conversations with officials of the municipality. "This is not Sofia," one of them reminded me at the end of one of our meetings. I was not sure if the statement was a threat or general provincial spite for the capital. I guess it was both, and it reminded me to tone down my questions in our conversations. My position in Bulgaria as a queer Albanian Muslim from Macedonia gave me some access and insight, but it changed from person to person, and it is still hard to draw a single coherent conclusion about how I was being perceived. Some white Bulgarians assumed familiar and trusting tones; others treated me with suspicion. One of the field administrators, responsible for "project assessment," by which he meant "visiting the neighborhood to make sure that the demolition contractors are delivering the work they were hired to do," asked me where I was from. Realizing I was from Macedonia, he assumed a familiar tone: "They multiply like cats. When they first arrived here, they were a couple of hundred; now they're in their thousands. You know is [sic] probably the same in Macedonia too." Probably not realizing I was Muslim, he went on to tell me that the fight that had taken place in June was waiting to happen: "They've become too arrogant since they get money and support from Muslim countries[,] and they are being told to have as many kids as possible to outnumber us."

Growing up in the Balkans means becoming familiarized with the conceptualization of the Roma as contaminating city landscapes, a normalized racism that has empowered postsocialist governments in particular to install and imagine the Europeanization and neoliberal modernization of their cities through the eradication of these neighborhoods that are assumed temporary in the first place. Such projects have been so common in the recent decade in Tirana, Belgrade, Sofia, and Skopje that it has resulted in the destruction of entire communities through evictions and the expropriation of land, forcing Roma communities to emigrate in mass. The sight of vacant and destroyed homes in Asenovgrad has become a familiar landscape throughout my fieldwork in Bulgaria. Similar scenes of destruction and displacement dominate the peripheries of Kazanlak, Sofia, and Plovdiv where Roma communities have lived for centuries despite the increased projection of these neighborhoods as recent "encampments" and "ghettos."

The demolitions in the summer of 2017 looked and felt different, however. Homes targeted for demolition did not appear random, messy, and sparse as they have in the recent past, where developers or the state start with a construction project that slowly but eventually evicts communities and expropriates their land. They seemed more serious and somewhat systematic. One of the members of the private demolition company contracted by the city of Asenovgrad told me it was instructed to first target the roof and then the walls to get people out immediately and return for the foundations and debris later, once the entire neighborhood had been vacated. Indeed, the public policy of the current government has been, "The stick should be longer and the carrot shorter" when dealing with Roma ghettos. This new tactic creates both a sense of depression and desolation in the neighborhood by placing residents in constant panic and anxious anticipation of whose house is next, while police control of the entrance and exit into the neighborhood makes residents feel a constant sense of living inside an enclosure under restricted movement, making it difficult for them to go into the city. The enclosure of the neighborhood therefore serves as a new form of expulsion, through which the Bulgarian state excludes Roma people from public life and the life of the city. Their presence in the city centers now on being closely policed.

Some residents have piled whatever material they could recover from the demolitions beside their former homes. Still in the neighborhood, they move from one neighbor, friend, or relative to the other, returning to their destroyed homes daily to take pictures with their smart phones or just roam around their ruined buildings. Members of the older generation keep their papers stored on their bodies, in interior pockets and undergarments, keen to attract the attention of anyone who shows interest in their *gaile* (worry, trouble). The demolition of the home is not just a material loss but also anticipation and constant angst about the possibility of displacement. Like Bosnians, Kosovars, and Palestinians who saved various fragments of their destroyed homes symbolically but also strategically to maintain claims to their homes, some people in Loznitsa dismantled their own homes to save the building material and store it in the neighborhood. I stopped to visit Navije, an elderly woman I had met in my previous visits. We smoked a cigarette together as her son and his wife were dividing the bricks from the clay blocks of her home that she had built after she had worked in Germany for nearly ten years. "I have seen enough to know the difference," she said. "This time they are really coming after the whole *mahalla* [neighborhood, community]." Navije and her family left Asenovgrad and moved to Sofia that summer, where, as they were told, things were somewhat better. Like many members of the community, she complained that her nephews could no longer go freely into the city center as the police continually agitated the youth by questioning them every time they left or returned home.

In conversation with the administrator of the city ordinance responsible for the demolitions, he claimed, like many white Bulgarians in town, that the Roma in Loznitsa were newcomers, that they only arrived there ten to twenty years before. Yet the papers that the residents carried were printed in socialist-era cadastral records, and residential permits were issued in the 1970s and 1980s. In casual conversations with the city administrator and the police, there was no denying the evidence of some permits having been issued during socialism, but most of the demolition was justified by delayed denationalization of property. To maintain the process "within 'legal' parameters," as one of the municipal employees involved in the process told me explicitly, land nationalized in Loznitsa during the socialist period was being offered back to their presocialist owners with prospects for development. In almost all instances, the presocialist owners were white Bulgarians. In the process, people who had been given residence permits during socialism to reside in the neighborhood—mostly Roma, Turkish, and Muslim families—were being evicted and the lands expropriated. A large, factory-like building had already been constructed, with none of the residents knowing who was behind the investment.

When I returned in August, the neighborhood was under stress as the municipality, prompted by the national government, had intensified thorough background checks for proof of residence and registration papers. As fall was approaching, residents were unsure if the city would stop demolishing homes during the cold months: "Winter here is cold; we nearly froze to death in 2009," said one of the neighbors congregating in front of the community's makeshift mosque. A wave of accounts of unchecked violence against Roma, migrant, and Muslim communities had intensified around the country, with the police participating in some of the violence. After a woman was raped in Varna at the beginning of August by an unknown offender, a few dozen police in civilian clothing beat up men from the nearby village of Kamenar, populated mainly by Roma Muslims. Angel Dzhambazki, a Bulgarian member of parliament from the cogoverning far-right Bulgarian National Movement party, had shown Roma boys aged ten to thirteen taking pictures with an ISIS flag in Asenovgrad and called for their execution through euthanasia. Mainstream and social media accounts of the Roma aggression protests conflated the "crisis" of Roma aggression with the demographic panic, with Islamization and the passing of refugees through Bulgaria in the last three years generating a fear-based political discourse of the country being "under siege."

Conspiracy theories of organized and intentional promotion of high births among Roma, Turks, and Muslims sponsored from the "Muslim world" or "Arab world" were normalized in almost all segments of Bulgarian society. Part of these conspiracies included the "Islamization of the Roma" theory, which presented the Muslim Roma population as a new phenomenon and part of the larger "Islamic" conspiracy against white Bulgarians, even though the majority of the Roma population in Bulgaria have been Muslim for centuries. Political commentators in particular argued that Roma aggression was intimately tied to their Islamization. Indeed, the terms *aggressive* and *arrogant* framed the national targeting of Roma and Muslim neighborhoods and communities in the 2017 rallies against Roma aggression and mirrored racist statements made by Simeonov earlier that year referring to Roma people as "arrogant, presumptuous and ferocious-like humanoids" whose demographic rise could be catastrophic for Bulgaria.[2] In his electoral campaign in 2016, Karakachanov had called for the control of the fertility rate among the Roma with parallel programs to confront their Islamization (Konstantinov 2016). Sensationalist stories circulating in mainstream media reiterated these threats. In September, the popular tabloid 24 Chasa reported that "the Islamization of the Gypsies" in Pazardzhik, Plovdiv, Asenovgrad, Haskovo, and Burgas was undertaken with an intent to "merge with the Muslim world." This trend, argued the report, was threatening the territorial integrity of the country with supposedly alarming rates of growth, giving unsubstantiated examples such as "the mosque of Gypsy Islamism is Iztok quarter in Pazardzhik, which had a few hundred Muslims in [the] early 21st century, now numbering over 15,000" (Bultimes 2017).

Borisov's governing coalition made the threat of demographic crisis and Islamic radicalism a question of national importance, frequently speaking of low birth rates among Bulgarians on the one hand and the rise of pensioners, Roma, and Muslims as the "bad human material" (Economedia AD 2009) on the other. Since his first election as prime minister in 2009, he pursued surveillance, raids, and trials of "Islamic radicals" as well as legislative measures to ban "radical Islam" and foreign funding of Islamic organizations (Nikolova 2016). Simultaneously, the government invited ethnic Christian Bulgarians from Macedonia, Ukraine, Moldova, and all other parts of the world to move to Bulgaria as a patriotic duty to confront the demographic crisis (Dumbrava 2019). Many Macedonians and Moldovans utilized the opportunity and registered as Bulgarians to obtain citizenship and, through it, access to the EU labor market. The claims of Bulgaria under siege by radical Islam and demographic crisis were further strengthened by two events in 2015: the European-wide refugee panic where Borisov presented Bulgaria at the front line of the "refugee crisis" at the EU-Turkish border and the release of the United Nations Population Perspectives showing that the population of Bulgaria, then around seven million, would decrease to 3.5 million people by 2100 (United Nations 2015, 18). Such demographic reports had first emerged in the 2000s, raising nationalist panic over the ensuing years that a "de-Bulgarianization" process had been set into motion that blamed anything from Azis's chalga pop-folk music to an imagined Muslim invasion. But de-Bulgarization was also a response to Muslim Bulgarians reclaiming the names and traditions that they were denied during late socialism when the Bulgarization process in 1989 forcefully changed the names of nearly one million Muslims and expelled to Turkey those who resisted. To most proponents of the demographic catastrophe, the question of de-Bulgarization was not simply in the declining numbers of the white Bulgarian population but also in the deterioration of Bulgarian culture through, as Peter Ivanov, the deputy chairman of the Demographic Policy Centre, wrote, a "widespread presence of the chalga and the entry into the politics of the gypsy mentality—of racism, theft and dishonesty" (Иванова 2010).

Amid the racist rallies of summer 2017, Azis released the single "Motel" on YouTube. Within a month of its release, the single had reached twenty-six million views (Azis Online 2017a). Azis takes the viewer on a different journey than that of the Bulgarian nationalist panic over refugees and rising Roma and Muslim demographics. Seated at the back of a bus driving through Sofia, Azis observes not so much a city that he would like to see but rather a city that is already in the making: queer characters sharing pictures with an old couple drinking *rakija*, moments of separation and intimacy between people in and out of love, everyday struggles for survival, and endless possibilities to redeem, re-exist, and reclaim what they are otherwise told are irreconcilable differences. The visuals do not erase the afterlives of racist violence and the ongoing silencing of Roma and Muslim people. Instead, by placing a Muslim couple at the center of the video, Azis puts on display that which the state denies, hides, and actively targets for destruction. The intersection of the Roma and Muslims conjures a particular kind of fear in the imagination of white Bulgarians, one where historically racialized communities in the margins converge to confront the color-blind borders of *Bulgarianness*, charting new liberation imaginaries and itineraries.

Invited to discuss his video on *Greetings Bulgaria* (Здравей България 2017), the hosts ask Azis whether he is aware of what is happening around Europe, an allusion to the ongoing European public debates about terrorist attacks and normalized racist panic over the integration of migrants and Muslims (Azis Online 2017b). Azis explains how keenly aware he is because when he travels to Europe, people avoid him in the streets because they think he is Muslim given the color of his skin. Surprised, the hosts try to convince Azis that his new trend of siding with Muslims is problematic given that he doesn't seem to realize that Muslims are actually a real threat. The hosts continue to argue that Azis is not taking into account the fact that Muslims arrived in Europe only in the last twenty to thirty years and that they continue to live in ghettos and refuse to integrate into European life, to which Azis responds with examples from his accounts of his childhood in Bulgaria. When he was young, his mother would dress him up in such a way that his dark skin color wouldn't be as prominent when they went to auditions. Despite all her efforts, people would shut the door in their faces because he was still too dark for the Bulgarian *estrada* pop music scene. "This is why they are in the ghettos," says Azis. But "European society is so tolerant and civilized," object the hosts, "they even accept gay marriage." "But they don't accept Muslims," retorts Azis.

I have thought through the reconstitution of Bulgarian postsocialist whiteness with Azis, not only because his music has been a constant companion on my travels around Bulgaria but also because his music disturbs Bulgarian and Balkan racist and homophobic imaginaries, all the while serving *realness* and dancing the postsocialist house down. As nationalist threats of sexual, racial, and religious differences enfold into one another, Azis troubles not only nationalist hetero-mythologies of ethnically clean pre-Ottoman Bulgaria but also the postsocialist nostalgia of the left whose recruitment of the socialist past as color blind finds lodging in the investment of EU-NATO in cultivating whiteness through its Euro-Atlantic integration project. In "Motel," Azis invites us all to get a on different bus and travel with the kind of self-affirmation and solidarity that is not as "neoliberal" as everything seems to be today but is directed at generating and empowering the antiracist imaginaries of Roma, queer, migrant, worker, and Muslim communities to love themselves, regardless of the repeated reactionary returns and enlargements of racism. In Balkan-style shade, Azis deploys what across the Balkans translates as, "Let the dogs bark, the caravan shall pass." His enormous popularity in Bulgaria and the Balkans across racial, religious, and class divides reflects the resonance he has been able to achieve with the undercommons (Harney and Moten 2013) by bringing back and bringing up ungendered genealogies and subjectivities of desire "narrowed" by (post)Ottoman and socialist modernity.

One way to challenge the "scope of the gender system of Eurocentered global capitalism," Maria Lugones suggests, is to start by understanding the "extent to which the very process of narrowing of the concept of gender to the control of sex, its resources, and products constitutes gender domination" (2008, 12). Azis provides an opportunity to consider "decolonial imagination," as defined by Monica Hanna, Jennifer Hardford Vargas, and José David Saldivar (2015, 8), in its local and peripheral manifestations that may not always be in direct conversation with larger decolonization movements but manifests itself in all its local Bulgarian and regional Balkan complexities and connectivities to the coloniality of power and gender. Because "dismantling ingrained modern and colonial structures of through and modes of being must occur at the creative and cultural level of the imagination" as a way of "envisioning into existence alternative worlds that have not yet been recognized" (Hanna, Hardford Vargas, and Saldivar 2015, 8). Nowhere has his interventions been more important than in confronting mixing fears.

The anxiety over the popularization of chalga in the last two decades and the spread of the "gypsy mentality" among Bulgarians are perceived as threats to a pure white and Christian Bulgarianness as they blur the historical color lines that have constituted it in the first place. This became particularly evident in 2018, when Azis released "Pozna Li Me?" (2018), which raised eyebrows in both the liberal left and conservative right circles since it featured the Bulgarian iconic actress Tsvetana Maneva, who delivers at the end of the song a short monologue about the political situation in Bulgaria, pointing out that "whenever something goes wrong, "the 'others' are already here to be blamed—they are not invented." Maneva then looks into the camera and asks, "Who decides that they are a mistake? Who? We reject them, we rebuke them; we scream at them . . . are we truly vile, ignorant and evil people or are we cruel because we have forgotten our true nature?" The reaction to the video and the song was not so much connected to the content of Maneva's monologue but to her audacity to appear on an Azis video, identify herself with chalga, and mix herself up with someone like Azis. The bigger mixing the Bulgarian cultural commentators were concerned with was her theater pedigree being thrown into the same bag as chalga. The issue became so prominent, and Maneva received so many accusations about being paid by Azis to do the video against her better judgement, that both Azis and Maneva released statements about their collaboration. In an interview with *168 Chasa*, Maneva said that "the accusation that I have blurred the border between chalga and the intelligentsia is stupid" and that she is against that kind of thinking that is atrocious and fascist (Markova 2018). Maneva could not resist pointing out her surprise that it was not the song or the message that people reacted to but the fact that she had reduced herself to chalga: "I really did not expect this kind of reaction to the video, especially since people are not discussing the song but whether [it] is chalga or not; all the while the fact is that the message of the song was to remind ourselves that we have not been behaving as human beings towards each other, animals or the environment for a while now, a common sensibility I share with Azis which is why I chose to participate in the video and I do not see why I should be embarrassed." Meanwhile, Azis posted on his Instagram:

> I have heard you as your screams of hatred broke ground. I did not pay Maneva to join me, I shared my ideas and she said yes. This song is not about Tsvetana Maneva supporting Azis or the music genre you have come to hate. Tsvetana supported the cause that she could not live in denial of. We did not have time with Tsvetana to talk about the kind of music she likes and supports. Because with Tsvetana we wanted to scream: We cannot go on like this! And this is her radical gesture of empathy. She's priceless and her worth is not measured with money. This is a gesture against hatred and denial. Something clearly unknown to you! I love you, Tsvetana Maneva![3]

Meanwhile, fans fired back at the negative reactions by recording themselves singing the song, which Azis posted on his YouTube channel. Some of them rendered the song in different styles to question the public outcry over the mixing of chalga with respectable Bulgarian music.

But the real reaction to mixing came in June 2019, when Azis released his new song "Ciganche" (Azis Online 2019) on his YouTube video about love and mixing. The song, translated as "Gypsy Boy," tells the story of, as Azis points out, "shame, both being shamed and feeling shamed" for being who he is, the shame that, as the lyrics of the song go, also falls on the white person in love with a Roma, a love that forces them to "hide it from everyone that you love the black one, the shabby, the poor boy," ending with, "Don't be ashamed of my skin color and what people would say!" In the video, Azis appears in a house resembling those destroyed by the Bulgarian police in Roma neighborhoods. Speaking about the song in various mediums, he has pointed out that the song addresses the racism and shame Roma people are made to feel and that one way to deal with the panic over integration is for more people to mix through love. Azis used the debates on music to expand his message by pointing out that he believed "the *kyuchek* [Romani Brass Band music] has to be transferred to the Bulgarian home, and folk music in the Gypsy. Mixing couples—Bulgarians and Romas—is the direct pathway to integration," concluding that "there must be more love between Bulgarians and Gypsies" (Flagman 2019). The comments on mass media and social media were overwhelmingly negative. One commentator noted that "Azis has an inferiority complex for being Roma and is therefore keen on changing the genetic pool of the gypsies," and one web portal commented how Azis had thrown another bomb of provocation (Flagman 2019).

In both "Pozna li me?" (Azis Online 2018) and "Ciganche" (Azis Online 2019), Azis weighs in on the intersection of the fear of demographic crisis, enclosure, and the displacement of Roma Muslims across Bulgaria and anxieties about the mixing of bodies, music, language, class, taste, and race. As a gender nonconforming chalga performer, Azis came to mediate the intensification and convergence of queerphobia, racism, and Islamophobia in Bulgaria over the last two decades, but his response to racist panic also continuously disrupts and destabilizes nationalist Bulgarian masculinities by engendering alternative intersecting imaginaries. He thus threatens not only heterosexuality but its coconstitutive and overlapping relations to race. As a Roma and a homosexual, Azis fits the scenario of the perfect enemy, which he himself has recognized on several accounts. In a *New York Times* interview, Azis noted that "being gay and being Roma are highly discriminated against in Bulgaria," and since "they're both words that people here hate . . . I'm carrying the burden of the two" (McClelland 2016).

For two decades now, Azis has been a formative figure in not only bringing forward Bulgarian and Balkan-wide antiracist imaginaries but in disrupting their attachments to heteromasculinity, the patriarchy, virility, reproduction, demographics, sexuality, and security. As mentioned in the introduction, the current political rise of Boyko Borisov to power as prime minister was partly due to his targeting of Azis. The removal of Azis's billboards when heated debates about Azis's bare backside facing that of the national hero Vasil Levski became a key feature of his electoral campaign for European Parliament, which he won in 2007 with his newly established political party GERB (Citizens for European Development of Bulgaria). In that opening campaign, Borisov, who had received the award the previous year for best political campaign, which had targeted Roma and queer communities, opened the electoral campaign by confronting the centrist government for its lack of reproach to the de-Bulgarization and Gypsification of the cities, promising his electorate that "we will fight them at this election, because with Azis's butt they will not be able to beat us" (Dnes 2007). In power for over a decade, Borisov followed through with his political promises of Bulgaria for Bulgarians again. An active campaign to change Arabic and Turkish toponyms around the country in 2018, for instance, had been regarded by commenters as a re-installment of the socialist-era Revival Process that sought to assimilate Muslims into Bulgarians. The Revival Process was also guided by demographic concerns of the Bulgarian Communist Party who feared the traditional lifestyle of Turkish, Roma, and Muslim communities resulted in higher birth rates than white Bulgarians (Eminov 1997). References to the revival period are common in conversations with older Muslims in Bulgaria and have more recently resurfaced again in public discourse. When visiting Sofia in June 2018, one of my friends, Madlen, drew reference between the socialist Revival Process that targeted Muslims for assimilation and a project called Направи го за България (Do It for Bulgaria), which targeted women with free in-vitro fertilization in return for the christening of their newborns. The organization behind the campaign, the Movement for National Cause (Движение за национална кауза), uses the shorthand днк, Bulgarian for DNA, and concerns itself with "the cause of demography and the DNA" of the Bulgarian nation. In addition to the campaign's racist undertones, various promotional posters on social media and the streets of Sofia targeted women with misogynist messaging such as "size C without silicone" to suggest that the benefit of enlargement of breasts through birth as opposed to silicone implants (see figure 5.1) or storks carrying the Bulgarian flag to celebrate March 3, the day of national independence from the Ottoman Empire. In the meantime, Borisov's cabinet members have unfolded multiple policy proposals on free-of-charge sterilization for Roma women.

Borisov's approach to tackling the "Roma problem" and the demographic crisis as well as the supposed Roma and Muslim youth's increased attraction to Islamist fundamentalism has presented in the appointment of key positions of people in government such as Valeri Simeonov and Krasimir Karakachanov, who have expressed explicit racist approaches to simultaneously physically enclosing and then displacing Roma urban communities. The political framing of these actions has been situated in the broader discourse about demographic and moral crisis, making the Bulgarian government a model for many far-right and fascist groups

ЧАШКА **C** БЕЗ СИЛИКОН

Направи го сега

СРЕДНО 5 МЕСЕЦА ОТНЕМА ЗАЧЕВАНЕТО ПРИ ЖЕНИТЕ 20+.
WWW.NAPRAVIGO.BG ☐ NAPRAVIGO.BG ☐ NAPRAVIGO

ДНК

НАПРАВИ ГО СЕГА

Средно 5 месеца отнема зачеването при жените 20+.

FIGURE 5.1. "Size C without silicone," Movement for National Cause (DNA) campaign "Do It Now." Sofia, Bulgaria, 2019.

around Europe who have come to see Borisov, Bulgaria, and the Balkans as examples of connecting unapologetic white supremacy to demography and border security.

In November 2018, fascist movements from around Europe gathered in Sofia, Bulgaria, to attend a forum called "The Movement for a Europe of Nations and Freedom," organized months after Steve Bannon established "the Movement" in Brussels as an infrastructure "for the global populist movement" (Thompson 2018). The goal was to coordinate electoral politics for the 2019 EU parliamentary elections. Sofia was not an accidental choice. Bulgaria has been the best example of what most far-right political parties in the EU aspire to: a governing coalition with like-minded parties; normalized relations with the EU, the United States, and Russia; demographic policies favoring white populations; the tracking and pushing back of refugees; and building a fence at Bulgaria's border with Turkey. Bulgaria's ability to conduct massive demolitions and to displace Roma communities, to legitimize and at times reward vigilante border patrols, to criminalize "radical Islam," and more recently to undertake a platform to Christianize all Muslim-sounding toponyms in the country has attracted the attention of Marine Le Pen enough that the French politician showed up in Sofia too. The far-right French Magazine *L'Incorrect* dedicated an edition to the rise of the far right in Eastern Europe in 2018, titled "The Sun Rises in the East."

European and US far-right parties have followed all these changes closely. To most of them, the mass resurgence of revanchist racist politics in Bulgaria, the Balkans, and Eastern Europe more broadly epitomize the fulfillment of a post–Cold War consolidation of a transatlantic enclosure of a white geopolitical gated community against a racial demographic threat. There was similar demographic panic circulating around the EU as well. In 2017, for instance, the Robert Schuman Foundation's report *Europe 2050: Demographic Suicide* (2018) noted that "the population of Africa will likely increase by a total of 1 billion and 300 million—130 million in North Africa alone. In other words, the migratory pressure on Europe will be greater than ever! This will be a demographic shock—implosion (inside Europe) plus explosion (outside the EU)." The authors then asked the readers to imagine

> a few million climate refugees from Asia or more political and economic refugees arriving from Africa and the Middle East. Also, let us point out that if 1% of the increase from the African population settled in France within the next 35 years (remember 1980 is barely 35 years ago), that would equal 13 million more inhabitants by 2050; i.e., 20% more. Recalling how shaken the fragile European Union was in 2015 when a million refugees (3/4 political refugees) arrived, we realize that Europe should start preparing now for these potential situations. . . . At the same time, the Old Continent should encourage its population to have more children. (Robert Schuman Foundation 2018)

The EU has carefully curated its differences from the United States in regard to race, refugees, and racism, frequently using US excess to renew its internal and international innocence in relation to critiques of the intensification of border regimes across its southern and eastern frontiers and the establishment of external border controls with authoritarian regimes across its (post)colonies in the Maghreb and the Sahel. In a blunt contradiction of the 2016 EU-Turkey deal, the EU commissioner for foreign affairs Federica Mogherini (2017) critiqued the US "Muslim ban," arguing that "this is not the European way" and that unlike the United States, the EU is open to hosting "Syrian refugees and others who are fleeing from war" (Mogherini 2017). Beyond various past and present strident rebuffs leveled reciprocally between the EU and the United States, the fortification of common Euro-Atlantic security remains a robust form of cooperation, with the Trump administration having increased its spending for the European Reassurance Initiative in 2018 (Pellerin 2018).

Interviewed by the *New Yorker* in January 2019 about his European allies, Steve Bannon, for instance, pointed out that he had not heard any of the movements he was dealing with "ever say that they want to leave the E.U." (Zerofsky 2019, 42). Indeed, parties like the Alternative for Germany and Lega Nord have shown full support for the trilateral US-EU-NATO alliance and consider the Euro-Atlantic integration of postsocialist peripheries into the alliance an opportunity to seal Europe's geopolitical borders. During the closing remarks of the far-right forum in Sofia, activists from the host Volya played a wildly criticized EU-enlargement commercial released in 2012, where Europe, presented as a white woman under assault by Black and brown men, defends herself by summoning up other white Europeans who eliminate the Black and brown assailants by encircling them. The ad, meant to promote EU expansion eastward, closes with the message, "The more we are, the stronger we are," a message that has resurfaced among EU officials in the Brexit context. This political projection of former socialist countries as a buffer zone around Europe, to be protected from Black and brown people, gains a localized meaning, where the racial other is not only lurking just across the borders waiting to come in but is already in and is already waging a demographic and cultural war on the nation. Like the regional positioning of Albanian and Muslim populations as weak links at the Euro-Atlantic geopolitical borders in the Balkans, in Bulgaria the threat is localized and ascribed to Roma and Muslim minorities. While most of these debates have projected postsocialist Muslim women as victims of an encroachment of Arab Islam, Muslim men are also projected as transformed by the infusion of radical Arab Islam.

In a much publicized trial in 2012 that started a criminalization process that has now been normalized, thirteen Muslims were accused of an "anti-democratic ideology expressed in opposition to the principles of democracy, the separation of powers, *liberalism*, statehood, the rule of law, basic human rights, the equality of men and women, and religious freedom."[4] The prosecution argued that the accused had been influenced by radical Islam from the "Arab world" that was not compatible with a supposed autochthonous Bulgarian Islam. Being interviewed about the trial in 2017, one of the key prosecutors, Nedelka Popova, urged the public to consider the trial a warning of what was to come:

> The purpose of this case is not only to be examined by court, but to raise awareness. It's to signal to the public that something is happening in Bulgaria. And for this we should not be silent. Because we see danger. At present, Muslims are 10–12% in Bulgaria. And we have no reason to think that their numbers will decrease. It's exactly the opposite. And with the arrival of Muslims from abroad in Bulgaria and the return of some of those who have been exiled to Turkey, with the encouragement of birth rates, the percentage will increase. When it's 30%, our country is already in jeopardy. They are a monolithic mass, easily manipulated in elections. They are almost like a militarized structure. When somebody tells them to go and vote, they go. (Bulgarian Presidency 2018)

The aim of "producing more Bulgarians" also centers on discussions about the alarming virility of Muslim and Roma men, the central figure announcing these threats as the male Roma Muslim. The policies of enclosing Roma neighborhoods were not enacted just a response to stop Roma aggression. The Asenovgrad incident is also about a Roma man saving a white Bulgarian woman from drowning (their proximity to the woman being perceived by the members of the kayaking team as a threat). These anxieties are also not separate from the larger political climate in the country, which intersects with the refugee and terrorist panic, with the contrast between active public anxiety surrounding fewer Bulgarians and the attention focused on the increasing number of undesirable Roma and Muslim subjects in Bulgaria constantly in the air. While the primary target of these reproductive polices and demographic designs is Roma and Muslim women who are projected as targets of Islamization from the Middle East as "birth machines," as the far right calls them, the Roma and Muslim male body has also become a target. This is part of a larger global trend since the war on terror. Jasbir Puar points out in *Terrorist Assemblages: Homonationalism in Queer Times*:

> Although feminist postcolonial studies have typically theorized women as the bearers of cultural continuity, tradition, and national lineage, in the case of terrorism, the line of transmission seems always to revert

to the male body. The locus of reproductive capacity is, momentarily, expanded from the female body to include the male body. This expansion does not mark a shift away from women as the victims of rape and pawns between men during wartime. But the principle and overriding emphasis on rape of women as a weapon of war can displace the importance of castrating the reproductive capacities of men. (2007, 98)

An Orientalizing and sexualizing gaze directed at young male Muslims and Roma entails the application of specific security measures to assure that their so-called *instincts* are kept in check. *Sexcurity* experts reject the "materialist" interpretations of terrorism that posit terrorism as a factor of economic and political deprivation, arguing rather that there is something inherent to Islam itself that makes young Muslim men imitate the Prophet Muhammad and commit atrocities. The Bulgarian translator of Foucault and former Bulgarian ambassador to the Holy See, Vladimir Gradev, for instance, argues that Mohammad serves as an example for "the terrorist wannabes" such that they grow their beards but shave their mustaches. Working with Hegel's interpretation of grooming as an everyday struggle of civilization against nature allows for a person to reveal their individuality. Gradev argues that growing a beard is a symptom of distancing oneself from European civilization and individual freedoms. Moreover, he argues, the grooming style is indicative of another problem inherent to Islam—an interplay between domination and subordination: bearded men dominate veiled women, and mustacheless men are subordinated to Allah (Gradev 2014). Afsaneh Najmabadi's *Women with Mustaches and Men without Beards* (2005) may confuse the Bulgarian "budget Foucault," to use a Junot Díaz phrase, but his interpretations have gained popularity. Along Gradev's analysis, the Bulgarian-language version of the German state-funded news outlet *Deutsche Welle*, for instance, has provided analysis of the Prophet Mohammad as a "sensitive and easily hurt outsider disappointed again and again by the world," his masculinity troubled because he was continuously "looking for a new refuge," his only "motherland" being the "battlefield" (Andreev and Abdel-Samad 2015). A more recent trope is that of the "gipsy gigolos" who earn their living working for sex in the West. The most desired, according to one such media account, are "youngsters up to 25 years old with a muscular fragrant body, a good 'package' and endurance." It's difficult to imagine, continues the author, how "our 'gypsy beggars' have captured the minds, hearts and groins of the blondes from the north, but some of our Roma have been able to take advantage of their benefactors fairly well" (Rezon Media 2017). These media imaginaries are then triangulated with additional stories of Roma and Muslim organized crime, drug and human trafficking, or the "crime-terror nexus."

In public discussions that concern Muslim men, self-representation is rare. When it does appear, it takes the form of representational governmentalities through the deployment of "good" Muslims who come to police their coreligionists who have gone astray. European far-right activists came to their support by giving them visibility as heroes and defenders of Europe.

The construction of the "good Bulgarian Muslim" is also racialized through class, ethnicity, and language. Bulgarian- and Turkish-speaking Muslims, while still considered a threat, are thought of as the better-assimilated Muslims while Roma Muslims are made to constitute the ultimate internal other and are then brought into association with newly arriving migrants from the Middle East. A racializing process that requires the disaggregation and differentiation of "white" Bulgarian Muslims from migrants and Roma Muslims has emerged at a time of heightened border securitization along the Balkan refugee route where the tentative alignment of Bulgarian Muslims with Europe works to simultaneously racialize and exclude new and old others.

On a local level, the male Muslim body is perceived and projected as a direct threat and a site of revulsion. Not only is such a body dangerous but it is also imbued with contaminating abilities. On a national level, the male Muslim body represents the Ottoman past that simply refuses to die, despite ongoing attempts in the present to destroy it. While such a body is increasingly perceived as suspect and criminal, its policing is no longer undertaken with the goal of expulsion or death, as was the case during most of the post-Ottoman period, but is rather targeted, as the current government describes it, with "carrots and sticks." I want to suggest that this new approach to targeting racialized minorities in order to gradually eliminate them, one where their slow destruction within the simultaneous logic of "let live" and "will not let die," in Puar's rendering, has to wield benefits such that the nondeath incentives of carrots do not allay the damage caused by the stick. In this way, the damage does not produce a dead body straightaway but generates instead an infrastructural industry of displacement and death making as witnessed in Asenovgrad. Expanding on Achille Mbembe's notion of *necropolitics* (Mbembe 2003)—war waged in order to debilitate the infrastructure that supports life—in relation to Zionist settler-colonial practices in Palestine, Puar argues that the Israeli Defense Force "policy of shooting to maim entails an incremental depopulation through the slow attrition of debilitation and incapacitation" (2015, 7). Maiming, Puar points out, "functions as slow but simultaneously intensive death-making, as targeting to maim is an accelerated assault on both bodily and infrastructural fronts. . . . If slow death is conceptualized as primarily through the vector of 'let die' or 'make die,' maiming functions as 'will not let die' and, its supposed humanitarian complement, 'will not make die.' Maiming masquerades as 'let live' when in fact it acts as 'will not let die'" (139).

Note here that maiming, or more specifically the necropolitical logic of "will not let die," can extend from conditions of postcoloniality to think through postsocialist necropolitical logic and technologies and that maiming regenerates national sovereignty, postnational European coloniality, and whiteness. The recent intensification of pressure on Roma Muslim populations works through legal means: through the eviction and expropriation of Roma Muslims from their homes, making their lives impossible. Although such policies fit into a long continuity stretching from socialism into postsocialism beginning with Bulgaria's integration into Euro-Atlantic structures, the legal evictions of Roma Muslim people from their homes has been undertaken as a way of pushing them out. As one of my Roma interlocutors reported, "When they remove us from our homes, we ask them, 'Where do we go?' 'Go to Europe,' they say. 'You can travel there now.' But in Europe they, too, don't want us."

While most research on the techniques of ethnic cleansing of Muslims in the Balkans has focused on the swift and violent expunging of white Muslims from Europe, known as the genocides of Bosnia and Kosovo, the cleansing of Roma populations in general and Roma Muslims in particular works via a protracted technique. These technologies of biopolitical management increasingly function through maiming, "as slow but simultaneously intensive death-making, as targeting to maim is an accelerated assault on both bodily and infrastructural fronts" (Puar 2017, 139). The biopolitical control of Roma Muslim populations in Bulgaria cannot be considered outside race or fragmented down to arguments about national particularities and interethnic conflict, for it is part of the global remaking of Cold War/post–Cold War categories of race and demarcations of borders in neighborhoods, nations, and postnational projects like the Euro-Atlantic enclosure.

I want to return to Azis, because his work functions not only as an influential counternarrative to Bulgarian racism but also because his queer and chalga aesthetics and sensibilities confront European and global homophobia, transphobia, and racism. Amplifying the voices of marginality and generating an actual and imagined futurity outside the Euro-Atlantic racist imaginary, Azis has used his international popularity to regularly refuse homo-nationalist invitations and itineraries. Instead, he prefers to attend to those bodies by sharing the experiences of embodied racialization, gesturing in a direction where "the break," as defined by Stefano Harney and Fred Moten (2013,) has already occurred. I want to suggest that Azis's challenging of gender through the creation of complex characters and performances avenges all queers—not just Roma and racialized bodies but all postsocialist bodies. Summoning sovereignty in the face of reoccurring assaults, agitations, evictions, and expropriations, he gives the historically marginalized people significance through his songs and politics.

Western European and American observers have been puzzled by how the supposedly macho audiences of the Balkans have embraced a gender-queer performer who seems to challenge all their essentialist notions of "Balkan butch masculinities" produced primarily by Marina Abramovic's *Balkan Baroque* and Emir Kusturica's misogynist and masochistic rendition of the Balkan body. But Azis is not so much queering gender from a presentist counter-hegemonic position as much as he is reactivating and reclaiming lost vernacular and virilities that send panic through the white-aspiring Bulgarian and Balkan hetero and racist gaze. Azis's aspirational politics of solidarity projected in "Motel" (Azis Online 2017a), "Pozna Li Me?" (Azis Online 2018), and "Cicanche" (Azis Online 2019) form part of a continual attempt by Roma and Muslim performers and activists in the Balkans to deinvest from whiteness and heteronormativity. More importantly, his work has questioned "gender" as an organizing principle of Roma and Muslim histories. He has influenced a new generation of queer artists who are not all about abandoning their communal memories to a universalized pop—artists like Božo Vrećo in Bosnia, whose queering of *sevdah* has transformed communal genocidal trauma into a Bosnian *kara-sevdah*, or tallava artists in Kosovo whose mournful lyrics expose what lurks in the deep unconsciousness of the Albanians,

Muslims, Bosnians, and Roma that the secular, modern redemption offered seems unable to articulate yet represses from public debate.

These new, emerging queer embodiments are a response to the repository of violent Balkan Christian and secular modern manhood, which once outlawed tallava and chalga and today seeks to police its renewal through a possessive search for authenticity and purity in the ethno-fold dances choreographed and purified to promote gendered fantasies of the ideal pre-Ottoman Christian Byzantine man and woman. But it is important to note that Azis does not denounce all of the socialist past but calls for its queer interrogation as opposed to hetero-nostalgia, masquerading the hammer and sickle in "Hop" (2011) but also throwing shade at Western gays to find eastern birds on "Myconos" (2014), Mykonos, Greece, being the iconic gay destination of wealthy Eurogays, where postsocialist and postcolonial queer refugees enact their Orientalist fantasies of premetrosexual manhood as bodies that come from a different space and time.

Afterword

I have worked on this book through expanding and contracting panicked anger that has unfolded over the last decade, at times moving swiftly with a severe and urgent need to write in the face of renewed revisionism and swelling waves of denial of our recent violent past that have coincided with intensified violent measures on refugees, Roma, and Muslim people along the Balkan route. At other times, I moved through callous slowdowns amid angst-filled dread and despair, mental illness, deaths of close ofriendships, post-traumatic stress, breakdowns of relationships, and precarious academic positions that have frequently amounted to debilitating doubt and debts. Part of the doubts had to do with the absence of vocabulary to address the complex constellations of race, coloniality, and whiteness in the Balkan context. While I was interested in what decolonial praxis along enclosures—be they built around Loznitsa in Asenovgrad or the larger regional enclosure built around the Balkan route—could mean about ongoing antiracist strategies and solidarity among peripheries, I was continuously confronted with a raceless levelling of violence on racialized communities in postsocialism as interethnic conflict. This required historical attention to the coloniality of race in the region while also observing and acknowledging the differences and shifts in the contemporary methods of racial violence.

In August 2019, I returned to Asenovgrad to find more demolished homes and the neighborhood reduced to a shadow of its former self. Surveillance had intensified, and additional homes had been demolished. In December 2017, the regional court had given six provisional sentences and five effective sentences against eleven defendants from the summer 2017 incident. I attended a somber evening *namaz* in a makeshift mosque in upper Loznitsa that has also been designated for demolition. After I inquired about the whereabouts of the arrested men, the imam, who had been taken into custody but released, told me that three of them were still serving their sentences and the rest who had returned were no longer going out or meeting people for fear of being framed again or attacked. I walked around the neighborhood for visits. References to the neighborhood becoming a prison with the police station and surveillance had emerged as new concerns:

> We are stopped every time we go in and out of Loznitsa: "Where are you going?" "What business you have to go downtown?" "Who are your parents?" "Let me see your papers" . . . . When we do make it downtown, some cafes now ask us for "membership cards" to sit down, even though we know these people, some of whom we went to school with, and we know that you don't need a membership card to sit there.

I visited several people I had interviewed in the municipality. Nearly all of them pointed out that one of the arrested men in the Asenovgrad incident was Stefan Dimitrov—or Tefik Hodjza, as he is known in the neighborhood. Hodjza had already been placed under surveillance by the police and had been arrested several times on charges of preaching Islamic radicalism but was never charged because of lack of evidence. A small mosque where Hodjza serves in Loznitsa has been locked and is being investigated as a "nest of Islamization."

In March 2020, Sofia municipal authorities received a directive by the district prosecutor to bring under tighter control the parts of the city "populated by people of different ethnicities, clearly demonstrating their unwillingness to comply with the restrictions" (Kolov 2020) of the pandemic. While this book was under review, the immunity imperative revealed what was already in the making: Roma neighborhoods and villages around Bulgaria are now encircled with police and military checkpoints on the ground, while thermal drone surveillance and airplanes from the sky surveil temperature and spray disinfectants. This racial mapping of the pandemic by targeting only Roma communities has been accompanied by various warnings of the danger citizens face when approaching "mixed areas." In the relatively short span of the pandemic, Roma communities have gone from being mediated as "Islamization nests" to "infection nests." The enclosure infrastructures that have been in the making for nearly a decade around Roma and refugee communities are now fully operational in all the countries along the Balkan route. As I have argued throughout this book, enclosures are neither new nor exceptional local or national provisory measures of containment for sorting populations designated to live and those actively pursued for damage and death. Their deployment and function in the colonial context—enslavement, internment, encampment, and genocide—are well documented but frequently enacted through narrow spatial and temporal concerns of race and coloniality that evade their refraction as regional and global regimes of violence. Like the walling of the US-Mexico border or the pushback on the Mediterranean passage, the enclosures built around Roma, refugees, and racialized communities around the Balkan route are not national particularities but interdependent Euro-American collaborative efforts of securing white demographics, wealth, and health.

The drive toward the impenetrability of claimed white territories by encircling their colonial/capitalist-accumulated wealth with walls, by wholesale surveillance and militarization, with endless funding for migrant policing and violence, through incarceration of communities of color inside the enclosure, and through sophisticated biometric and drone control across their geopolitical borderlands points to the enclosure as a final act to safeguard white supremacy in the face of disintegrating Euro-American coloniality/modernity. If we think of the European transatlantic project from the fifteenth to the twentieth century as defined by the transatlantic slave trade, settler colonialism, Christian crusades, and Reconquista mapping of colonial/capitalist European frontiers to the south and north, their refashioning and redeployment in the Euro-Atlantic at the beginning of the twentieth century to integrate the "rest of the white people" from former Eastern Europeans suggests an ending of enclosure through transatlantic coloniality. But enclosure may also be a way of buying time to shift the now quaint narratives of global "growth" and "progress" toward cataclysmic crisis to secure another collective commitment to "save the world" by saving Euro-American coloniality/modernity. It is also how racial capitalism extracts value from crisis, whose political utility is then deployed to coerce, stifle, or fold resistance into its reactionary center. Nowhere is the latter more obvious than in the nostalgic cries of European and US liberals over the supposed recent rise of racism that merges with reactionary calls for the restoration of a more reasonable regime of white supremacy/coloniality.

The most predictable of all being the apocalyptic sighs that "we are all in this together." We are not. But that cry does seem to capture how white Western panic still aspires to lure the world into thinking that the loss of their world is the end itself. It is of course not. What is interesting to witness, however, from a decolonial vantage point, is how truly desperate those concerns have become in the last year. Attempts to mobilize knowledge production and academic policy to censor decolonial praxis and critical race theory as antiwhite and Islamo-leftist ideologies, as the infamous *Manifeste des 100* illustrated in November 2020, just as police infrastructures moved to arrest Black Lives Matter activists, have faced an inescapable drive toward abolition and decolonization.[1] Calls for reparations that accompanied the toppling of statues of Western heroes on horses from Bristol to Bangalore to Bridgetown have drawn attention across the world. The unfinished work of decolonization does not remain a postcolonial alternative but a worldwide imperative. Peripheral divestment from whiteness, political support for racialized communities inside the Euro-American enclosure, and migrants at its borderland are now more important than ever. As are collaborative lines of flight, exchanges of strategies, and methods and routes to decoloniality.

When Achille Mbembe notes that "our world remains a 'world of races,' whether we admit it or not" and that "the racial signifier is still in many ways the inescapable language for the stories people tell about themselves, about their relationships with the Other, about memory, and about power" (2017, 55), he not only calls attention to race as a malleable instrument of modernity but also as regulatory regime of power in the world coordinates of coloniality. From this angle, formations of a modern/colonial white supremacy are redistributed across world peripheries to serve different purposes of reactivating more sedimented racial b/orders. Part of this redistribution of racial typologies and hierarchies across postcolonial and postsocialist peripheries today works toward the fragmentation of peripheral solidarity and simultaneous reinforcement of global racial hierarchies. From a decolonial perspective, the (post) socialist world still cannot seem to resolve this epistemic and simultaneously (geo)political predicament of being in pact and proximity with Euro-American coloniality or its product of defying periphery. When Albanian students protested the neoliberalization of universities in 2019, one of the slogans that gained visibility read, "European Prices, African Salaries, Aryan Race, Taliban Standards, Miserable Albania." The politics of the protests was not at all comparable to the racist "Roma aggression" rallies in Bulgaria. Although a more thorough analysis of the student protests is beyond the scope of this project, I bring this up here because it illustrates how the geopolitical imaginaries that govern colonial/capitalist racial hierarchies inform the postsocialist position in relation to them. What the sign articulates is an indignation of an "Aryan race" vis-à-vis the premise of privileged relations promised by the racial politics of postsocialist Euro-Atlantic white integration. The use of the symbolism of the Aryan race and similar claims to whiteness that are visible across eastern and southeastern European spaces, as I have illustrated in this book, are not exclusive to the far right but permeate the entire political spectrum. What the above illustrates is that coloniality isn't just about regional repertoires of denial and ignorance over racism and colonialism but that coloniality is complicit in the larger Euro-American anti-Black vison of a post–Cold War global color line.

Instead of appropriating postsocialism, a product of Cold War Euro-American-area studies is to speak about former Eastern European grievances as peripheral to Euro-American power, of economic and labor exploitation, of unfair or unequal treatment of "eastern" partners in the European Union, or of not being anthologized in the academic Euro-American annals of knowledge. Academically, this political positioning calls for an interrogation of internal European inequality through decoloniality, while simultaneously offering some necessary difference as "East" European to the neoliberal discourse of diversity. For this narrative to work, all critique must be lodged in the postsocialist present, since more protracted histories could reveal complicity with coloniality/modernity, as the work of Madina Tolstanova illustrates. Decoloniality would mean thinking about the region from its margins. I am not suggesting that decoloniality should transform into a standard to be streamlined across global peripheries but should deepen knowledge of situated histories of coloniality as a way of forging sharper lines of solidarity.

Tracing the genealogies of the colonial/modern methods of racial violence as well as the histories of decolonization movements across occluded spaces of coloniality remains necessary as a way of connecting trans-local struggles to confront the resurgence of an emboldened yet still unpredictable Euro-American revanchist white supremacy. I hope that sketching the broader terrain of de/coloniality in the Balkans in relation to geopolitical race making and border making, its embodied consequences, and resistance in racialized and refugee populations along the Balkan route is less a conclusion on the regional complicity with infrastructures of white supremacy and more of an opening to rethink past and present political alliances, leanings, and most of all, positions locally but also regionally and globally. I want to hope that antiracist and decolonial movements in the Balkans are increasingly becoming part of larger geographies of liberation and a growing network of decolonial movements that are neither nostalgically mourning the passing of socialism nor celebrating the pseudosocialist politics of the Euro-American left but are working toward abolition and the building up of the decolonial international.

Notes

INTRODUCTION

1. For more on the histories of white international battalions, see Sweeney (2019) as well as Burke (2018).

2. I'm thinking of borderization along Achille Mbembe's conceptualization as "the process by which certain spaces are transformed into uncrossable places for certain classes of populations who thereby undergo a process of racialization, where speed must be disabled and the lives of a magnitude of people judged to be undesirable are meant to be immobilized if not shattered." Mbembe (Universitaet zu Koeln 2019) argues that these processes are ghettoizing entire regions of the world and contribute to the reclassification and refraction of bodies through fertility and mortality, with population politics becoming a new approach to georacial designs, "towards contraction, towards containment, towards enclosure; and various forms of encampment, detention and incarceration; typical of this logic of contraction being the erection in countless parts of the worlds of all kinds of walls and fortifications, gates and enclaves . . . of off-shoring and fencing of wealth . . . whose function is to decelerate movement, to stop it for certain classes of people in order to manage risk."

3. The response to refugees from the invasion of Ukraine by Russia in February of 2022, where audiences around the world were reminded that these were not Black and brown refugees coming from the Middle East or Africa but "relatively" civilized and relatively European people being the more recent examples of the racial border regimes that dominate European refugee policies. For more on this, see Nachescu (2022).

4. For more on this, see Chang and Rucker-Chang (2020).

5. Needless to say, these were processes that were tied to larger economic interests; the case of the Trepça mine in Kosovo is illustrative of this. Following Kosovo's colonization, the Serbian state gave the mine, under a fifty-year concession, to Alfred Chester Beatty of Selection Trust Ltd., who had similar colonial concession agreements across Africa and Asia.

6. It should be noted that it was not just nationalist movements that supported the Reconquista policies of (post)Ottoman nation-states in the Balkans. The founder of the socialist movement in Serbia, Svetozar Markovic, would note in 1867 that "everyone alive knows that there is no other way for the resolution of the Eastern Crisis but a war for life and death between Muslims and Christians" (Markovic 1987, 31).

7. In Europe, such ideas were famous among pan-Europeanists like Richard von Coudenhove-Kalergi, the founder of the pan-European movement, as well as the head of the former Habsburg Empire, Otto von Habsburg. The latter would become the president of the pan-European movement from 1973 to 2004 and play an important role in the post–Cold War Euro-Atlantic integration of Central and Eastern Europe.

8. For more on this, see Marušiakova and Popov (2000).

9. Josip Broz Tito, known as Tito, was the former president of the Socialist Federal Republic of Yugoslavia.

CHAPTER ONE. NONALIGNED MUSLIMS IN THE MARGINS OF SOCIALISM

An earlier version of this chapter was previously published as "The Politics of Postcolonial Erasure in Sarajevo," *Interventions: International Journal of Postcolonial Studies* 20, no. 6 (2018): 930–45.

1. Halil, like most "Oriental" others in Yugoslav films, never speaks. He communicates through gestures and monosyllabic words. Halil utters only one word repeatedly, asking for "su," which is not Albanian but Turkish for "water."

2. For more on the details of the outbreak, see Bura (2012).

CHAPTER TWO. HISTORICIZING ENCLOSURE

An earlier version of this chapter was previously published as "Imperial Inventories, 'Illegal Mosques,' and Institutionalized Islam: Coloniality and the Islamic Community of Bosnia and Herzegovina," *History and Anthropology* 30, no. 4 (2019): 477–89.

1. *Sarajli* is local Bosnian term for Sarajevan.

2. Sassja is a female hip-hop artist from Tuzla who had become popular that year with her 2015 debut album *Taktički Praktično*.

3. For more on this, see, for instance, Burke (2014).

An earlier version of this chapter was previously published as "Unmapping Islam in Eastern Europe: Periodization and Muslim Subjectivities in the Balkans," in *Eastern Europe Unmapped: Beyond Borders and Peripheries*, edited by Irene Kacandes and Yuliya Komska (New York: Berghahn, 2017), 53–78.

1. For more on the International Commission of Control, see Schmidl (1999).

2. The Malami order was spread in the Balkans in the late nineteenth century through the teachings of the Egyptian sheikh Muhammad Nur al-Arabi, who had settled in Skopje. For more on this, see Harry Thirlwall Norris (1993) and Robert Elsie (2001, 177).

3. For more on the transformation, see Puto (1987, 597).

4. For more on this, see Puto (1978).

5. Wilson remains one of the most revered US presidents in Albania and Kosovo. A statute is dedicated to his strategically linking old and new Tirana, as he is understood to be the savior of securing a new Albanian state after the Ottoman Empire. Both publications encouraged the Albanian diaspora to buy World War I bonds, tying them directly to their homeland's future. Words from Fan Noli's poem "Jepni Per Nenen" would become a popular song among Albanian migrants in the United States and Europe: "Hithni, hithni tok dollarë . . . Mbahu, Nëno, mos kij frikë / Se ke djemtë n'Amerikë" (Give, dollars together . . . don't worry mother / your sons are in America).

6. Donald Trump (@realDonaldTrump), "Another great day for peace with Middle East," Twitter, September 4, 2020, https://twitter.com /realDonaldTrump/status/1301924019147616257.

1. Bejtexhis were Ottoman-era poets who wrote (and frequently performed) Albanian poetry in Arabic script. They were known and celebrated for their for their cross-gender and homoerotic verses, some of which they dedicated to their same-sex lovers.

2. Dylbers were admirers of the bejtexhi poets and frequently their inspiration. Aheng is a musical evening or a poetic gathering.

3. See, for instance, one of the most noted Albanian bejtexhi poets Nazim (Frakulla) Berati, who, in the late eighteenth century, writes to his dylber, "I am Ferhad, you are Shirin / You're a falcon, I'm a rock dove / I am Muslim, you are Islam / I'm the faithful, you are imam" (Kycuku and Frakulla 1824, 127). For more on Nezim Berati, see Abazi-Egro (2009).

4. A *qefin* is a Muslim burial garment.

5. While the term *Islamic* or *Muslim sexualities* is used here to illustrate the construction of Orientalist Muslim male sexuality, this is by no means an

endorsement of the terms but rather, as Puar reminds us, a "pernicious inhabitation of homosexual sexual exceptionalism [that] occurs through stagings of U.S. nationalism via a praxis of sexual othering, one that exceptionalizes the identities of U.S. homosexualities vis-à-vis Orientalist constructions of 'Muslim sexuality'" (Puar 2017, 4). See also Éwanjé-Épée and Magliani-Belkacem (2013).

CHAPTER FIVE. ENCLOSURE DEMOGRAPHICS

1. The Nationalist United Patriots coalition blocked key checkpoints at the Bulgarian-Turkish border to prevent Bulgarian Turks who lived or worked in Turkey to vote in local elections.

2. Simeonov frequently uses the term *humanoids*, also used by European colonizers in the nineteenth century, to refer to Indigenous populations.

3. Azis, "Чух ви!" (I heard you!), Instagram, September 8, 2018, https://www.instagram.com/p/BndYf_khPp6/.

4. Pazardzhik District Prosecutor's Office v. S.M.M. et al. 2014, case нохд no. 330/2012, http://www.court-pz.info/2014_1/0070f512_33031914.htm; italics mine.

AFTERWORD

1. *Manifeste des 100* is a manifesto signed by one hundred French academics who claim that the study of racism, colonialism, and decoloniality spreads "Islamo-leftist" ideology and "anti-white hatred." The signatories asked for the French Ministry of Higher Education to protect secularism. For more on the debate, please see the manifesto ("Le Manifeste des 100," accessed March 29, 2022, https://manifestedes90.wixsite.com/monsite) and one of the many responses to the manifesto (Alana Lentin and Co-Signatories, "Open Letter: The Threat of Academic Authoritarianism—International Solidarity with Antiracist Academics in France, *Open Democracy*, November 5, 2020, https://www.opendemocracy.net/en/can-europe-make-it/open-letter-the-threat-of-academic-authoritarianism-international-solidarity-with-antiracist-academics-in-france/).

References

Abazi-Egro, Genciana. 2009. *Divani Shqip*. Tirana, Albania: Botimet Toena.

Abdou, Mohamed. 2019. "Queer Muslims: Identity and Sexuality in the Contemporary." PhD diss., Queen's University. http://hdl.handle.net/1974/26101.

Abu-Lughod, Lila. 2002. "Do Muslim Women Really Need Saving? Anthropological Reflections on Cultural Relativism and Its Others." *American Anthropologist* 104 (3): 783–90.

Ahmed, Sara. 2007. "A Phenomenology of Whiteness." *Feminist Theory* 8 (2): 149–68.

Al-Ahmad, Jalal. 2015. *Occidentosis: A Plague from the West*. Pennsauken Township, NJ: BookBaby.

Al-Bahloly, Saleem. 2013. "The Persistence of the Image: Dhākira Hurra in Dia Azzawi's Drawings on the Massacre of Tel Al-Zaatar." *ARTMargins* 2 (2): 71–97.

Albanian American Civic League. 2013. "DioGuardi: Winning Sen. Biden's Support on Kosova Part 3 04-28-2002." YouTube video, 9:59. May 29, 2013. https://www.youtube.com/watch?v=GDe9vFVgmJU.

Aleksandrova, Dayana. 2016. "The Bulgarian Chalga Phenomenon." *Post Pravda*, November 26, 2016. https://www.postpravdamagazine.com/bulgarian-chalga-phenomenon.

Alessandri, Emiliano. 2010. "The Atlantic Community as Christendom: Some Reflections on Christian Atlanticism in America, circa 1900-1950." In *Defining the Atlantic Community*, edited by Marco Mariano, 55–78. New York: Routledge.

Alkalaj, Sven. 2007. "Speech of Sven Alkalaj, Minister of Foreign Affairs of Bosnia and Herzegovina." Speech at the Proceedings of the International Conference "Islam in Europe," Vienna, March 23.

Alloula, Malek. 1986. *The Colonial Harem*. Translated by Myrna Godzich and Wlad Godzich. Minneapolis: University of Minnesota Press.

Amato, Giuliano, Carl Bild, Avis Bohlen, Jean-Luc Dehaene, Kemal Dervis, Mircea Geoana, Kiro Gligorov et al. 2005. "The Balkans in Europe's Future." International Commission on the Balkans. http://pdc.ceu.hu /archive/00001501/01/Report.pdf.

Amir-Moazami, Schirin. 2011. "Dialogue as a Governmental Technique: Managing Gendered Islam in Germany." *Feminist Review* 98 (1): 9–27.

Amzi-Erdogdular, Leyla. 2013. "Afterlife of Empire: Muslim-Ottoman Relations in Habsburg Bosnia Herzegovina 1878–1914." PhD diss., Columbia University. https://doi.org.10.7916/D8N01DR4.

Andreev, Alexander, and Hamed Abdel-Samad. 2015. "Параноите на пророка Мохамед" (The paranoias of the prophet Muhhamed). *Deutsche Welle*, September 9, 2015. https://www.dw.com/bg/параноите-на-пророка -мохамед/a-18731463.

Anzaldúa, Gloria, 1987. *Borderlands: The New Mestiza*. San Francisco: Aunt Lute.

Armstrong, D. Heaton. 1995. *Prince Vidi: Gjashtë muaj mbretëri*. Tirana, Albania: Tiranabook.

Arsenijević, Vladimir. 2007. "Naše crnje" (Our Blacks). *Pescanik*, September 20, 2007. https://pescanik.net/nase-crnje-2.

Asad, Talal. 2003. *Formations of the Secular: Christianity, Islam, and Modernity*. Stanford, CA: Stanford University Press.

Atanasoski, Neda. 2013. *Humanitarian Violence: The U.S. Deployment of Diversity*. Minneapolis: University of Minnesota Press.

Avramopoulos, Dimitris. 2017. "The Western Balkans and Their European Path." *European Western Balkan*, January 17, 2017. https:// europeanwesternbalkans.com/2017/01/17/avramopoulos-the-western -balkans-and-their-european-path-2/.

Azis Online. 2017a. "AZIS—MOTEL / Азис—Мотел (Official Video)." YouTube video, 5:02. June 26, 2017. https://www.youtube.com/watch?v=v _ici9SWJ-Y.

Azis Online. 2017b. "Азис за песента 'Мотел' в "Здравей България."" YouTube video, 24.02. July 20, 2017. https://www.youtube.com/watch?v =qCdOpe22owo&t=1066s.

Azis Online. 2018. "AZIS—Pozna li me? / Азис—Позна ли ме? (Official Video)." YouTube video, 6:10. September 7, 2018. https://www.youtube.com/watch ?v=Smdc5GcCM-A.

Azis Online. 2019. "AZIS—Ciganche / АЗИС—Циганче (Official Video)." YouTube video, 4:36. June 7, 2019. https://www.youtube.com/watch?v=i _mPzU2_72E.

BalkanWeb. 2015. "Parada e LGBT-Ve, Lame: U Spastruan Historitë Me Dylberë e Çuna Të Bukur." May 19, 2016. https://balkanweb.com/parada-e-lgbt-ve

-lame-u-spastruan-historite-me-dylbere-e-cuna-te-bukur-pinderi-dje-i
-hanin-duart-sot-foli-me-b/.

Barnes, J. S. 1918. "The Future of the Albanian State." *Adriatic Review* 1 (1): 66–82.

Bassichis, Morgan, and Dean Spade. 2014. "Queer Politics and anti-Blackness." In *Queer Necropolitics*, edited by Jin Haritaworn, Adi Kuntsman, and Silvia Posocco, 191–210. New York: Routledge.

Baudrillard, Jean. 1995. "Asserbissement occidental." *Libération*, July 3, 1995. https://www.liberation.fr/tribune/1995/07/03/asserbissement-occidental_138651/.

Baudrillard, Jean. 1996. *The Perfect Crime*. Translated by Chris Turner. New York: Verso.

BBC. 2015. "Austria Passes Controversial Reforms to 1912 Islam Law." *BBC*, February 25, 2015. https://www.bbc.com/news/world-europe-31629543.

Bhattacharyya, Gargi. 2018. *Rethinking Racial Capitalism: Questions of Reproduction and Survival*. Lanham, MD: Rowman and Littlefield.

Bhattacharyya, Gargi. 2019. "Other Internationals: World-Making Counter-Projects beyond the State." Lecture presented at the 44th Annual Conference of the British International Studies Association, London, June 13, 2019.

BIRN (Balkan Investigative Reporting Network). 2008. "Kosovo: World's Most Optimistic Country." *Balkan Insight*, December 19, 2008. https://balkaninsight.com/2008/12/19/kosovo-world-s-most-optimistic-country/.

Blumi, Isa, and Gëzim Krasniqi. 2014. "Albanians' Islam(s)." In *The Oxford Handbook of European Islam*, edited by Jocelyne Cesari, 475–516. Oxford: Oxford University Press.

Blushi, Ben. 2008. *Të Jetosh Në Ishull: Roman*. Tirana, Albania: Toena.

Blushi, Ben. 2009. *Otello, Arapi i Vlorës: Roman*. Tirana, Albania: Toena.

Borba. 1979. November 26, 1979.

Böröcz, József, and Melinda Kovács, eds. 2001. *Empire's New Clothes: Unveiling EU Enlargement*. Telford, UK: Central Europe Review.

Böröcz, József, and Mahua Sarkar. 2017. "The Unbearable Whiteness of the Polish Plumber and the Hungarian Peacock Dance around 'Race.'" *Slavic Review* 76 (2): 307–14.

Bouteldja, Houria. 2016. *Whites, Jews, and Us: Towards a Politics of Revolutionary of Love*. Los Angeles: Semiotext(e).

Boym, Svetlana. 2008. *The Future of Nostalgia*. New York: Basic.

Branch, Taylor. 2010. *The Clinton Tapes: Wrestling History in the White House*. New York: Simon and Schuster.

Bulgarian Presidency. 2018. "Prosecutor Calls Muslims a Threat to Bulgaria's Security." March 29, 2018. http://bulgarianpresidency.eu/prosecutor-calls-muslims-a-threat-to-bulgarias-security/.

Bultimes. 2017. "Ислямизацията на циганите върви по оста Пазарджик—Пловдив—Асеновград" (The Islamization of the gypsies goes along

the Pazardzhik-Plovdiv-Asenovgrad axis). https://bultimes.com
/Ислямизацията-на-циганите-върви-по-ос/.

Bura, Nikola. 2012. *Bez Obdukcije* (Without autopsy). Belgrade: Prometej.

Burke, Edmund. 2014. *The Ethnographic State: France and the Invention of Moroccan
Islam*. Berkeley: University of California Press.

Burke, Kyle. 2018. *Revolutionaries for the Right: Anticommunist Internationalism
and Paramilitary Warfare in the Cold War*. Chapel Hill: University of North
Carolina Press.

Cashman, Greer Fay. 2019. "Holocaust Main Subject of Conversation between
Rivlin and Croatian President." *Jerusalem Post*, July 31, 2019. https://www
.jpost.com/israel-news/holocaust-main-subject-of-conversation-between
-rivlin-and-croatian-president-597095.

Chang, F. B., and S. T. Rucker-Chang. 2020. *Roma Rights and Civil Rights: A Transatlantic Comparison*. Cambridge: Cambridge University Press.

Christides, Giorgos, Lüdke, Steffen, Popp, Maximilian, and Statius Tomas. 2022.
"Stürzt der Frontex-Chef doch noch über den Pushback-Skandal?" (Will
the Frontex boss fall over the pushback scandal?) *Der Spiegel*, March 17, 2020.
https://www.spiegel.de/ausland/frontex-skandal-warum-fabrice-leggeri-doch
-noch-stuerzen-koennte-a-c5af6fff-2e06-4908-b252-205b356bc5ee.

Council of the European Union. 2017. "EU—Western Balkans Justice and Home
Affairs Ministerial Forum—Joint Press Statement." October 27, 2017.
http://www.consilium.europa.eu/en/press/press-releases/2017/10/27/eu
-western-balkans-justice-and-home-affairs-ministerial-forum-joint-press
-statement/.

Čubrilović, Vasa. 1937. *Исељавање Арнаута / Iseljavanje Arnauta* (The expulsion of the Albanians). Belgrade: Institute of Military Archives of the
Former Yugoslav Army (Arhiv Bivše Jugoslovenske Vojske).

Dabashi, Hamid. 2015. *Can Non-Europeans Think?* London: Zed Books.

Dako, Kristo. 1919. *Albania, the Master Key to the Near East*. Boston: Grimes.

Daulatzai, Sohail, and Junaid Rana. 2015. "Left." *Critical Ethnic Studies* 1 (1):
39–42.

De Genova, Nicholas, ed. 2017. *The Borders of "Europe": Autonomy of Migration,
Tactics of Bordering*. Durham, NC: Duke University Press.

De Gruyter, Caroline. 2016. "Habsburg Lessons for an Embattled EU." Carnegie Endowment for International Peace. September 23, 2016. https://
carnegieendowment.org/2016/09/23/habsburg-lessons-for-embattled-eu
-pub-64658.

Deutsche Welle. n.d. "Jihad Made in Kosovo." Accessed August 24, 2014. http://
www.dw.de/jihad-made-in-kosovo/a-17874069.

Dezfuli, César. 2018. "51st State: Kosovo's Bond to the US—Photo Essay." *Guardian*, February 16, 2018. https://www.theguardian.com/artanddesign/2018
/feb/16/51st-state-kosovos-bond-to-the-us-photo-essay.

Dnes. 2007. "Борисов: Няма как да ни бият с дупето на Азис напред" (Borisov: There is no way they can beat us with Azis's ass). April 22. https://dnes.dir.bg/archive/-1600549.

Donchev, Anton. 1964. *Време разделно* (Time apart). Sofia, Bulgaria: Bulgarski Pisatel.

Dowler, Lorraine, and Joanne Sharp. 2001. "A Feminist Geopolitics?" *Space and Polity* 5 (3): 165–76.

Dumbrava, Costica. 2019. "The Ethno-Demographic Impact of Co-Ethnic Citizenship in Central and Eastern Europe." *Journal of Ethnic and Migration Studies* 45 (6): 958–74.

Džanko, Muhidin. 1993. "Sarajevski novi primitivizam—Pokret za destrukciju muslimanskog nacionalnog bića." United Bosnia and Herzegovina. Accessed August 10, 2008. https://haler.blogger.ba/2008/10/08/sarajevski-novi-primitivizam-pokret-za-destrukciju-muslimanskog-nacionalnog-bica/.

Economedia AD. 2009. "Бойко Борисов недоволен от лошия човешки материал в България" (Boyko Borissov dissatisfied with the bad human material in Bulgaria). *Dnevnik*, February 5, 2009. https://www.dnevnik.bg/bulgaria/2009/02/05/669511_boiko_borisov_nedovolen_ot_loshia_choveshki_material/.

Economist. 2019. "Emmanuel Macron in His Own Words." November 7, 2019. https://www.economist.com/europe/2019/11/07/emmanuel-macron-in-his-own-words-english.

Elsie, Robert. 1997. *Kosovo: In the Heart of the Powder Keg.* Vol. 478. Boulder, CO: East European Monographs.

Elsie, Robert. 2001. *A Dictionary of Albanian Religion, Mythology, and Folk Culture.* New York: New York University Press.

El-Tayeb, Fatima. 2008. "'The Birth of a European Public': Migration, Postnationality, and Race in the Uniting of Europe." *American Quarterly* 60 (3): 649–70.

El-Tayeb, Fatima. 2011. *European Others: Queering Ethnicity in Postnational Europe.* Minneapolis: University of Minnesota Press.

El-Tayeb, Fatima. 2016. "Creolizing Europe." *Manifesta Journal* 17:9–12. http://www.manifestajournal.org/issues/creolizing-europe-0#.

Eminov, Ali. 1997. *Turkish and Other Muslim Minorities in Bulgaria.* London: Routledge.

Erickson, Charles. 1914. *Albania: Key to the Moslem World.* Princeton, NJ: Princeton University Press.

Esposito, John, and Vali Nasr. 2000. "Rethinking US Foreign Policy and Islam after Kosovo." *Georgetown Journal of International Affairs* 1:15–25.

European Union External Action Service. n.d. *Stigma.* Accessed March 1, 2016. https://www.youtube.com/watch?v=RZBz6EkoTt8.

European Western Balkans. 2016. "Launch of Cultural Year 2016 in Sarajevo."
European Western Balkans, February 9. https://europeanwesternbalkans
.com/2016/02/09/launch-of-cultural-year-2016-in-sarajevo/

Éwanjé-Épée, Félix Boggio, and Stella Magliani-Belkacem. 2013. "The Empire
of Sexuality: An Interview with Joseph Massad." *Jadaliyya*, March 5, 2013.
http://www.jadaliyya.com/pages/index/10461/the-empire-of-sexuality_an
-interview-with-joseph-m.

Fallowell, Duncan. 2006. "Will the Real Mr. Kadare Please Stand Up?" *Telegraph*, April 23, 2006. https://www.telegraph.co.uk/culture/books/3651778
/Will-the-real-Mr-Kadare-please-stand-up.html.

Fanon, Frantz. 1963. *The Wretched of the Earth*. Translated by Constance Far-
rington. New York: Grove.

Feministički antimilitaristički kolektiv. 2019. "No to Further Militarization of
Security Forces—Use the EU Money to Improve Humanitarian Conditions of the People on the Move!" Change.org. http://chng.it/jzwxpqRV.

First-Dilić, Ruža. 1985. "Prostorna Stabilizacija i Udomaćivanje Roma." *Sociologija i prostor* 87–90:23–53.

Flagman. 2019. "Азис хвърли бомба: Кючекът трябва да влезе в българския
дом, за да се интегрират ромите" (Azis drops a bomb: Kyuchek must
enter the Bulgarian home to integrate the Roma people). June 10, 2019.
https://www.flagman.bg/article/189272.

Flood, Alison. 2009. "'I Am Not a Political Writer' Says Ismail Kadare." *Guardian*, March 24, 2009. https://www.theguardian.com/books/2009/mar/24
/ismail-kadare-political-writer.

Fluri, Jennifer L. 2009. "Geopolitics of Gender and Violence 'from Below.'" *Political Geography* 28 (4): 259–65.

Fuchs, Brigitte. 2011. *Health, Hygiene, and Eugenics in Southeastern Europe to 1945*.
Budapest: Central European University Press.

General Secretariat of European Council. 2015. *EU Western Balkan Counter-
Terrorism Initiative: Integrative Plan of Action*. Brussels: European Union.
https://www.statewatch.org/media/documents/news/2015/dec/eu-council
-western-balkans-antiterrorism-13887-15.pdf.

General Secretariat of European Council. 2018. *European Council Meeting (28
June 2018)—Conclusions*. Brussels: European Union. https://www.consilium
.europa.eu/media/35936/28-euco-final-conclusions-en.pdf.

Ghitis, Frida. 2016. "A Muslim Country That Loves America." CNN Opinion.
March 30. https://www.cnn.com/2016/03/30/opinions/why-albania-loves
-america-ghitis/index.html.

Golubović, Milka, and Slavka Dimitrijević. 1967. "Zdravstveno stanje i
ponašanje stanovnika sela Čabra" (Health condition and behavior of the
inhabitants of the village of Čabra). *Sociologija i prostor* 16:62–67.

Gilmore, Ruth Wilson. 1999. "Globalisation and US Prison Growth: From Military Keynesianism to Post-Keynesian Militarism." *Race and Class* 40 (2–3): 171–88.

Gradev, Vladimir. 2014. "Theology of Delirium." Pentimento.bg, October 10, 2014. https://www.pentimento.bg/page/?p=5483#more-5483.

Grosfoguel, Ramón. 2011. "Decolonizing Post-Colonial Studies and Paradigms of Political Economy: Transmodernity, Decolonial Thinking, and Global Coloniality." *Transmodernity* 1 (1): 1–36.

Hage, Ghassan. 2017. *Is Racism an Environmental Threat?* Hoboken, NJ: Wiley.

Hajdarpasic, Edin. 2015. *Whose Bosnia? Nationalism and Political Imagination in the Balkans, 1840–1914.* Ithaca, NY: Cornell University Press.

Hall, Catherine. 2018. "Doing Reparatory History: Bringing 'Race' and Slavery Home." *Race and Class* 60 (1): 3–21.

Hanna, Monica, Jennifer Harford Vargas, and José David Saldívar, eds. 2015. *Junot Díaz and the Decolonial Imagination.* Durham, NC: Duke University Press.

Haritaworn, Jinthana. 2015. *Queer Lovers and Hateful Others: Regenerating Violent Times and Places.* London: Pluto.

Harney, Stefano, and Fred Moten. 2013. *The Undercommons: Fugitive Planning and Black Study.* New York: Minor Compositions.

Hellsberg, Clemens. 2014. "Concert in Sarajevo." Wiener Philharmoniker, June 29, 2014. https://www.wienerphilharmoniker.at/en/magazin/concert-in-sarajevo/5753.

Hernández, Roberto D. 2018. *Coloniality of the US/Mexico Border: Power, Violence, and the Decolonial Imperative.* Tucson: University of Arizona Press.

HKW (Haus der Kulturen der Welt). 2013. "After Year Zero—Geographies of Collaboration since 1945 | Interview with Kodwo Eshun." YouTube video, 16:50. October 10, 2013. https://www.youtube.com/watch?v=Wx_BvPxYDjY.

Hoti, Avdulla. 2020. "Remarks by President Trump, President Vučić of Serbia, and Prime Minister Hoti of Kosovo in a Trilateral Meeting." September 4, 2020. Trump White House Archives. https://trumpwhitehouse.archives.gov/briefings-statements/remarks-president-trump-president-vucic-serbia-prime-minister-hoti-kosovo-trilateral-meeting/.

Hosaflook, David. 2019. "Preface." In Kristo Dako, *Albania: The Master Key to the Near East*, vii–xxii. Tirana, Albania: Institute for Albanian and Protestant Studies.

Hruby, Denise. 2019. "Their Homes Were Burned Down in Racist Violence: Then Officials Told Them to Flee." CNN, May 2019. https://edition.cnn.com/interactive/2019/05/world/roma-bulgaria-violence-eu-elections-cnnphotos/.

Iğsız, Aslı. 2018. *Humanism in Ruins: Entangled Legacies of the Greek-Turkish Population Exchange*. Stanford, CA: Stanford University Press.

Imre, Anikó. 2005. "Whiteness in Post-Socialist Eastern Europe: The Time of I Gypsies, the End of Race." In *Postcolonial Whiteness: A Critical Reader on Race and Empire*, edited by Alfred J. López, 53–78. Albany: State University of New York Press.

InterSoft. 2006. "Ars Aevi izložba: 'Greetings for Europe' Kurt & Plasto." *Klix*, March 4, 2006. https://www.klix.ba/magazin/kultura/ars-aevi-izlozba -greetings-for-europe-kurta-plaste/060304001.

Ismaili, Astrit. 2014. "Trashformation." Vimeo video, 7:28. January 22, 2014. https://vimeo.com/84777939.

Istrefi, Era. 2014. "Era Istrefi ft. Mixey—E dehun." YouTube video, 3:40. May 17, 2014. https://www.youtube.com/watch?v=yddX5MB9vig.

Izetbegović, Alija. 1980. *Islam between East and West*. Oak Brook, IL: American Trust Publications.

Izetbegović, Alija. 1990. *Islamska deklaracija* (Islamic declaration). Sarajevo: Bosna. http://www.vakat.me/wp-content/uploads/2017/01/Islamska -Deklaracija-knjiga-o-islamizaciji-muslimana-Alija-Izetbegovic.pdf.

Izetbegović, Alija. 2002. *Izetbegović of Bosnia and Herzegovina: Notes from Prison, 1983–1988*. London: Greenwood.

Jackson, Abdul Hakim Sherman. 2005. *Islam and the Blackamerican: Looking toward the Third Resurrection*. Oxford: Oxford University Press.

Jordan, David Star. 1918. "The Balkan Tragedy" *Journal of Race Development* 9 (2): 120–35.

Jovanović, Vladan. 2015. "Rekonkvista Stare Srbije: o kontinuitetu teritorijalne i demografske politike na Kosovu" (Reconquista of old Serbia: On the continuity of territorial and demographic policy in Kosovo). In *Figura neprijatelja: preosmišljavanje srpsko-albanskih odnosa*, edited by Aleksandar Pavlović, Adriana Zaharijević, Gazela Pudar Draško, and Rigels Halili, 95–116. Belgrade: IFDT & KPZ Beton.

Kadare, Ismail. 1999. "Konkurs bukurie për burrat në Bjeshkët e Namuna" (Beauty pageant for men in the Accursed Mountains). In *Vjedhja e Gjumit Mbretëror* (The theft of the royal sleep), 117–55. Elbasan, Albania: Onufri.

Kadare, Ismail. 2006. *Identiteti evropian I shqiptarëve: sprovë* (Evidence: The European identity of Albanians). Tirana, Albania: Onufri.

Kadare, Ismail. 2009. *Viti I Mbrapshtë: Roman* (The bad year). Tirana, Albania: Onufri.

Kakissis, Joanna. 2018. "Welcome to the Country with the Biggest Crush on America." NPR, February 24, 2018. https://www.npr.org/sections/parallels /2018/02/24/588250164/welcome-to-the-country-with-the-biggest-crush -on-america.

Kancler, Tjaša. 2016. "Body-Politics, Trans* Imaginary and Decoloniality." Paper presented at the 4th Nordic Transgender Studies Symposium, I Centre for Gender Studies, Karlstad University, Sweden, October 11–13. https://www.academia.edu/31557368/Body-politics_Trans_Imaginary_and _Decoloniality.

Kapidžić, Hamdija, ed. 1973. *Naucne ustanove u Bosni I Hercegovini za vrijeme austrougarske uprave* (Scientific institutions in Bosnia and Herzegovina during the Austro-Hungarian rule). Vol 6. Sarajevo: Arhiv Bosne i Hercegovine.

Karagozov, Konstantin. 2017. "Валери Симеонов: Изгонихме 843 цигани от Асеновград" (Valeri Simeonov: We expelled 843 Gypsies from Asenovgrad). *Fakti*, July 11 2017. https://fakti.bg/bulgaria/247827-valeri -simeonov-izgonihme-843-cigani-ot-asenovgrad.

Karbowski, Martin. 2004. "Азис, проф. Иван Славов—Полемика за задник" (Azis, prof. Ivan Slavov—Controversy over the ass). YouTube video, 35:45. March 25, 2016. https://www.youtube.com/watch?v=8WBYSLCoKXI.

Karbowski, Martin. 2015. "Защо 'Хабиби'?" YouTube video, 6:53. November 20, 2015. https://www.youtube.com/watch?v=xcqHNY2KW1g.

Kavazović, Husein. 2016a. "Address by the Grand Mufti." In *The Islamic Community in Bosnia and Herzegovina and the European Union: Main Policy Recommendations*, edited by Grand Mufti Husein Kavazović, Razim Čolić, Senaid Kobilica, Dževada Šuško, Muhamed Jugo, Muhamed Fazlović, and Muhamed Jusić, 5–12. Brussels: Representative Office of the Islamic Community in Bosnia and Herzegovina to the European Union. https:// www.academia.edu/30663000/The_Islamic_Community_in_Bosnia_and _Hercegovina_and_the_EU.

Kavazović, Husein. 2016b. "Rijaset predstavio izvještaj o razgovorima sa nelegalnim džematima" (The Riyaset issues a report on talks with illegal congregations). *Islamska Zajednica u Bosni i Herzgovini*, April 23, 2016. http://www .islamskazajednica.ba/vijesti/aktuelno/23732-rijaset-predstavio-izvjestaj-o -razgovorima-sa-paradzematima.

Khanna, Neetu. 2020. *The Visceral Logics of Decolonization*. Durham, NC: Duke University Press.

Kifner, John. 1993. "In Sarajevo, a Different Kind of Islam." *New York Times*, December 15, 1993. https://www.nytimes.com/1993/12/15/world/in-sarajevo -a-different-kind-of-islam.html.

Kika, Ardit. 2018. "The Sounds of Tallava." *Prishtina Insight*, January 22, 2018. https://prishtinainsight.com/the-sounds-of-tallava-mag/.

Kirn, Gla. 2014. "The Mass Popular Uprising in Bosnia-Herzegovina: 20 Years After the War." *LeftEast*, February 27. https://lefteast.org/popular-uprising -bosnia-20-years-after/.

Kobilica, Senaid. 2016. "The Contributions of Bosnian Muslims to Greater Openness and the Visibility of Muslims in Europe." In *The Islamic Community in Bosnia and Herzegovina and the European Union: Main Policy Recommendations*, edited by Grand Mufti Husein Kavazović, Razim Čolić, Senaid Kobilica, Dževada Šuško, Muhamed Jugo, Muhamed Fazlović, and Muhamed Jusić, 22–24. Brussels: Representative Office of the Islamic Community in Bosnia and Herzegovina to the European Union. https://www.academia.edu/30663000/The_Islamic_Community_in_Bosnia_and_Hercegovina_and_the_EU.

Kolov, Božidar. 2020. "Pritisak Na Roma u Bugarskoj: Ksenofobija kao Stredsvo Protiv Korone" (Pressure on Roma in Bulgaria: Xenophobia as a means against the corona). *Romi.hr*, April 3, 2020. https://romi.hr/fokus/hrvatska/ksenofobija-kao-sredstvo-protiv-korone.

Konstantinov, Kaloyan. 2016. "Каракачанов ще се бори с циганизацията и ислямизацията на България" (Karakachanov will fight the Gypsyization and Islamization of Bulgaria). *Offnews*, April 12, 2016. https://offnews.bg/izbori/karakachanov-shte-se-bori-s-'tciganizatciata-i-isliamizatciata-na-balga-637384.html.

Kosovarja. 2018. "Vargjet e Shahirave Shqiptarë Që Adhuronin Homoseksualët." (Verses of Albanian singers who admired homosexuals). October 10, 2018. https://new.kosovarja-ks.com/vargjet-e-shahirave-shqiptare-qe-adhuronin-homoseksualet/.

Krstić, Đorđo. 1928. *Kolonizacija u južnoj Srbiji* (Colonization in southern Serbia). Sarajevo: Đ. Krstić.

"Kuasa Sunia: Satu Bantahan Bagi Siasah." 1914. *Majalah al-Islam* 6 (6): 188–96.

Kurt & Plasto. 2005. *Greetings for Europe*. Sarajevo: Kurt & Plasto.

Kwon, Heonik. 2018. "Sites of the Postcolonial Cold War." In *Ethnographies of US Empire*, edited by Carole McGranahan and John F. Collins, 214–26. Durham, NC: Duke University Press.

Kycuku, Muhamet, and Nezim Frakulla. 1824. *Erveheja dhe Vjersha të Tjera*. (Erveheja and other poems). Tirana, Albania: Albanian National Library.

Limbong, Andrew. 2022. "Why Ukrainians Are Being Treated Differently than Refugees from Other Countries." NPR, February 28, 2022. https://www.npr.org/2022/02/28/1083580981/why-ukrainians-are-being-treated-differently-than-refugees-from-other-countries.

Lugones, María. 2007. "Heterosexualism and the Colonial/Modern Gender System." *Hypatia* 22 (1): 186–219.

Lugones, María. 2008. "Coloniality and Gender." *Tabula Rasa* 9:73–102.

Lugones, María. 2010. "Toward a Decolonial Feminism." *Hypatia* 25 (4): 742–59.

Lutovac, Momčilo S. 1977. *O Romima u Crnoj Gori* (On the Roma of Montenegro). Belgrade: Glasnik Etnografskog instituta SANU.

Mahmood, Saba. 2004. *Politics of Piety: The Islamic Revival and the Feminist Subject.* Princeton, NJ: Princeton University Press.

Maldonado-Torres, Nelson. 2007. "On the Coloniality of Being: Contributions to the Development of a Concept." *Cultural Studies* 21 (2–3): 240–70.

Marí, Cristina. 2014. "Modern Family Is Not Only a TV Show: Kosovo 2.0 Talks to One." Kosovo 2.0. July 4. http://www.kosovotwopointzero.com/en/article/1273/modern-family-is-not-only-a-tv-show-kosovo-20-talks-to-one.

Markova, Hydrangea. 2018. "Цветана Манева: Не съжалявам!" (Tsvetana Maneva: I'm not sorry!). *168 Chasa*, September 12, 2018. https://www.168chasa.bg/article/7052405.

Marković, Goran, dir. 1982. *Variola Vera.* Yugoslavia: Aleksandar Stojanović.

Marković, Milovan. 1974. "Relativno Duže Održavanje Porodičnih Zadruga U Albanaca Na Kosovu" (Relatively longer maintenance of family cooperatives in Albanians in Kosovo). *Sociologija i prostor* 43:95–100.

Markovic, Svetozar. 1987. *Celokupna dela.* Book 1. Belgrade: Narodna knjiga.

Marušiakova, Elena, and Veselin Popov. 2000. "The Bulgarian Gypsies–Searching Their Place in the Society." *Balkanologie: Revue d'études pluridisciplinaires* 4 (2). https://doi.org.10.4000/balkanologie.323.

Massad, Joseph A. 2008. *Desiring Arabs.* Chicago: University of Chicago Press.

Massad, Joseph A. 2015. *Islam in Liberalism.* Chicago: University of Chicago Press.

Massaro, Vanessa A., and Jill Williams. 2013. "Feminist Geopolitics." *Geography Compass* 7 (8): 567–57.

Massey, Doreen. 2005. *For Space.* London: Sage.

Mbembe, Achille. 2003. "Necropolitics." Translated by Libby Meintjes. *Public Culture* 15 (1): 11–40.

Mbembe, Achille. 2017. *Critique of Black Reason.* Durham, NC: Duke University Press.

McClelland, Mac. 2016. "25 Songs That Tell Us Where Music Is Going." *New York Times Magazine*, March 10, 2016. https://www.nytimes.com/interactive/2016/03/10/magazine/25-songs-that-tell-us-where-music-is-going.

Mestrovic, Stjepan, ed. 2013. *Genocide after Emotion: The Post-Emotional Balkan War.* London: Routledge.

MIA (Macedonian Information Agency). 2016. "Austrian FM Concerned over Rising Islamic Radicalization of Balkans." September 19. https://www.mia.mk/en/Inside/RenderSingleNews/208/133347690.

Mignolo, Walter D. 2002. "The Geopolitics of Knowledge and the Colonial Difference." *South Atlantic Quarterly* 101 (1): 57–96.

Mignolo, Walter D. 2007. "Delinking: The Rhetoric of Modernity, the Logic of Coloniality and the Grammar of De-coloniality." *Cultural Studies* 21 (2–3): 449–514.

Mignolo, Walter D., and Catherine Wash. 2018. *On Decoloniality.* Durham, NC: Duke University Press.

Miller, Brenna. 2017. "Faith and Nation: Politicians, Intellectuals, and the Official Recognition of a Muslim Nation in Tito's Yugoslavia." In *Beyond Mosque, Church, and State: Alternative Narratives of the Nation in the Balkans*, edited by Theodora Dragostinova and Yana Hashamova, 129–50. Budapest: Central European University Press.

Mills, Charles W. 2015. *Global White Ignorance*. London: Routledge.

Miñoso, Yuderkys Espinosa, Diana Gómez Correal, and Karina Ochoa Muñoz, eds. 2014. *Tejiendo de otro modo: Feminismo, epistemología y apuestas descoloniales en Abya Yala* (Weaving from another world: Feminism, epistemology and de-colonial stakes in Abya Yala). Popayán, Columbia: Editorial Universidad del Cauca.

Mishra, Pankaj. 2017. *From the Ruins of Empire: The Intellectuals Who Remade Asia*. New York: Farrar, Straus and Giroux.

Missiroli, Antonio, Jan Joel Andersson, Ido Bar, Martin Breitmaier, Florence Gaub, Nicu Popescu, Zoe Stanley-Lockman, John-Joseph, Samar Batrawi, Dimitar Bechev, Cameron Johnston, Predrag Petrović, and Stanislav Secrieru. 2016. *Strategic Communications East and South*. Paris: EU Institute for Security Studies. https://www.iss.europa.eu/sites/default/files/EUISSFiles/Report_30.pdf.

Mitra, Durba. 2020. *Indian Sex Life: Sexuality and the Colonial Origins of Modern Social Thought*. Princeton, NJ: Princeton University Press.

Mitrović, Aleksandra. 1985. "Brak i porodični odnosi Roma kao činilac njihova društvenog položaja" (Marriage and family relations of Roma as a factor in their social position). *Sociologija i proctor* 23 (87–90): 81–97.

Mogherini, Federica. 2017. "Remarks by Federica Mogherini Following the Meeting with the Minister of Foreign Affairs of Norway, Mr. Børge Brende." Commission Européenne. January 30. https://eeas.europa.eu/headquarters/headquarters-homepage_fr/19488/.

Momentum Worldwide. 2016. "You Have No Idea by Selma Selman." Vimeo video, 29:33. Uploaded June 16, 2016. https://vimeo.com/170964709.

Morgan, Peter. 2011. "Greek Civilization as a Theme of Dissidence in the Works of Ismail Kadare." *Modern Greek Studies (Australia and New Zealand)* 15:16–32.

Moten, Fred. 2003. *In the Break: The Aesthetics of the Black Radical Tradition*. Minneapolis: University of Minnesota Press.

Mufaku, Muhamed (Arnauti). 2009. *Lidhjet Letrare Shqiptare—Arabe*. (Arab-Albanian literary relations). Tirana, Albania: Qendra Shqiptare për Studime Orientale.

Nachescu, Ileana. 2022. "Ukraine: Beyond the Postsoviet: The War Is Shaped by Global Neoliberalism, Sexism, and Racism—Not Just Cold War Dynamics." *Boston Review*, March 4, 2022. https://bostonreview.net/articles/ukraine-beyond-the-postsoviet/.

Najmabadi, Afsaneh. 2005. *Women with Mustaches and Men without Beards: Gender and Sexual Anxieties of Iranian Modernity*. Berkeley: University of California Press.

National Assembly of the Republic of Bulgaria. 2017. " ТРИДЕСЕТ И ТРЕТО ЗАСЕДАНИЕ София, сряда, 5 юли 2017 г. Открито в 9,01 ч" (Thirty-third session Sofia, Wednesday, July 5, 2017 Opened at 9:01 am). July 5, 2017. http://www.parliament.bg/bg/plenaryst/ns/52/ID/5785.

NATO. 1999. "A Defining Moment for NATO: The Washington Summit Decisions and the Kosovo Crisis." *NATOReview* 57 (Summer). https://www.nato.int/docu/rev-pdf/eng/9902-en.pdf.

Nikolova, Madlen Ivanova. 2016. "Islam on Trial: Normalisation of Islam in Bulgaria and the Role of Intellectuals." Master's thesis, Central European University, Budapest.

Norris, Harry Thirlwall. 1993. *Islam in the Balkans: Religion and Society between Europe and the Arab World*. Columbia: University of South Carolina Press.

Obradović, Milovan. 1981. *Agrarna reforma i kolonizacija na Kosovu (1918–1941)* (Agrarian reform and colonization of Kosovo [1918–1941]). Priština, Kosovo: Institut za istoriju Kosova.

Office of Public Communication. 1989. *The Department of State Bulletin*. Washington, DC: Office of Public Communication, Bureau of Public Affairs.

Oslobođenje. 1983a. "Aveti prošlosti u teroristčkom plaštu" (Ghosts of the past in a terrorist coat). August 14, 1983.

Oslobođenje. 1983b. "Mračni refreni neprijateljske grupe" (The dark refrains of an enemy group). August 13, 1983.

Pack, Doris. 2011. "Motion for a European Parliament Resolution on Sarajevo as a European Capital of Culture 2014." European Parliament, May 2. https://www.europarl.europa.eu/doceo/document/B-7-2011-0281_EN.html.

Papantonopoulou, Saffo. 2014. "'Even a Freak like You Would Be Safe in Tel Aviv': Transgender Subjects, Wounded Attachments, and the Zionist Economy of Gratitude." *Women's Studies Quarterly* 42 (1/2): 278–93.

Parajanov, Sergei, dir. 1989. *Ashik Kerib*. Tblisi, Georgia, Soviet Union: Kartuli Pilmi.

Pearson, Owen. 2004. *Albania and King Zog: Independence, Republic, and Monarchy, 1908–1939*. New York: New York University Press.

Pellerin, Cheryl. 2018. "Budget Request for European Reassurance Initiative Grows to $4.7 Billion." US Department of Defense. June 1. https://dod.defense.gov/News/Article/Article/1199828/2018-budget-request-for-european-reassurance-initiative-grows-to-47-billion/.

Prguda, Abid. 1990. *Sarajevski Proces*. Visoko, Bosnia: PGD Iskra.

Pribićević, Adam, Čedomir Višnjić, and Božidar Vlajić. 1996. *Od gospodina do seljaka* (From gentleman to farmer). Vol. 2. Zagreb, Croatia: Prosvjeta.

Puar, Jasbir K. 2007. *Terrorist Assemblages: Homonationalism in Queer Times*. Durham, NC: Duke University Press.

Puar, Jasbir K. 2015. "The 'Right' to Maim: Disablement and Inhumanist Biopolitics in Palestine." *Borderlands* 14 (1): 1–27.

Puar, Jasbir K. 2017. *The Right to Maim: Debility, Capacity, Disability*. Durham, NC: Duke University Press.

Puto, Arben. 1978. *Pavarësia Shqiptare dhe Diplomacia e Fuqive të Mëdha: 1912–1914* (Albanian independence in the diplomacy of great powers: 1912–1914). Tirana, Albania: 8 Nëntori.

Puto, Arben. 1987. *Çështja shqiptare në aktet ndërkombëtare të periudhës së imperializmit* (The Albanian question in international acts in the age of imperialism). Vol. 2. Tirana, Albania: 8 Nëntori.

Quijano, Aníbal. 2000. "Coloniality of Power and Eurocentrism in Latin America." *International Sociology* 15 (2): 215–32.

Račevskis, Kārlis. 2002. "Toward a Postcolonial Perspective on the Baltic States." *Journal of Baltic Studies* 33 (1): 37–56. https://doi.org10.1080/01629770100000201.

Radovanović, Borislav. 1964. "Reproduction of Agricultural Households in Kosovo and Metohia." *Sociologija Iroctorr* 4:47–52.

Rao, Rahul. 2020. *Out of Time: The Queer Politics of Postcoloniality*. Oxford: Oxford University Press.

Regional Cooperation Council. 2016. *Initiatives to Prevent/Counter Violent Extremism in South East Europe a Survey of Regional Issues, Initiatives and Opportunities*. Sarajevo: Regional Cooperation Council. https://www.rcc.int/pubs/38/initiatives-to-preventcounter-violent-extremism-in-south-east-europe-a-survey-of-regional-issues-initiatives-and-opportunities.

Reinl, James. 2018. "Islam Takes Backseat in Kosovo Politics as Country Pushes for EU Membership." *Middle East Eye*, July 10, 2018. https://www.middleeasteye.net/news/islam-takes-backseat-kosovo-politics-country-pushes-eu-membership.

Republic of Austria, Federal Ministry of the Interior. 2016. "Declaration: Managing Migration Together." February 24, 2016. Vienna. https://www.bmeia.gv.at/fileadmin/user_upload/Zentrale/Aussendungen/2016/Westbalkankonferenz_Draft_Declaration_Letztfassung.pdf.

Rexhepi, Piro. 2019. "Imperial Inventories, 'Illegal Mosques' and Institutionalized Islam: Coloniality and the Islamic Community of Bosnia and Herzegovina." *History and Anthropology* 30 (4): 477–89.

Rezon Media. 2017. "БГ циганин, жиголо в Швеция, мечтае за семейство с мъж и замък" (BG gypsy, gigolo in Sweden, dreams of a family with a man and a castle). *Fakti*, October 6, 2017. https://fakti.bg/bulgaria/263813-bg-ciganin-jigolo-v-shvecia-mechtae-za-semeistvo-s-maj-i-zamak.

Ristić, Kosovar. 1958. "Kolonizacija i kolonistička naselja u ravni Kosova" (Colonization and colonial settlements in Kosovo). *Glasnik: Srpskog Geografskog Drustva* 38 (2).

Robert Schuman Foundation. 2018. "Europe 2050: Demographic Suicide." December 2, 2018. https://www.robert-schuman.eu/en/european-issues/0462 -europe-2050-demographic-suicide.

Robinson, Cedric J. 2020. *Black Marxism: The Making of the Black Radical Tradition.* 3rd ed. Chapel Hill: University of North Carolina Press.

Rodríguez, Encarnación Gutiérrez. 2018. "The Coloniality of Migration and the 'Refugee Crisis': On the Asylum-Migration Nexus, the Transatlantic White European Settler Colonialism-Migration and Racial Capitalism." *Refuge* 34 (1): 16–29.

Rutazibwa, Olivia U. 2020. "Hidden in Plain Sight: Coloniality, Capitalism and Race/ism as Far as the Eye Can See." *Millennium* 48 (2): 221–41.

Ruthner, Clemens. 2008. "Besetzungeng: A Post/Colonial Reading of Austro-Hungarian and German Cultural Narratives on Bosnia-Herzegovina, 1878–1918." In *WechselWirkungen: The Political, Social and Cultural Impact of the Austro-Hungarian Occupation of Bosnia-Herzegovina, 1878-1918*, edited by Clemens Ruthner, Diana Reynolds Cordileone, Ursula Reber, and Raymond Detrez, 221–42. New York: Peter Lang.

Sabadoš, Mirna Radin, Dorota Gołuch, and Sue-Ann Harding. 2017. "Fanon in the 'Second World': Yugoslavia, Poland and the Soviet Union." In *Translating Frantz Fanon across Continents and Languages*, edited by Kathryn Batchelor and Sue-Ann Harding, 151–95. London: Routledge.

Sabaratnam, Meera. 2017. *Decolonising Intervention: International Statebuilding in Mozambique.* London: Rowman and Littlefield.

Salaymeh, Lena. 2020. "Women and Islamic Law: Decolonizing Colonialist Feminism." In *The Routledge Handbook of Islam and Gender*, edited by Justine Howe, 310–17. London: Routledge.

Samardžić, Radovan, and Milan Duškov, eds. 1993. *Serbs in European Civilization.* Belgrade: Nova, Serbian Academy of Sciences and Arts, Institute for Balkan Studies.

Sarajevo Times. 2017. "Doris Pack: This Islam Is a European One, Muslims Aren't a Danger for Us." November 9, 2017. https://sarajevotimes.com/doris-pack -islam-european-one-muslims-arent-danger-us/.

Sayyid, Salman. 2016. "Muslims and the Challenge of Historiography: An Interview with Salman Sayyid (Part One)." By Junaid S. Ahmad. *Jadaliyya,* April 1, 2016. http://www.jadaliyya.com/pages/index/24190/muslims-and -the-challenge-of-historiography_an-int.

Sayyid, Salman. 2018. "Islamophobia and the Europeanness of the Other Europe." *Patterns of Prejudice* 52 (5): 420–35.

SBSCMES. 2013. "A Moveable East? North African and Middle Easter Community, Education, and Media in Modern Europe." YouTube video, 50:18.
   May 15, 2013. https://www.youtube.com/watch?v=8EOu3Uo6gso&t=378s.

Schmidl, Erwin A. 1999. "The International Operation in Albania, 1913–14."
   International Peacekeeping 6 (3): 1–10.

Scott, Joan Wallach. 2019. *Sex and Secularism*. Princeton, NJ: Princeton University Press.

Sessmus, Kevin. 2016. "Stop the Violence: LGBT Rights under Assault in Eastern Europe and the Balkans." *Huffington Post*, February 2, 2016. http://www
   .huffingtonpost.com/kevin-sessums/LGBT-rights-eastern-europe-balkans
   _b_1594916.html.

Shilliam, Robbie. 2019. "Other Internationals: World-Making Counter-Projects
   beyond the State." Lecture presented at the 44th Annual Conference of
   the British International Studies Association, London, June 13, 2019.

Silova, Iveta, Zsuzsa Millei, and Nelli Piattoeva. 2017. "Interrupting the Coloniality of Knowledge Production in Comparative Education: Postsocialist
   and Postcolonial Dialogues after the Cold War." *Comparative Education
   Review* 61 (S1): 74–102. doi:10.1086/690458.

Singh, Nikhil Pal. 2017. *Race and America's Long War*. Berkeley: University of
   California Press.

Smith, Sara. 2017. "Gendered and Embodied Geopolitics of Borders, Marginalization, and Contingent Solidarity." *Journal of Middle East Women's Studies* 13
   (3): 350–53.

Smith, Sara, and Pavithra Vasudevan. 2017. "Race, Biopolitics, and the Future:
   Introduction to the Special Section." *Environment and Planning D: Society
   and Space* 35 (2): 210–21.

Smith, Shawn Michelle. 2020. *Photographic Returns: Racial Justice and the Time of
   Photography*. Durham, NC: Duke University Press.

Sontag, Susan. 1994. "Waiting for Godot in Sarajevo." *Performing Arts Journal* 16
   (2), 87–106.

Spritzer, Dinah. 2007. "Kosovo Nationhood: Problem for Israel?" Jewish Tele-
   graphic Agency, December 18, 2007. https://www.jta.org/2007/12/18/israel
   /kosovo-nationhood-problem-for-israel.

Staikov, Ludmil, dir. 1988. *Време на насилие* (Time of violence). Sofia, Bulgaria:
   Nu Boyana Film Studios.

Stanković, Slobodan. 1982. "Danger of Pan-Islamism in Yugoslavia?" Radio Free
   Europe, August 26, 1982.

Statovci, Pajtim. 2019. *Crossing*. New York: Penguin Random House.

Stoler, Ann Laura, ed. 2013. *Imperial Debris: On Ruins and Ruination*. Durham,
   NC: Duke University Press.

Stoler, Ann Laura. 2016. *Duress: Imperial Durabilities in Our Times*. Durham, NC:
   Duke University Press.

Subotić, Jelena, and Srdjan Vučetić. 2019. "Performing Solidarity: White-ness and Status-Seeking in the Non-aligned World." *Journal of International Relations and Development* 22 (3): 722–43. Doi:10.1057/s41268-017-0112-2.

Sulstarova, Enis. 2006. *Arratisja nga Lindja* (Escape from the east). Chapel Hill, NC: Globic Press.

Sweeney, Matthew. 2019. "Bring the War Home: The White Power Movement and Paramilitary America." *Democracy and Security* 15 (2): 200–202.

T7. 2018. "Edhe rapsodët shqiptarë ju këndonin burrave me preference të ndry-shme seksuale" (Albanian rhapsody sung to men with different sexual desires). YouTube Video, 3:14. October 11, 2018. https://www.youtube.com/watch?v=pTWwYeDHXvs.

Tahir, Sevim. 2017. "Prisoners of Image: The Representation of Bulgarian Muslims (Pomaks) during the Communist Regime and Its Legacy." *Memo-Scapes: Romanian Journal of Memory and Identity Studies* 1 (1): 76–84.

Telegraph. 2009. "Mayor of Sofia Brands Roma, Turks and Retirees 'Bad Human Material.'" February 6, 2009. https://www.telegraph.co.uk/news/worldnews/europe/bulgaria/4531391/Mayor-of-Sofia-brands-Roma-Turks-and-retirees-bad-human-material.html.

Thobani, Sunera. 2020. *Contesting Islam, Constructing Race and Sexuality: The Inordinate Desire of the West.* London: Bloomsbury.

Thompson, Isobel. 2018. "Steven Bannon, Patriot for Hire, Says 'Vaffanculo' in Italy." *Vanity Fair*, June 1, 2018. https://www.vanityfair.com/news/2018/06/steve-bannon-says-vaffanculo-in-italy.

Times (London). 1914. "Protecting Prince William." June 5, 1914.

Times of India. 1914. "The Albanian Revolt." June 23, 1914.

Times of Israel. 2020. "Netanyahu: Kosovo to Be First Muslim-Majority Nation to Open Jerusalem Embassy." September 4, 2020. https://www.timesofisrael.com/netanyahu-kosovo-to-be-first-muslim-majority-nation-to-open-jerusalem-embassy/?fbclid=IwAR2QoD5ZH_RT6ohtr-YQlOnJbLZCsz7I-_N9OdqUfuPMajgobm4W_dBE_dg#gs.fqxozh.

Tlostanova, Madina. 2012. "Postsocialist ≠ Postcolonial? On Post-Soviet Imagi-nary and Global Coloniality." *Journal of Postcolonial Writing* 48 (2): 130–42. doi:10.1080/17449855.2012.658244.

Tlostanova, Madina. 2013. "Post-Soviet Imaginary and Global Coloniality: A Gendered Perspective." Interview. Kronotop.org. July 2013. http://www.kronotop.org/folders/post-soviet-imaginary-and-global-coloniality-a-gendered-perspective-madina-tlostanova/.

Tlostanova, Madina. 2015. "Can the Post-Soviet Think? On Coloniality of Knowledge, External Imperial and Double Colonial Difference." *Intersec-tions: East European Journal of Society and Politics* 1 (2): 38–58. doi:10.17356/ieejsp.v1i2.38.

Tlostanova, Madina. 2017a. "Transcending the Human/Non-Human Divide: The Geo-Politics and Body-Politics of Being and Perception, and Decolonial Art." *Angelaki* 22 (2): 25–37. doi:10.1080/0969725X.2017.1322816.

Tlostanova, Madina. 2017b. *Postcolonialism and Postsocialism in Fiction and Art: Resistance and Re-Existence.* New York: Palgrave Macmillan.

Tlostanova, Madina. 2018. *What Does It Mean to Be Post-Soviet? Decolonial Art from the Ruins of the Soviet Empire.* Durham, NC: Duke University Press.

Tlostanova, Madina. 2019a. "What Does It Mean to Decolonize?" Lecture presented at the Swedish Royal Academy, Stockholm, May 28.

Tlostanova, Madina. 2019b. "The Postcolonial Condition, the Decolonial Option and the Post-socialist Intervention." In *Postcolonialism Cross-Examined: Multidirectional Perspectives on Imperial and Colonial Pasts and the Neocolonial Present,* edited by Monika Albrecht, 165–78. New York: Taylor and Francis.

Todorova, Maria. 2009. *Imagining the Balkans.* New York: Oxford University Press.

Tribune (Lahore). 1914. "A Pan-Islamic Movement in Albania." June 14, 1914.

Tudor, Alyosxa. 2017. "Queering Migration Discourse: Differentiating Racism and Migratism in Postcolonial Europe." *Lambda Nordica* 22 (2–3): 21–40.

Tudor, Alyosxa. 2018. "Cross-Fadings of Racialisation and Migratisation: The Postcolonial Turn in Western European Gender and Migration Studies." *Gender, Place and Culture* 25 (7): 1057–72.

United Nations. 2015. *World Population Prospects: The 2015 Revision; Key Findings and Advance Tables.* New York: Department of Economic and Social Affairs, Population Division. https://esa.un.org/unpd/wpp/publications/files /key_findings_wpp_2015.pdf.

Universitaet zu Koeln. 2019. "Bodies and Borders // Achille Mbembe // AMP 2019." YouTube video, 45:50. July 18, 2019. https://www.youtube.com /watch?v=JqreV_1FqtU.

US Embassy Pristina Kosovo. 2014. "Judge Ted Weathers and Family Discuss LGBT Issues in Kosovo." YouTube video, 3:58. July 11, 2014. https://www .youtube.com/watch?v=NgNwrJRZrcw.

US Embassy Tirana. 2016. "25th Anniversary of Secretary of State James A. Baker III's Historic Visit in Albania." Medium, June 22, 2016. https:// medium.com/u-s-embassy-tirana/25th-anniversary-of-secretary-of-state -james-a-baker-iiis-historic-visit-in-albania-c2d363b9954e.

USKINFO PROMOCIJA d.o.o. 2015. "Kurz: Europe Needs Islam as Practiced in BiH." USKinfo, June 18, 2015. http://www.uskinfo.ba/vijest/kurz-evropi -treba-islam-kao-sto-se-prakticira-u-bih/13644.

Vekerdi, József. 1988. "The Gypsies and the Gypsy Problem in Hungary." *Hungarian Studies Review* 15 (2): 13–26.

Verli, Marenglen. 2014. *Shqiptarët në optikën e diplomacies Austro-Hungareze (1877–1918): Studime, Analiza, Dokumente* (Albanians in the optics of the

Austro-Hungarian diplomacy [1877–1918]: Studies, analysis, documents). Tirana, Albania: Klean.

Vitalis, Robert. 2015. *White World Order, Black Power Politics: The Birth of American International Relations.* Ithaca, NY: Cornell University Press.

Walsh, Catherine E. 2018. "Insurgency and Decolonial Prospect, Praxis and Project." In *On Decoloniality: Concepts, Analytics, Praxis,* edited by Walter D. Mignolo and Catherine E. Walsh, 33–56. Durham, NC: Duke University Press.

Wang, Jackie. 2018. *Carceral Capitalism.* Cambridge, MA: Semiotext(e).

Zerofsky, Elizabeth. 2019. "Viktor Orbán's Far-Right Vision for Europe." *New Yorker,* January 7, 2019. https://www.newyorker.com/magazine/2019/01/14/viktor-orbans-far-right-vision-for-europe.

Здравей България. 2017. "Азис: Хората обърнаха внимание на таланта ми—Здравей, България (30.06.2017г.)" (Azis: People paid attention to my talent—Hello, Bulgaria). YouTube video, 23:53. June 30, 2017. https://www.youtube.com/watch?v=B5UXc9DTlr4.

Иванова, Ива. 2010. "2050-а у нас—3.5 млн. Цигани, 1.2 турци, 800 хил. Българи." *Newsbg* (2050 in our country—3.5 million Gypsies, 1.2 million Turks, 800 thousand Bulgarians). November 22, 2010. https://news.bg/bulgaria/2050-a-u-nas-3-5-mln-tsigani-1-2-turtsi-800-hil-balgari.html?sort=desc&page=6.

Направи го за България (Do It for Bulgaria). n.d. Accessed August 7, 2018. https://www.napravigo.bg/index.php.

Index

Note: page numbers followed by *f* indicate figures.

zens for European Development of
Bulgaria); Izetbegović, Alija; Maneva,
Tsvetana; National Front for the
Salvation of Bulgaria (NFSB); Revival
Process; white Bulgarians
Bulgarian Communist Party, 23, 141
Bulgarian government, 4, 23f, 36, 141
Bulgarian National Movement Party
(IMRO), 3-4. See also Karakachanov,
Krasimir
Bulgarianness, 136; Christian, 138
Bush, George W., 98, 102

capitalism, 22, 28, 40, 65, 76, 114, 137;
carceral, 35; critique of, 49; racial, 5-6,
10, 35, 38, 153 (see also coloniality)
chalga music, 26, 135-36, 138-40, 149-50.
See also Azis
Chechnya: Muslims of, 21; separatism
in, 121
Christianity, 8, 14-16, 95, 118
Christian missionaries, 15, 95, 112. See also
Erickson, Charles Telford
Clinton, Bill, 102; administration of, 99
Cold War, 19, 21, 61; aftermath of, 102;
decolonial praxis and, 47; decolonization and, 31; Kosovo and, 98-99;
Yugoslav Muslim activists and, 46
colonial difference, 9; double, 13
colonialism, 5, 38, 105, 114; coloniality
and, 155; Habsburg colonial sites and,
71; Hegel and, 51; indemnity of, 53;
Izetbegović on, 57; Manifeste des 100
and, 160n1; in the Middle East, 49;
Muslims and, 68; Salihbegović on, 56;
settler, 37, 153; Western European, 13
coloniality, 9, 33, 70, 155; arrested developments of, 92; of the Bosnian Islamic
Community, 83; of built environments, 71; Cold War and, 19, 41; enclosures and, 93; Euro-American, 34,
121; Euro-Atlantic, 8-9; European, 12,
32, 148; of gender, 34, 65, 138; Hungary
and, 14; metropolitan, 36; of migration, 5, 30; Muslim positionality and,
40; of power, 10, 65, 138; of race, 151;

race and, 29, 153-54; racial capitalism
and, 6, 38; racism and, 28; of secular
states and subjectivities, 123; socialist
states and, 46; sovereignty and, 106;
transatlantic, 102, 153; whiteness and,
8, 106, 148; Yugoslavia and, 21. See also
coloniality/modernity; modernity/
coloniality
coloniality/modernity, 89, 106, 114, 153,
155
colonial matrix of power, 70, 92
colonial sites, 32, 69, 71, 73; Habsburg,
70, 81; salvation of, 72
Croatia, 5, 62-63; border with Bosnia,
6, 61
cross-dressing, 27, 109

de-Bulgarianization, 3, 135
decoloniality, 12, 154-55, 160n1
decolonial movements, 22, 156
decolonial praxis, 10, 28, 46, 151, 154
decolonization, 19-20, 28, 31, 39, 138,
154-55; Albania and, 100; Cold War and,
40; decolonial school of thought and,
70; Izetbegović and, 53; Salihbegović
and, 43, 48; Yugoslavia and, 18, 21, 51
demography, 17, 26, 36, 141-42
demolition of homes, 1-3, 35, 128, 130-34,
142, 151-52
desire, 36, 53, 137; Bulgarian, 25; disciplin-
ing of, 109; mandates of, 114; same-sex,
112
development, 2, 43, 50-52, 133; capitalist,
10, 53; postconflict, 88. See also GERB
(Citizens for European Development
of Bulgaria)
displacement, 133, 147; Muslim, 23, 29,
140; Roma, 2-3, 10, 35, 132, 140
dylbers, 107-8, 112-13, 116, 159nn2-3
Dzhambazki, Angel, 3, 134

Eastern Europe, 9; coloniality, 12-13;
racism 14, 46; refugees, 63; Muslims, 99; far-right 143; area studies,
155;
El-Tayeb, Fatima, 12, 41, 98

enclosure, 71, 153, 157n2; of borders, 34; fugitive flights from, 11; integration of Eastern Europeans and, 13; logic of, 8; Muslim populations and, 31; regional politics of, 33; transatlantic, 143; violence of, 36; white, 9, 12. *See also* Balkan route: as enclosure; Euro-Atlantic enclosure; Loznitsa neighborhod: enclosure of

enclosures, 6–7, 28, 31, 153; decolonial praxis along, 151; global white, 72; racialized, 69; of whiteness, 9, 37, 70, 131

Erickson, Charles Telford, 95–96, 99

Euro-Atlantic alliance, 8, 92, 99, 102

Euro-Atlantic enclosures, 6, 13, 28–30, 39, 70, 92–93, 106, 123–24, 143, 149, 154; fascist and vigilante groups and, 5; policies, 8; of Roma neighborhoods, 35; sexuality and, 115; whiteness and, 100, 131; white supremacy and, 32

Eurocentrism, 40, 53, 72

Europeanization, 87–88, 132; of Albanian gender and desire, 112; of Bulgarian society, 24

Europeanness, 123; of Albanians, 118; of Bosnian Islam, 83; Bosnia's, 64; crisis of, 13; heterosexuality and, 106; of Serbs, 14

Europeans, 76; Albanians as, 95, 99, 115; Balkan Muslims as, 66, 69; Bosnian Muslims as indigenous, 30; Eastern, 13–14, 153; Islam and, 59, 71; Roma and Muslim population as tainted, 13; Sarajevo and, 75; white, 13, 30, 35, 144

European Union (EU), 14, 127, 142, 144; Albanian organized crime and, 99–100; asylum policies, 5; Balkan Muslims and, 66; Bosnia and, 61–62, 64, 72–74, 80, 82; Bosnian Muslims and, 30; Bulgaria and, 3–4, 7; "Challenging Homophobia in Kosovo," 120–21; Council of the, 4, 63; deal with Turkey (2016), 4, 85; Habsburg colonial sites and, 70–71, 74–77, 81; Kosovo and, 103, 124–25; Kurz and, 84–85; labor market, 135; LGBTQI+

rights and, 121, 124; membership, 9, 63; Muslims and, 123–24; postsocialist integration and, 38; racism and, 143; rapid border intervention and, 5–6; refugee crisis, 4, 61–62; whiteness and, 5; white supremacy and, 8. *See also* Islamic Community of Bosnia and Herzegovina

Fanon, Frantz, 39, 51; *The Wretched of the Earth*, 105

far right, 145, 155; Bulgarian, 4; in Eastern Europe, 143; groups, 141

fascism, 76, 98

fascist groups/formations, 2, 5, 36, 141

Foucault, Michel, 120, 146

Frontex (European Border and Coast Guard Agency), 5–6

gender, 11, 27–28, 80, 126; Albanian, 112, 125; capitalism and, 137; coloniality of, 34, 65, 138; decolonial praxis and, 10; deviance, 106, 112; Ottoman modernization and, 108; queering, 149; rights, 114. *See also* Azis

genocide, 50, 153; Bosnian, 8, 32, 63–64, 148; Kosovo, 148; on Muslim populations, 13, 38, 58, 63; of Roma, 38; Srebrenica, 58

geopolitics, 92; Euro-American, 12; post–Cold War clash of civilization, 68; race and, 40, 46

GERB (Citizens for European Development of Bulgaria), 4, 140

Greece, 14, 16f, 17–18, 150; ancient, 80, 119

green transversal, 20, 61–63

Gutiérrez Rodríguez, Encarnación, 5, 29, 65

Habsburg empire, 14, 33, 71; colonial administration, 75, 78, 83. *See also* colonial sites: Habsburg; Islamic Community of Bosnia and Herzegovina; Vijećnica

hajj, 23, 60

Hayes, Carlton, 15, 17, 97

Hernández, Roberto, 7, 33

heteronormalization, 24, 112
heterosexuality, 25, 119, 140; Albanian,
    34, 106, 112, 118; white, 11. *See also* Azis
Hoffman, Ross, 15, 97
homoemancipation, 121–22; Euro-, 35;
    white, 120
homophobia, 113, 120, 149
homosexuality, 113, 119–20; U.S., 160n5
Hungary, 5, 14

incarceration, 6, 122, 157n2; of communi-
    ties of color, 153
Indigenous people, 41, 45, 102
integration, 84, 87, 91, 122; Bulgaria's,
    148; Euro-Atlantic, 9–10, 13, 17, 30,
    38, 46, 62, 65, 68, 88, 126, 137, 144,
    155, 158n7; European, 28, 120; mixing
    couples and, 140; of Muslims, 13, 123,
    136; panic over, 139; post–Cold War
    transatlantic, 37; postsocialist, 5, 8–9,
    34, 38, 45, 88, 155; Roma communities
    and, 4, 13; of western Balkans, 74.
    See also Kurz, Sebastian
International Control Commission,
    33–34, 92–93, 95, 100, 106, 110, 112;
    soldiers of, 109
internationalism: liberal, 98; under-
    stated, 31
international relations, 17, 40
Iranian Revolution, 20, 44, 68
Islam, 11, 48, 52–55, 59, 112, 146; Albanians
    and, 100, 105–6, 114–15; Arab, 140;
    Austro-Hungarian empire and, 69;
    Bosnian, 54, 64, 66, 82–88; Bulgarian,
    145; conservative, 64; converts to, 24;
    decolonial, 40; European institutions
    of, 72; Europeanization of, 87; Hegel
    and, 51; institutionalization of, 54, 83,
    86–88; Kurz and, 84; local practices
    of, 32; militant, 62; moderate, 71, 84,
    88; modernization and, 20; racial
    differentiation of, 30; radical, 26, 71,
    82, 84, 99–100, 135, 142, 144; return
    of, 67; sexuality and, 112, 114, 118–19,
    123, 159n3. *See also* Izetbegović, Alija;
    Salihbegović, Melika; Shariati, Ali

Islamic Community of Bosnia and Her-
    zegovina, 30, 54, 71, 82–83, 85–88
Islamic fundamentalism, 3, 21, 46, 54, 56,
    65, 82, 141
Islamic life, 44, 68
Islamic threat, 20, 31, 46, 59, 131
Islamization, 36, 66–67, 134; of Bos-
    nians, 64; of knowledge, 52 (*see also*
    Izetbegović, Alija); Loznitsa and, 152;
    of Roma, 134–35, 145
Islam Law (Austria), 83, 85
Islamophobia, 13, 140; globalization of,
    21, 90; internalized, 100, 105
Ismaili, Astrit, 124–25
Israel: enclosures and, 6; Grabar-
    Kitarović's visit to, 62; Trump and, 104
Izetbegović, Alija, 45–46, 49–50, 53–57;
    followers of, 48; *Islam between East and
    West*, 49; *Islamska deklaracija* (Islamic
    declaration), 22, 31, 44, 46, 52, 54; pan-
    Islamist praxis of, 21

Jordan, David Starr, 15–16

Kadare, Ismail, 101, 115–19
Karakachanov, Krasimir, 3–4, 135, 141
Karbowski, Martin, 25–26
Kavazović, Husein, 30, 83–84
Kobilica, Senaid, 30, 87
Kosovo, 29, 33, 102–3, 113, 125, 158n5;
    Albanians in, 3, 18, 23, 56, 103, 105; Kurz
    and, 65; Habsburg expansion into, 78;
    genocide in, 148; homoemancipation
    in, 120–21; Muslim integration in, 123;
    Muslims in, 67; queer artists in, 124;
    settler colonization of, 14; sovereignty
    in, 32, 34, 39; student protests in, 21;
    tallava artists in, 149; Trump and,
    103–4; United States and, 91–92; war,
    8, 38, 46, 60, 66, 90, 98–99, 101, 106;
    Wilson and, 159n5. *See also* NATO;
    Thaçi, Hasim; United Nations Mis-
    sion in Kosovo (UNMIK); *Variola Vera*;
    Vetëvendosje
Kurz, Sebastian, 65, 82–85
Kusturica, Emir, 47, 74, 149

League of Communists of Yugoslavia, 43–44
League of Nations, 17, 98
Le Pen, Marine, 58, 143
liberalism, 64, 144
Lippmann, Walter, 15, 97
Loznitsa neighborhood, 1, 6, 9, 128–29, 131, 152; enclosure of, 130; enclosures and, 151; Roma in, 133
Lugones, María, 11, 65, 137
Lunacek, Ulrike, 120, 124

Macedonia, 36–37, 131; Christian Bulgarians from, 135; Habsburg expansion into, 78; Islamic radicalization and, 65; oppression of Albanians in, 56; rapid border intervention and, 6; rejection of EU membership for, 63
Maneva, Tsvetana, 138–39
Marubi, Pietro/Pjetër, 107–8, 109f, 110, 111f
masculinity, 115, 146; heteronormative European, 117; heterosexual, 118, 140; secular, 11
Mbembe, Achille, 7, 105, 148, 154; borderization and, 157n2
media, 77, 131; Albanian, 113; Bosnian war and, 59; imaginaries, 147; Iranian Revolution and, 20; Kosovo and, 90, 104; refugees and, 3–4; Roma and, 19, 134–35; Salihbegović trial and, 45; social, 26, 61, 73, 140–41
Middle East, 7, 20, 27, 49; migrants from, 147; *muhacirs* and, 29; nonaligned decolonial movements in, 22; radical Islam and, 84; refugees from, 103, 143, 157n3; Trump and, 104–5
migrants, 61–66, 68, 72, 147, 154; Albanian, 159n5; Balkan route and, 6–7, 25, 30; Europe and, 5; Gulf War (1990) and, 37; integration of, 136; Kurz on, 85; Muslim, 7, 26, 56; racist attacks on, 14; torture of, 129
migration, 10, 36; African, 7; coloniality of, 5, 30; Euro-American regimes of, 65; management, 4, 62
military corporatism, 6, 34

minorities, 14, 59; racialized, 147; Roma and Muslim, 144; Turkish, 3; violence on, 129
Mitterrand, François, 38, 63
Mladi Muslimani, 21, 48
modernity, 12, 33, 115, 154; Albania and, 116; Euro-Atlantic, 38; in the Muslim world, 52; performances of, 126; second-world, 39; socialist, 10, 48, 137
modernity/coloniality, 7, 11–12, 19, 28, 34, 68
Montenegro, 6, 16f, 65, 95
Moten, Fred, 37, 149
multiculturalism: of the Habsburg empire, 83; liberal, 121–22
Muslim activists, 44–46, 49, 53. *See also* Sarajevo Process
Muslim peasants, 47–48, 53
Muslim populations, 11, 31, 144; assimilation and expulsion of (Bulgaria), 20; erasure of, 13; genocide of, 63; Islamic radicalization and, 65; Ottoman, 83; post-Ottoman, 29, 106; Roma, 148
Muslims, 1, 5, 8, 65, 86, 95, 136–37, 150, 158n6; Albanian, 48, 91–92, 104–5; Arab, 66, 81; in Austria, 82; Balkan, 66–67, 71, 99–100, 112, 114, 123–24; Baudrillard on, 58–59; birth rates and, 134–35; Bosnian, 20, 30, 74, 80–81, 87; Bulgarian, 21–23, 26, 49, 145, 147; coloniality and, 40; expulsion of, 15f, 136; extermination of, 38; forced conversion of, 60; from Greece, 17; male, 146–47; memory and, 72; political struggles of, 31; Pomak, 19, 24, 27; racialization of, 58; Roma, 2, 6, 19, 48, 134, 140, 145, 147–48; Revival Process and, 141; structural subordination of, 53; Trump and, 90, 104–5; Turkish, 24, 27; whiteness and, 13, 67; in Yugoslavia, 20–22, 44–49, 51–56, 68. *See also* Azis; Islamic Community of Bosnia and Herzegovina

National Front for the Salvation of Bulgaria (NFSB), 4, 128–29

refugees (continued)
Herzegovina and, 85; from the Middle East, 103, 157n3; Muslim, 26–27, 29; panic around, 71, 136; queer, 27, 150; racialization of, 67; Syrian, 3, 62, 143; trans, 27; Ukrainian, 63, 157n3; violence against, 151; whiteness and, 13, 72

revanchism, 13, 41

Revival Process, 22–23, 27, 59, 141

rights, 124–25; civil, 122; communist and twentieth-century, 55; equal, 76; human, 59, 144; LGBTQI+, 120–22, 124; rhetoric of, 9; sexual, 11, 34, 114, 126

Roma, 3–4, 8, 41, 132, 144, 149–50; Bulgarian kayaking team and fight with, 1, 128, 145; in Czechoslovakia, 56; eviction of, 1, 36, 130, 134, 148–49; genocide of, 38; in Loznitsa, 133; memory and, 72, men, 145–46; music, 24, 126 (see also Azis; chalga music); Muslims, 2, 6, 19, 48, 134, 140, 145, 147–48; Muslim women, 23; racialization of, 19, 22, 149; racism against, 1, 35–36, 127, 129–30, 134–36, 139, 147, 155; refugees, 27; sterilization of, 3, 56, 141; survival, 36

Roma communities, 2, 4, 35, 130; antiracist imaginaries of, 137; COVID pandemic and, 152; displacement of, 10, 35, 140–42; enclosure of, 6, 35, 131–32, 140, 153; lifestyle of, 141

Roma neighborhoods, 2, 19, 130, 132, 134, 139, 145, 152; enclosure of, 35. See also Asenovgrad, Bulgaria; Loznitsa neighborhood

Roma populations, 1, 13, 134, 148; high birth rates among, 23; racialization of, 19

Salihbegović, Melika, 31, 43–45, 47–57, 68, 77–79

Sarajevo, 44, 47–49, 66, 74–75, 79–80, 87; Austrian presence in, 82; liberation of, 73; polemics about pan-Islamism in, 20; protests in, 76f; as seat of Habsburg southern expansion, 78; siege of, 32, 58; Sontag and, 81. See also neoprimitivism; Vijećnica

Sarajevo Process, 21, 45–46, 74

saving, 15; of Albanians, 106; of gendered and sexed bodies, 66; of the LGBTQI+ community, 120–21, 123; missions, 11, 89

Sayyid, Salman, 13, 40

second world, 13, 19

secularism, 34, 67, 82, 105, 160n1; critiques of, 39

secularization, 44; of the Albanian male, 106

security, 140; Balkans as site of, 15; border, 5, 19, 33, 36, 62–63, 66, 142; Bulgarian national, 3; enclosure and, 13; Euro-American, 72, 99–100; Euro-Atlantic, 5, 11, 19, 62–64, 144; infrastructures of, 28; in Loznista neighborhood, 1; Muslims as threat to, 56, 61; North Atlantic Pact and, 17; transatlantic, 74; white, 36. See also Azis

Serbia, 14, 16f; ethnic cleansing and, 58; Islamic radicalization and, 65; Kosovar popular-culture defiance to, 125; Kosovo and, 100; persecution of Muslims and, 95; rapid border intervention and, 6; refugee panic and, 62; socialist movement in, 158n6; Trump and, 103–4

Serbs, 58–59; Bosnian, 74; Europeanness of, 14

sex, 11, 34, 12, 137, 146; anal, 25; rights, 114

sexual deviance, 11, 106

sexuality, 11–12, 28, 106, 115, 120–21, 126; Albanians and, 34; Eurocentric inscriptions of, 27; homoerotic, 118; Islam and, 114, 123; Islamic, 117, 119–20, 123–24; Muslim, 119, 159n5; (post) Ottoman politics of, 24; postsocialist, 25; queer, 117, 119; in Viti i Mbrapshtë (Kadare), 116. See also Azis; gender; heterosexuality; homosexuality

Shariati, Ali, 39, 46; Red Shi'ism, 44

Simeonov, Valeri, 128–31, 134, 141, 160n2

Skopje, Macedonia, 37, 132, 159n2

whiteness (continued)
7, 9, 35, 72; Islamic "queer" sexualities and, 119; Muslim, 71; NATO and, 137; the West and, 68, 70, 88–89, 91. *See also* Azis; Europeanness

white race, 15–16, 34

white supremacy, 8–9, 12, 28, 32, 36, 40, 142, 153–56

Wied, Wilhelm zu, 93, 115

Wilson, Woodrow, 16–17; Albania and, 91, 96–98, 102, 159n5

workers, 2, 24; aid, 5; exodus of Bulgarian, 3; Muslim, 49; postsocialist, 14; white Eastern European, 9

World War I, 15, 17, 91, 97; bonds, 159n5; centennial of, 71, 74–75, 83, 88. *See also* Paris Peace Conference

World War II, 4–5, 17–18, 73, 98

Yugoslavia, 18–19, 39, 47, 51; Albanians in, 3, 23, 48; colonial sites in, 73; influence of Iranian Revolution in, 20, 68; Muslims in, 21–22, 44–45, 48–49, 52, 54–56; Roma in, 23, 48; tribalism in, 121. *See also* Izetbegović, Alija; League of Communists of Yugoslavia; Salihbegović, Melika; Tito, Josip Broz; Union of Writers of Yugoslavia; *Variola Vera* (Marković)